CATHERINE'S LIEUTENANT

CATHERINE'S LIEUTENANT

MARY WARD MORTENSEN

atmosphere press

Table of Contents

Introduction

This book is dedicated to Frank Ward Junior, my father and hero, and to Mary Catherine Ward, my mother, who in her own right was a hero as well.

This book is for my sister, Terry Lynn (Ward) Green and my children, Stacey (Adcock) Happe and Gregory Adcock, and for my grandchildren. I've written this story so that you may learn about your family, who fought to protect our freedoms in World War II. We and generations to come are not allowed to forget their sacrifices. You can be proud of Frank and Catherine, as they were part of that generation which saved the very way of life that we now cherish. Now it is our turn to make the world a safer and kinder place to live.

*****

One day in 1951, in the dim light of our garage in Whittier, California, I noticed a trunk stashed way up high in the rafters. I had seen the trunk many times during my childhood and had always known it belonged to my Daddy. We had moved many times over the years, and the trunk was always with him wherever we moved: Los Angeles, Whittier, San Francisco, San Mateo, Fullerton, and Brea, California, and Henderson, Nevada.

"Daddy, what's in that trunk?" I asked, pointing way above my head.

"Oh, that's the trunk where I store letters from my time in the Army—letters from the war," he replied.

"Letters from who, Daddy?" I asked.

"Oh! They're from your Mommy, Mama Ward, Papa Ward, and Uncle Clint." "Oh, OK, Daddy," I said a little glumly, disappointed that there was nothing for me to play with in his special trunk.

I never thought about the letters again until October 16, 2001, when he passed away in Las Vegas, Nevada. In the midst of all of the chaos of a family in grief, I found myself going through his things ... and there was his trunk. For 56 years, he had kept the letters in that trunk. *Why?* I wondered. *Did he leave them for his family? Or was it simply a sentimental attachment to a cherished vestige of that very special time in his life?*

Suddenly my mind flashed back to a moment in Orange County, California. I was helping him move to Henderson, Nevada when we once again came across the trunk. "What do you want me to do with this trunk?" I asked. I was only concerned with the logistics of the move at that moment; the trunk represented one more decision.

"Kay, my *life* is in that trunk—in those letters—please put it on the moving truck."

On that day in October 2001, I knew I would always keep that trunk.

Like so many of our heroes of WWII, my father never spoke of the realities of the war. However, in spite of the fact that he never spoke of them, the memories that he could not shake remained a heavy burden on his heart for the rest of his life. It would have been agonizing for him to share stories about his "brothers in war" who had lost their lives in the battles of WWII. He and many other veterans protected their families, friends, and loved ones from the gruesome details of the carnage of war while, at the same time, asking themselves, *Why did I come home?*

After his death in 2001, it took me years to decide to go through his letters—the letters that are now the substance of this book. In 2014, when I finally mustered the courage to read them and discovered Frank and Catherine's very personal story of love during the war, I found the story to be an amazing one—and at that moment, I knew that it was a story that must be shared.

In his letters, Dad traces his journey, which began at Camp Roberts, California, where he did his basic training. He attended Officer Candidate School at Fort Benning, Georgia, and, within a few months, was commissioned as an officer with the 17th Airborne at Camp Mackall, North Carolina. In November 1943, he was deployed overseas to North Africa. After a short stint on the rocky northern coast of Africa, he subsequently served in Sicily, Italy, southern France, and England. His final stop in the European theater was in the Ardennes Mountains, where he fought and was wounded in the Battle of the Bulge in Flamierge, Belgium.

As his older daughter, I feel compelled to tell the story of his experiences during the war—the one he could not or would not voice. Yes, the love story that blossomed between Frank and Catherine is a story wrapped in the history of WWII.

This is for you, Dad!

The Childhood Days of Mary Catherine Oliver

The Olivers from 1919 to 1938
Charlotte, North Carolina

Mary Catherine Oliver was born in Pittsburg, Pennsylvania on February 26, 1919, but grew up in Charlotte, North Carolina. For the most part, she went by "Cath" or "Cat," as it is customary in the South to use the middle name as the primary name. However, her friends—the folks she knew at school and church – all knew her as "Cathy." She may have been born in Pittsburgh, but she never thought of herself as a "Yankee," and she didn't like to admit that she was born in the North.

Oh, yes! Catherine was proud of her North Carolina upbringing and proud to be a "Southern lady." Occasionally, she would forget her "ladylike" demeanor, but for the most part, she was sweet. Her charms were warm and sincere, along with her sweet, relaxed Southern accent—or, as she liked to call it, her "North Carolina accent." "Those people in the Deep South, well, they just talk *flat*," she would say. She did like to be a little naughty at times—but even in her naughty moments, she did everything in a lady-like way. Catherine also had a fiery side and was not in the least afraid to show her displeasure when she felt strongly about something. A bit like a sparkler on the Fourth of July, she was quick to flare, but the 'fire' also went out fast. It's a little curious to me now that she often sounded like a feminist with a Southern accent—definitely a woman ahead of the times.

In the 1920s, the Olivers lived in a lovely, simple home with all of the necessities of life. They were comfortable but not rich by any means. Then came the crash of 1929 ...

The Great Depression was hard on children, and especially hard on this child and her siblings. First, they lost the home they had loved so much. The family had to move to an old rental, which was small, cold, and drafty, and Catherine wore dresses that her mother had made of flour sacks. For weeks on end, the menu at their table consisted of biscuits and fatback gravy made from the flour and fatback (salt pork) donated by their church or the Assistance League. No one but the rich and the politicians managed to live well during the Depression. Jobs were nonexistent, and the unemployment rate was up to fifty percent—sometimes even higher.

Her sister, Margaret Rebecca, was two years younger than Catherine. Although their father loved all of his children, it was no secret that Becky was his favorite, and he made no bones about it. In spite of the fact that he loved his blond, blue-eyed Rebecca the most, which left deep scars in Catherine's heart, the two sisters had a close, loving relationship and never spoke of the favoritism out loud. Catherine and Becky both had a "prickly" side, but they were the best of friends for their whole lives.

Papa Oliver had made a good living as a plumber before the Depression, but now he was unemployed. He tried desperately to support his family with miscellaneous jobs, but it was hard to find work, and the extra income he earned proved to be slim to none. There were no unemployment benefits or welfare checks in the 1930s, and the soup lines were long. After long months of hard struggle, Papa Oliver made the hard decision to go out of state to work with the Conservation Corps, which was part of President Franklin Roosevelt's "New Deal." It was not until after the start of World War II, when the manufacture of war machines became a new element in the bedrock of the US economy, that the situation began to improve. At that point, the common worker was able to have steady work as he took up his role in support of the war effort.

Catherine also had an older brother, James William Oliver, who went by "Bill." When he was sixteen years old (around 1934–35), he lied about his age and joined the Navy, which guaranteed him three square meals a day, job training, and most of all, a check, which he sent home as often as he could. In 1944, he saved his ship, the destroyer-class USS *Wilson*, from sinking in the South Pacific and received a Silver Star for his heroism. He stayed in the Navy until the early 1960s and retired as a Chief Petty Officer.

Catherine's baby sister, Betty Jean, was born fourteen years after Catherine, in 1933. Mama Oliver was overweight for her small frame, and she almost died in childbirth with Betty Jean. She never fully regained her health after Betty Jean was born, and from then on, Catherine assumed the primary responsibility for the household chores during the Depression years: the cooking, cleaning, and the care of her baby sister. There's no getting around it: life is hard.

As her mother was ill, Catherine worked hard to keep the household clean and the family fed. The only source of heat was a wood-burning stove, and Catherine's first task each day was to get the fire going for her family so that they would wake up to a warm house. I picture her as an undernourished young child who was thin, pale, and unhappy. From an early age, she was convinced that she was the little girl no one loved—a feeling which, sadly, stayed with her for the rest of her life.

The Olivers loved their oldest daughter, but the family was poor, and times were hard. Dora May was sickly, and most of the time, she was just doing the best she could. In spite of the fact that they had a strong faith and religion played a large part in their daily life, the Oliver household was not warm, loving, or supportive. Dora May was a firm believer that Jesus would love her youngsters if they were good Christian children, but when Catherine asked, "Am I pretty, Mama?" her mother would either tell her, "Pretty is as pretty does," or she would quote a verse from the Bible. For a little girl who felt unlovable, those words were hard to hear and not very comforting.

Catherine's feelings of inferiority and her need for love plagued her all of her life. Once the Depression of 1929 had left the family poor and destitute, she never had more than two dresses at one time, and her coats and shoes were all second-hand. At school, the other children teased her because her shoes were too small and her clothes were almost rags.

In 1938, Catherine graduated from Central High School and was finally able to enter the workforce. Her first job was in a hosiery store. From there, she moved to Associated Transportation, a large transport company in Charlotte, where she traced lost shipments. Now that she had her own paycheck, she vowed never again to "go without." A real "clothes horse," she was never without a full wardrobe again. She sewed her own clothes and spent much of her paycheck on keeping up with the latest trends. She understood colors and fabrics, and with her sharp sense of style and an eye for classic contours with suave lines, she always managed to be dressed in the newest fashions.

By 1938, Catherine had grown into a beautiful young woman with olive skin like her father's. She was a natural beauty, used very little makeup, and had a freshness about her. The picture of innocence and honesty, she had shoulder-length hair and deep-set eyes of green and amber, which often sparked whether she was happy or angry. A little self-conscious about her narrow forehead, she pulled back her thick brunette curls and styled them in the fashion of the day. Painfully aware of her mother's weight and health problems, she was always careful to watch her figure and dressed to the nines whenever she could. She knew that her figure was striking, and she had a natural instinct for those fashions which accentuated her best features. This helped her regain some of the confidence and self-esteem that she had missed as a child growing up.

In the years following the Depression, the Olivers were, to some extent, able to recover from the bleak years of poverty. However, they never again lived in the kind of comfort they had known in the 1920s before the Depression hit. Papa Oliver was finally able to resume his profession as a plumber in the late 1930s, but for the most part, even those jobs took him out of town. Once Catherine and Rebecca graduated from high school in 1938 and 1939 and Bill was in the Navy, everyone contributed to the household expenses, and their standard of living gradually improved. Slowly, the US economy was beginning to rebuild, but salaries remained low. It wasn't until the United States entered WWII that the economy was able to return to its full swing.

As a young woman of eighteen, Catherine was happy, but the scarring from the 1930s was ever-present. For the first time in her life, she had many friends and nice clothes, and she was having loads of fun. She loved to help people, and she considered going into nurse training. However, in 1939–1940, the nurse-training program was in a major teaching hospital where the student nurses lived on-site. This was a problem for a couple of reasons. First, Catherine did not want to leave her family. In addition, the cost of the program was high. She was already doing what she could to help her family financially, and this program cost more than either Catherine or the Olivers could afford. There were no student loans in those days, and scholarships went to star athletes, not to nurses.

The Olivers 1919-1939

Mary Catherine Oliver
1938 High School Pictures

The Childhood Days of Francis Royal Ward Junior

The Wards from 1922 to 1938
Salt Lake City

On the other side of the country, Francis Royal Ward Jr. was born on June 5, 1921, in Salt Lake City, Utah. His mother called him Francis, but most people called him Frank. His older brother, Clinton, twelve years his senior, called Frank "the Kid" for most of Frank's childhood.

His mother, Anna Ethelda Crockett, was a niece to Davy Crockett of American folklore. One of four girls and a boy in the Crockett family, she was born on April 13, 1891, in Midway, Utah.

His father, Francis Royal Ward Sr. was second-generation Irish, the second of two boys. Shortly after the Ward family came to the US from Canada, Francis Sr. was born in Clinton, Iowa, in 1882.

Life was good in the 1920s, and the Ward family was happy. They lived in a modest home in Salt Lake City near friends, family, and their Protestant Church. Yes, although they had many good friends and family who went to the Latter-day Saints (LDS) Church, they were not Mormon. Anna Ethelda had been raised in the LDS church but had changed her religion to Protestant when she married Frank Sr.

Mama Ward was the thread that tied the Wards together. The youngest of five children, she never received an education past the fifth grade, which was not uncommon at that time.

After her mother had died at a young age, she moved from one relative to another in Park City and Salt Lake City, Utah. On July 6, 1908, at age seventeen, she and Francis Royal Ward Sr. were married in Salt Lake County, Utah. Papa Ward was a great student with an eidetic memory, and so from the time they were first married, Mama Ward began to educate herself with her husband's help.

Papa Ward worked for the Ford Motor Company until the crash of 1929. When he was unable to find employment after the crash, he supported his family in any way he could. At one point, he was fortunate to find work with the Civilian Conservation Corps, where he worked on projects like the Hoover Dam. Unfortunately, this also meant that he was often gone for long months at a time. Nevertheless, the New Deal saved many families from acute financial distress, and Frank Sr. was grateful to have work.

The differences between Catherine and Frank's experiences during childhood were striking. He was the beloved (but surprise!) second child of older parents who adored him. During his early years, he had a large, fun-loving family of aunts, uncles, and cousins, and there was always something fun going on. The Wards often jumped into their Ford Model T and took off for an impromptu camping trip. Often choosing their destination after they had already hit the road, they would then end up in Yellowstone, Bryce, and Zion National Parks or other places of natural beauty in the mountains of Utah.

Frank was a handsome, happy-go-lucky young man with thick black hair and navy blue eyes. He was mischievous, loving, very smart, and blessed with a good dose of self-confidence mirrored with kindness. In 1938, the world was his oyster. By the time he graduated from South High in Salt Lake City, Utah, with a diploma in commercial art and business, he had also completed two years of ROTC training.

Frank was born into a generation that did not have to

wonder if something was right or wrong. The values that served as the bedrock of the family were clear—and he just knew.

Going West
Los Angeles 1938–1941

Like so many Americans, the Wards went west to California during the Great Depression, looking for a new life. Los Angeles was a pristine, gorgeous city in the late 1930s with streetcars, no smog, and snow-covered mountain ranges, which enclosed the city like a treasured jewel.

Frank's older brother, Clinton, was the first to leave for Los Angeles, where he found a job in the bookkeeping department of the Challenge Creamery Company. Soon after the family's move, Frank Ward Sr. acquired a position at Challenge Creamery as well, where he continued to work until he retired in the 1960s. In 1938, the working man did not think in terms of having a career; folks just worked at any job they could find, hoping to survive.

Life in Southern California was a complete change for this family from Utah. They fell in love with the warm weather and the sunny outdoor lifestyle. The Los Angeles streets were so safe that they were able to walk to church, to the market, and to visit friends. Sometimes, this meant walking through back alleys between long blocks at night, and yet they still felt safe. They were thrilled with outdoor life and often hosted "backyard evening suppers" for friends and family.

From the time they first moved to Los Angeles, they always had someone living with them. Between the Crocketts and the Wards, there were many relatives who wanted to share in this sunny Shangri-La called Los Angeles. There was work for many, and all were welcome.

Frank had many friends, some of whom had also moved from the Salt Lake area to sunny California. He often met his friends at the beach, where they spent the afternoons enjoying the sun and the surf and topped it off with a beach picnic. As the tall and buff member of the group, Frank was always the center pillar when his buddies created a human pyramid on the sand.

All the girls were crazy about this tall Irishman, and he was always surrounded by a handful of young ladies who wanted to be more than just friends. Many a sweet little thing hoped to tickle his desires and win his heart during Frank's teen years, but he was never interested in getting tied down. At age seventeen, he was young, full of great dreams, and going places.

The Wards found a "back house" at 916 ½ West 53rd Street in Los Angeles, which they rented from their front neighbors and property owners, Mr. and Mrs. Hughes. The two-story home looked like an old Craftsman kit house, a design that was common in the early 1900s. They also had two cars: a 1934 Plymouth and a 1935 Chrysler.

Yes, the Wards were happy to be in Los Angeles. They were not rich in money, jewels, or property, but they were wealthy with love for each other. It was this love, and a happiness rooted in their genuine faith in God, which sustained them through thick and thin and carried them through the most challenging times in their lives.

During his early adult years, Frank held down a few different jobs and tinkered with the idea of making military service his career. At one point, he worked for three years as a stock clerk with Bernstein's Original Fabrics. His natural interest in textiles was rooted in his great eye for color and his sharp sense of style. He was always well-dressed and never hesitated to tell you if your colors didn't match!

During the years just before WWII, Frank was busy exploring different opportunities and defining the man he was going to be. A happy-go-lucky young man—a boy-man—he loved to play and to enjoy life, just the way life was supposed to be.

Salt Lake City Home

Frank, 1924
A boy and his dog

Frank's High School
Senior Picture 1938

Camp Roberts Basic Training

December 7, 1941
Los Angeles, California

The weather for this Sunday morning in December was sunny, with temperatures hovering in the mid-seventies. That was probably the best thing about this day, as this was the day the Empire of Japan bombed Pearl Harbor.

It was approximately 8:00 a.m. The Wards were just about to eat breakfast and were looking forward to their short walk to the Presbyterian Church at the corner of their block. Papa Ward worked nights at the Challenge Creamery, so it was a bit of a hardship to rise so early. But he had been a lay preacher back in Utah, and he didn't like to miss church.

The Ward family lived in Los Angeles, California, in a rented home on West 53rd Street. It was a sprawling, two-story house with large rooms. The spacious kitchen had always been the hub of their home: center stage for much of their family time together. Most days, the room was filled with California sunshine: natural light came streaming through the tall white curtains at the windows and was amplified by the unusually high vaulted ceiling above. Their huge kitchen table was always so inviting with its colorful tablecloth—often one which had been lovingly hand-embroidered by Mama Ward or one of her sisters—a fitting centerpiece in this comfortable, homey kitchen.

Papa took a deep whiff of the bacon as he walked into the kitchen and kissed his wife. Lovely church melodies greeted him from the family radio, which was just around the corner in the living room. He smiled at the familiar sounds of the church choir as he sat down at the table. As a family, they tried never to forget the Sabbath and always kept it holy. They all loved the old hymns. Within the next few minutes, Anna Ethelda would be frying up some eggs in the bacon fat and flipping a few flapjacks to serve on the side. He smiled, knowing that Mama loved cooking for him and their two strapping sons.

A few hours later, they were home from church, and dinner was prepared. Suddenly, Clinton rushed into the kitchen, gasping, "Hurry! Something is on the radio!" Within minutes, the whole family had huddled around the radio, listening to the Associated Press news release. The first reports were sketchy and incomplete but offered enough detail to send the family into a state of shock and disbelief. Was it possible? Could they really believe what they had just heard? The Empire of Japan had bombed Pearl Harbor!

Frank Jr. sat up on the sofa and kept listening, unable to believe his ears. "Mother, this means war for sure," he said in a quiet, deliberate voice. He sat there for another moment in a kind of stupor, as if he were trying to more fully grasp the meaning of this news. Then he looked up at her again, and in a voice that was somewhere between muted and angry, he declared more forcefully, "We are at war!"

"Now, Francis," she said, "let's just listen." Mama Ward was always a glass-half-full kind of person – always waiting for the good side of things to emerge in any situation. However, on this day, there would be no "good side" to the news. Shortly after the initial report, CBS followed up with more details as they trickled their way through the news stations. Was it possible? The entire Pacific Naval Fleet had been destroyed in the early morning raid while the men lay sleeping in their quarters!

The Wards all looked at each other as the reality of it all began to settle in. What a black day for the US. At least 2400 men had been killed, and eight battleships along with 150 planes had been lost in the attack.

That day, Ethelda's glass would quickly sink to empty.

One major concern in California was that the Japanese would just come over to the California coast, attack the San Francisco shipping lines and the ports at Los Angeles and San Diego, and then help themselves to the refineries. With this as a very real fear, the West Coast went dark with blackouts as quickly as it could. As it happened, the big California attack that they so feared never did materialize to any significant extent, but some experts believe that the Japanese could indeed have done major damage if they had attacked because the US was so poorly prepared for war.

Everyone who was alive on December 7, 1941, remembers exactly where they were when they heard the news of the bombing. Suddenly, the fear of an attack on US soil was real. At this point, if we didn't enter the war, there was a very real fear that the bullies of the century—Hirohito and Hitler – would soon be on our shores, meeting up in Omaha! Americans all felt an unbelievable need for revenge and retaliation for this evil attack. In response to the collective anger that had so suddenly gripped the whole nation, President Franklin Delano Roosevelt made a momentous decision. On the morning of December 8, 1941, he addressed the nation with his "Day of Infamy" speech and resolutely declared that we were at war with Japan. However, before he finished his address, he added a note of stern reassurance, letting every American know that "We have nothing to fear but fear itself."

According to the "Selective Service Training Act," passed by Congress and put into effect in 1940, all men between the ages of 21–45 were required to sign up with the local draft board. As Frank was only twenty, he was not required to sign up. But he wanted to serve. The day following Roosevelt's speech, he arose early and called his boss at the textile company, saying that he would not be coming in. Within the hour, he was standing in one of the long lines that snaked around the block, leading to the doors of the Army Draft Board.

Frank was interested in serving in the Army Air Corps, the branch of the service that is now known as the Air Force. The draft board told him the first step would be to sign up for active duty in the National Guard. He resigned his position at Bernstein Textiles and, for the next nine to ten months, was stationed with the National Guard at the Presidio in San Francisco, where one of his duties was to guard and protect the Golden Gate Bridge.

Papa Ward was too old to serve, and Clinton (then 32) suffered from high blood pressure, which meant that he was classified as 4F. (High blood pressure had always been the Wards' curse.) This added to Frank's determination to stand up and serve.

In the months that followed, Frank served in the National Guard, waiting for the opportunity to accept a position and training in the Air Corps. His dream was to be a pilot—or at least to fly. Finally, in September 1942, he was drafted and sent to Camp Roberts, California, for six weeks of basic training. He wasn't particularly happy to be going to Camp Roberts, as he had applied to be a cadet in the Army Air Corps training program, a special program that trained young men without college degrees to be navigators, flight engineers, bombardiers, and pilots. In spite of the fact that he did qualify in every category, he received a letter in mid-1942 which read: "You have not been chosen at this time for the USAAC Cadet program." He was seriously disappointed but still anxious to do his duty. So, he left for Camp Roberts.

Interim Thoughts

Frank was honorably discharged from the National Guard a few weeks before he was drafted into the "Army Infantry." He then reported to Camp Roberts in September 1942. The letter below is the first one Frank wrote to his family while in the US Army.

*****

September 3, 1942
Camp Roberts, California

Dear folks,

Well, we finally arrived, but don't ask me how. When we boarded the train Friday evening we went straight to bed, expecting the train to pull out. As it happened, the train did not pull out until 5:00 a.m. the next morning and we didn't arrive at Camp until 1:00 p.m.! When we arrived, the company we were assigned to issued orders that we were not to write home until further notice. (This is the 'further notice.') That Saturday we were restricted to the company area for the whole day. On Sunday we were given the freedom of the post and I made the most of it. We started walking right after breakfast and kept it up until just before lunch.

As for a few of the more interesting details about Camp Roberts ... It covers an area of 58 square miles. With a drill field 4100 feet long and 1200 feet wide, it has one of the largest drill fields in the country. Each battalion has a recreation hall where fellows can play pool and buy soft drinks and beer. That's where I'm writing from now. They have table tennis, reading material, screens for shows, and a jukebox with the latest tunes—and plenty of tables where we can write. Ironically, it is called the "Hideout." So you can see that Uncle Sam is taking good care of his nephews! Each company has its own mess, and the grub is excellent. Our company was given a banner for the best mess. This honor was bestowed on Company A by the old man himself: the "Colonel." Just as we did at Fort Mac (The Presidio, in San Francisco) we go to bed at 9:00 p.m.

and rise at 5:45 a.m.

They have (or shall I say, *I* have) discovered my talents for military life; I have been put in charge of a squad of men!

We will only be here for 6 weeks. Where we go from here, even the good Lord wouldn't know. Incidentally, I'll be able to take a lot of pictures and film is plenty cheap: only 25 cents a roll.

I went to the Holiday Inn the other night, and it was very good. The only problem is that the base is so damn far from any town of any size. They allow weekend passes to about 40% of the companies, based on merits. For instance: Is your bed wrinkled at any time? How is your conduct? Is your personal appearance neat? and so forth. I'm not as worried about that as I am about transportation. Unless you are able to get reservations on the "daylight" (train), you won't get into LA until midnight. But so much for that.

I trust that each and every one of you is in the best of health. As for me, I'm disgustingly so.

In the morning we are going on a hike with a light field pack, bayonet, and rifle. Wow ... tomorrow night I can just hear the moans and groans of fellows with tired and aching feet!

Camp Roberts is not half as bad as I had it built up to be. Yes, it's hot, it's dry, and it's dusty, and also rather barren. But all in all, taking in its good features and its bad, you find that the good will hold the balance. They have four theaters here, and each has the latest and best pictures. They also have what they call a guest house where people can visit a soldier here in camp. The price of the lodgings is 50 cents per night with a maximum stay of three days. So there again, you can see that Uncle Sam is looking out for our interests.

Well, folks, I guess that will be all for right now. Please excuse the writing—I am in a hurry to get this in the mail. Please write soon. Oh yes—they have mail call two times a day here!

As ever,
Frank Jr.

*****

Private Francis R. Ward 195
T.O.P.S. Camp Roberts, California

Dear folks,

Well, today is Thanksgiving, and I am giving thanks for the fact that I have at last found time to sit down and write a letter.

I have been at this camp now for 4 days and I think I'm going to like it, outside of a few inconveniences such as no hot water, no air conditioning and the fact that we are miles away from the main camp. An average day goes as follows: reveille at 0630, breakfast at 0700, and at 0800 we fall out for an inspection with rifles and shoes. The shoes look like a Negro's heel. We are inspected by our upperclassmen, and they don't mind giving out merits and demerits. At 0830 we go to class. We have several different types of classes: lectures, conferences, and practical work. Our professors take more interest in us than a college professor would. A college professor would take interest simply because it is his duty. Here at camp, they put much importance on honor, duty, and country.

One doesn't have much time to do anything outside of studying, shining shoes and cleaning rifles. I think more time is spent on shoes than anything else!

I have to write a summary about myself and my life so far—it's for possible OCS

Did Willie get the car back home OK? After I got to camp I began to wonder if I had left her enough gas … a fine time to think about it!

Have you seen Don?

I got a nice present from the camp. I received notice that I'll be a table waiter for Thanksgiving. Damn it.

Incidentally, I'm running out of razor blades. I've got enough for 5 more days.

How is everything down there? I'll tell you more about camp in my next letter, or when I see you all again. The noon dinner is ready, so here I go again!

Adios,

Frank Jr.

An Autobiography of Francis Royal Ward Junior, 1942
Frank was 21 years old.

In my brief span of 21 years, one might say that my life has neither lacked experiences and thrills, nor has it been filled with them. I have been Mr. Average Man in an average walk of life.

I was born in Salt Lake City, Utah, on June 5, 1921, the second of two boys. My father was born of Irish descent in 1881 in Clinton, Iowa, and my mother was born in Midway, Utah in 1892, of French descent. They were married on July 6, 1908, and my brother Clinton came along on June 9, 1909. So I was 12 years his junior. My father worked for the Ford Motor Company from 1923 to the Crash of 1929, at which point he lost his job. Times were hard, and he was unable to secure another permanent position until we moved to California in 1938.

As a young kid in Salt Lake City, I attended Hawthorne Grammar School. I later attended South High School, where I graduated with a Commercial Business Course Diploma in 1938.

The following year I started my business career in Los Angeles, California with a Textile Jobbers firm. My beginnings with this firm are of little significance, but in the three years of my employment there I grew with the establishment and gained invaluable knowledge of the textile field in general.

My military experience had started during high school with the ROTC, where I was a Platoon Sergeant. In 1942 I resigned my textile job and volunteered for active duty. I was assigned to the California National Guard, where I received invaluable training. After nine months with the Guard, I was honorably discharged, drafted into the Army, and went to basic training at Camp Roberts. I have been considering a career in the military because I like the order and discipline of the service.

I am humbled and proud of my ancestors who a few centuries ago settled this continent and brought forth the American way of life. They have since fought many times to preserve our freedoms and peace. Once again we have taken up the sword and sallied forth to meet the ugly foe. And now I am proud to be one of millions of American men who are fighting so that we may someday go home and resume our American way of life.

I am of the opinion that the world doesn't owe me a living. It is up to me to make my trail over life's highway, picking from the pieces of life's jigsaw puzzle of my life. One of the pieces is Success. One of the essentials for success is Friendship. If a man is a millionaire and has no tried and trusted friend, he has nothing. My life would be of little value without friends. Another piece of the puzzle is Happiness; for the world would be colorless and drab without happiness. In order to obtain happiness, a person must have love and live by and understand the golden rule. Success is not necessarily measured in wealth or fame. If a man has friends and completes his goal, along with love and happiness, he will be able to look back on his life's journey as a success.

O.C. Francis R. Ward 148

Thoughts for "Camp Roberts Basic Training"

The letter dated November 25, 1942, was written during Frank's first Thanksgiving in the Army—the first time he had ever been away from his home and family on the holiday. He loved this all-American holiday, and during every Thanksgiving celebration, he made a point to speak of the things he was thankful for. He celebrated three Thanksgivings during his time in the service: one at Camp Roberts and the other two overseas. In his letters, he spoke of being thankful to be in the present, to be safe, and to be eating well (as opposed to consuming C-rations in a foxhole somewhere).

When he was still in basic training, Frank was accepted into OCS, Officer Candidate School. He knew that he would be moving from base to base over the next few years of his Army career and that he wouldn't need a car while in training. In the above letter written on Thanksgiving (no date), he asked if his girlfriend, Wilma (or Willie, as she was called), had gotten the car back OK. She had taken him back to Camp Roberts in Plymouth after a family leave and had then driven his car back to the Wards in Los Angeles. Willie was mentioned a lot in Frank's letters during those months—until he met a certain Southern gal in Charlotte, North Carolina.

In the early days of the war, following Roosevelt's declaration on December 8, 1941, it was quickly discovered that there were not enough officers or leaders to take our troops into battle. Men who demonstrated leadership abilities were tested, and many of them went on to be "ninety-day wonders." We do not know whether Frank was selected for OCS before or after he was at Camp Roberts.

OCS Training

Fort Benning Georgia
December 1942

To Frank's family from Frank:
December 12, 1942
Fort Benning, Georgia

Dear Folks,

Well, I have finally been assigned to a class (Class 191 by name) and I'm now known as O.C. (Officer Candidate) Francis R. Ward. My new address is:

O.C. Francis R. Ward 39530129
22nd Company 3rd S.T.R.
4th Platoon, Ft. Benning, Ga.

The S.T.R. stands for Student Training Regimen. As I have previously stated, most of my time will be taken up with studies. But until today I didn't realize how true that statement was. Last night I studied from 7:00 p.m. until 9:30, and I still have not finished. We get up at 6:45 a.m. Our first formation is at 7:05 a.m., breakfast is at 7:30, and our first class usually starts about 9:00 a.m.

This morning I was appointed as platoon leader guide. I will hold that rank for a week, and then I will either become company commander or I'll be a man in the ranks. The men here all had ranks when they entered the program, but now that they are here, they are considered soldiers without a rank and are simply called candidates so and so. Next week I will be able to tell you more about it. We go to bed at 10:00 p.m. on weekdays and 11:00 on the weekends. Tomorrow being Sunday, I'll have a busy day.

You asked me what I would like for Christmas. Well, if I began to list my needs I'd fill this tablet and another one—twice! But for one thing, a pair of slippers and it would be great if Client could make me some bookends. I have about a dozen ¾ books and no means of supporting them. Could you find out how much my foot locker weighs, and then figure out how much it would cost to ship it? If it doesn't cost over $5.00 or $6.00, I would like you to send it—and I mean collect, not prepaid. Otherwise, forget it. I'm also sending my camera home. It's illegal to have them on the post and you get a $5,000 fine if you're caught with one. If you can find a recent publication of the officer's guide I wish you'd send it; they are very scarce around here. Oh—and there is a little package coming for you and Dad. Half of what's in it goes to Uncle George and Aunt Virginia.

I'm afraid that particular package will be a little late due to unforeseen circumstances. In another package, I have enclosed one item which I understand it is hard to get as a civilian. You poor civilians should join the Army and have a steak!

The other day when we first came in, there were a bunch of "old timers" watching us. The general theme of their shouts was, "You will be sorry!" Seems that is the byword around O.C. School.

Well, folks, it's back to map reading and personal hygiene, two more hours of study, then to bed.

Love to all,

Frank

p.s. Please send my watch—it's indispensable. If I think of anything else, I'll airmail you.

Adios! (Incidentally: no fair peeking until Christmas!)

*****

To Frank's family from Frank:
January 10, 1943
Fort Benning, Georgia

Dear Folks,

Have you ever heard the sound a bullet makes when it goes over your head at about 2200 feet per second? Sounds like a bee—only I'll guarantee that the sting is considerably worse! We were on the machine gun tactical range this last week learning all about where to place an M.O. in combat and the advantages of life in an M.O. squad—it was all very interesting. We fired a lot of trace ammunition and now I can understand why they set it up to fire low rather than too high. If you can't get the enemy with a straight fire and your bullet's low, it's almost certain that the bounces will finish the job. We finished off the week with a nice GT (general test), and as far as I can ascertain, I missed just two questions.

Yesterday we were on the hand grenade court. The instructor was demonstrating how to take the proper stance for throwing the grenade and how to pull the safety pin. When taking the proper position, the thrower flings his grenade hand to the rear. When the instructor was doing this, he dropped the grenade. Well, you should have seen a bunch of scared OCS freeze in their seats! It turns out that it was a practice grenade which doesn't make any more noise than a firecracker—but the effect was tremendous!

As I have already told Clint, I received your package on the 27th of December and I sure was pleased with its contents. The shave cream was an item to be relished—it's impossible to get it here. Thanks a million for everything!

Well, today is Sunday and I know you can't guess what I did, so I will tell you. I arose at the early hour of 9:00, dressed in my best duds, secured my pass and headed for Columbus.

We arrived there about 10:00, had breakfast at the USO, and from there we went to church. I saw them holding up the portal (elaborate gateway) as I went in. All in all, it was a good sermon. After church, I went to one of the cafeterias and had a very nice lunch which consisted of steak and potatoes, and topped it off with pie à la mode.

They've got me behind the eight ball and I have to rate 32 fellows in the order in which I think they would be good officers. I don't like to do this because I'm afraid that I'll underrate somebody. But everyone has to do the same, so there are about 220 fellows that are behind the same 'ball.'

I am glad to hear that you approved of my selections of gifts. I sure was up a stump as far as knowing what to get (also on the financial end).

Have you heard from Don since Thanksgiving? If you do, tell him that I am just as busy as he is, and I'll find time to write when I can.

Surprise of the month: I have not seen a show since Camp Roberts—I just haven't had time.

How did the Crocketts like the picture? If they don't like it, tell them they can give it back. I got my eye on a cute little southern gal.

After all of my promises to send money home this month, I am finding it an impossibility. I received exactly $15.00 on the 31st and I spent $6.00 for coveralls, $4.00 for books and $3.50 for my radio. I received a partial payment for December so they still owe me part of the December pay. I also raised my pay reservation to $10.00. Sometime in February, you ought to receive a couple of bonds and if you don't, let me know. They are made out in both mom's and my name. If you ever get in a pinch for funds, I want you to use them.

Well, in about 5 minutes I am going in for an interview with my tactical officer. I am not very worried about it because everyone in the platoon is being interviewed.

Well, folks, that is about all for now. I'll write soon—you do the same.

Adios, Frank

p.s. I just had a meeting with my tactical officer. He said I was doing good.

*****

From Frank Senior to Frank Junior:
January 6, 1943
Los Angeles, California

Dear Frank:

Well, now that the holiday season is no more, we can probably settle down to the business of living again. For no matter how we may enjoy them, it is always a relief to see them safely in the rear. Everything considered, it has been an enjoyable season for us, barring your absence from home and some few deprivations forced on us by the war conditions.

So you finally received your package. It was not as long in transit as we feared it might be. Too bad we could not have sent it a week earlier. I hope you found everything in good condition.

So far it looks like we are going to have another of those dry winter seasons like we had a year ago. We have only had slight rains and everything is quite dead. We need a lot more rain in order to help out the crops.

I do not know of much news that might be of interest. We are having our regular January slump and everything is quite dead. The main topic of interest is the extensive rationing move which is scheduled to start February 1st. It will include all canned stuff, dairy products, clothing, and a lot of other items.

The car is running OK, but we do not use it much. Clint has a "B" book of gas ration coupons, so now we are not worried about gas. However, the Chrysler has developed some carburetor trouble and Clint can't get the necessary repair parts. So he may have to use the Plymouth for a while.

We have had several bad fires here recently, and some of them were undoubtedly sabotage. The toll for the past week has included a magnesium plant and two fish canneries. Also, Bing Crosby's home burned with a loss of $250,000. Luckily no one was injured.

We are all fairly well here at home, although Addie has had another one of her attacks, a light one, however.

We do go out, but very little nowadays, and we are becoming quite proficient in the art of conservation—not only of rubber and gas but of money as well. We do not have any trouble getting what food is necessary, but the variety is of course somewhat restricted. And mother sometimes has to go to several shops before she can get enough meat for a meal.

We have been trying to write often enough so there will always be a letter in the mail for you and will continue to do so, but I do not always get enough time at one sitting to write much. I have spent three nights writing this one.

Well, Frank, we will keep you posted on things in general but don't feel that you have to answer every letter individually, as I know you don't have a great deal of time. However, we will be glad to hear from you whenever you can drop a line.

We would particularly like to know about Georgia and its climate. We have perhaps been wrong in thinking it is about like California.

Well, Frank, I will sign off here as I want to get this letter in the morning mail and I will try to write to you at least once a week. Take care of yourself and watch out for the Georgia peaches that we read so much about.

Au Revoir and best wishes,

From, Dad

*****

To Frank's family:
February 3, 1943
OCS, Fort Benning, Georgia

Dear Folks,

Another week has slipped by. I'll only have to say that 5 or 6 more times and I'll be out of here.

The other night we went to study hall and not for the purpose of studying. The Captain decided that it was about time we had a chat. So Class 191 and the Captain had a chat. It was one of those one-sided conversations which wasn't dull. First of all, he talked about officer uniforms. Told us what we needed to graduate in, what we would need after we leave here, and what we wouldn't need, such as Sam Browne belts.

Next on his list, he had a little bad news for us. Due to the fact that the Army is greatly overstocked in 2nd Lieutenants, the infantry school has raised its academic standards and has clamped down on regulations in general. The way things are right now, they'd just as soon flunk a guy out as look at him. We have one factor that is in our favor. The Captain is intent on getting as many officers over the last hurdle as he can. And boy, he's sure trying! Last Monday there was a GI (General Inspection) on the mortar, and boy! Was it a "lulu"! (It had more curve balls than a major league baseball game!) I think I missed about 8 questions—extremely high for me. My average is about 2% which is about a high B. (A new way now of grading ABCD, etc.)

Saturday we fired up the 37 mm anti-tank gun. Boy, was it fun! Our class broke the school record in qualifications on this weapon. When a fellow fires this piece, there is just one thing to remember: watch out for the recoil!

On Sunday, instead of my usual trip into Columbus, I stayed in Camp for the purpose of buying myself a uniform. I bought a very nice blouse—green in color—and a very beautiful exquisite pair of "Pinks" (trousers). Next, I bought a domestic felt Garrison hat, two shirts of khaki color, one shirt which was a green wool gabardine, one pair of green pants to match the blouse, 2 sets of insignias, 1 belt, and a few other incidentals. Grand total to date is $93.02 with a balance of $156.98 that I still have to buy: leggings, raincoat, shorts, a coat, shoes, and a few other miscellaneous items. Maybe I am being an optimist, but I am not. It is just a safety measure to ensure a uniform—if and when we graduate.

There is a little rhyme going around school here that is rather cute. I thought I would pass it on:

Here lie the bones of Lieutenant Jones
A mighty man was he
But he dies on the night of his very first fight
Using the school's solutions

Moral of the story, obvious: don't use the school's solutions!

Now to answer your questions (the ones I can remember): I attend the First Presbyterian Church in Columbus. No, I don't want you to subscribe to the Reader's Digest for me—I can get it in the post here for 15 cents.

Enclosed herein is a meager amount for you to use the way you see fit. Get a new pair of shoes, or a new dress or some records or books ... Oh, hell—just use it!

Adios,

Frank

p.s. Is southern money good in California? Ha! Ha!

*****

From Clinton to Frank:
February 5, 1943
Los Angeles, California

Dear France,

Well in the daily grind and rush I find that right about here on this beautiful warm sunny day I have time to drop you a small note. I think it's my turn to write but even if it isn't, there's no harm done. It is just two thirty, on this the fifth day of February. I'm gazing out the window, as usual, wondering when the company is going to close up. But I hardly think they will, as there is too much invested to do that. So they will just hang on and hope.

Tomorrow is Saturday, and I do hope it remains warm and sunny, as I am starting to paint the Plymouth. I have already painted one wheel, just sort of a test run, and boy, it looks great! It shines like a mirror and the paint dries as hard as steel. I sure wish you were here to try shooting another kind of gun. It's sure fun, but rather expensive for ammunition, tho! If the Plymouth turns out, then I will tackle the Chrysler.

Another sport we "poor civilians' ' are engaging in is to go out and smell out something to eat. That is, we get watery at the mouth visualizing huge steaks smothered in onions, steaming hot strong coffee and other such goodies. After getting into such a frenzied state, and having our sense of smell very acute, we cruise among the markets till a familiar odor is detected like fresh beef, coffee, ham, or bacon—and then the battle is only half won. We have to convince the baron butcher that we are starving. (I usually have a hard time convincing anyone that I'm hungry because of my rotund figure.) I've learned a quick little trick, though: over at the Mexican market and the Latin Quarter there are a great many markets and due to the fact that their patrons can't afford or don't want fresh beef, veal, and other meats, they usually have plenty. Just over the river from the plant here is a large Mexican Central—and in it, huge markets like Vons. Believe it or not, I've been able to obtain steak and roasts for the past three weeks! I was over there today and proceeded without any trouble to get a huge seven-pound rump roast and three pounds of beautiful steak. Boy! I hope not too many others catch on ... The only difficulty is that the butchers are Mexican and therefore we don't understand each other very well. But by the flashing of money and a little sign language, we get along.

Well, everyone is alright. Dad has grown increasingly sleepier. He sleeps all the time except at night—then he has to work. Mom is alright; the only thing I don't like about her condition is that she gets so utterly tired all of the time. Addie's holding up fairly well and Essie is alright. But the only money Essie now has is just what Janice gives her, and that isn't very much. I suppose we'll have to keep her pretty soon, too. What gripes me is that she could be working and making her own way as she isn't getting any younger.

The two cats, Mickey and Maize, seem to be the only sensible ones; they never worry, never pay taxes, always find plenty to eat, and are petted and pampered.

I'm feeling very good and am looking forward to seeing you. You know, after your last letter explaining about the air fare, etc., you had me worried—if you don't show up now, well, it will just break Mom and Dad, and the rest of us won't feel so good either.

Well, brother, the hour is now close to quitting time and I must hurry home to show the folks the beautiful meat I obtained and watch their eyes pop out.

How's everything there with you? Are you ready to make an announcement about graduating from OCS yet? Do you think you are over the hump at OCS? When you come home on your furlough will it be before or after you pass?

Well, brother, I think that is all on the home front tonight. So write soon,

As always, your brother,

Clinton

*****

From Anna Ethelda (Mama Ward) to Frank:
February 10, 1943
Los Angeles, California

Dear Francis,

It was sure good to receive your letters. I got one letter Monday and one today (Wednesday). I feel so happy when I get a letter from you—although your letter Monday had me a little bit worried. I couldn't imagine what you were going to do with "pink trousers," but when Clint came home, he straightened me out. He said you meant "Pinks," which is slang for dress trousers ... is that correct? If not, please explain. I think you are going to look like a million in your new outfit and I can hardly wait to see you in them. Say, what colors are your Pinks anyway? You have me guessing. Thanks, dear, for the twenty—it was sure welcome, but I felt guilty keeping it. Please don't run short.

We sent you a box Monday. You ought to get it by the end of the week. Don't think I was stingy with the shrimp—sometimes we can't even get one can. Saturday, we went to three different markets but could not find any more. I had one can on hand. Let us know how they arrive. I made the cookies—hope they are good.

Clint painted Plymouth Sunday. It looks really nice. He takes it to work most of the time.

Prue was down this weekend, and where do you think she persuaded Clint to take her? You can never guess so I will tell you: to the Russian Ballet! What a man won't do for love! So Monday night he took me to see Bambi. I would not say anything about ballets.

Mrs. Wolf was over a little while ago and told me that Cleo had just graduated and they were resending him to another school. He made it in six weeks! And I thought *you* were smart! You never can tell about some people.

We have been having some cold weather here the past few days with a nice frost on the roofs in the mornings.

I am glad you go to church when you can. One needs the church and what it stands for now more than ever.

Frank, I haven't a doubt in the world but what you will

graduate, and with high marks, too. So I think you're perfectly safe in buying your outfit. Just when is the great day? Or is it a secret? Do they have graduating exercises like West Point, or do they just kick you out when they are through?

How much do you weigh? I am so anxious to see you. Well dear, I guess I have told you all about it. I can't think of anything else. Dad and Clint are both going to write and I know their letters are interesting so I guess I will say so long for today.

God bless you, dear.

with love from,

Mother

p.s.—Please excuse the mistakes. I don't know why I make them—I just do.

*****

March I, 1943

Fort Benning, Georgia

Dear Mom,

Well, I count the days on my hand. There's 10 more days left. Next week we have 3 graded tests. The 1st one on general tactics, the 2nd a general test, and the 3rd is one that has us all shuddering—it's on logistics. We have them 3 days in a row. So here's for another busy week. The schedule for this week is really a tough one. And just to make it a little tougher, at the end of the week we have a 36-hour problem. We go out firing at night and won't get back until Saturday night at about midnight. So as I said before, here's for another busy week.

We finished school that Saturday. We have nothing to do but lay around until the following Wednesday when we graduate. We lost 40 fellows at the board meeting. And, as the saying goes, we expect the ax to fall to the tune of another 30 fellows before it's all over. The innocent bystanders are always the ones who get hurt.

Well, I finished (reluctantly) the last of those cookies. I wished I had more, but the time is short. You know, maybe I shouldn't come home. If you can't find enough to feed the family, then you surely can't find enough to feed me! Oh well, I guess I could starve for a few days. After all, I could stand to lose a little weight. I only weigh 190 pounds.

Last night I was in town to get some luggage and clear up a few miscellaneous details. I also got a pound of cheese and a box of crackers. Boy, I felt like a thief. I hope not.

Well, I've got an hour before church, so I guess I can write a little more if I can think of something else.

I also went down to make reservations on the train, but it seems that I can't make reservations unless I take the Pullman and the Pullman is a little too much. But they told me that I'd be able to get a train alright. So if things go right, I ought to make the connection.

Mom, you know a lot depends on where I'm stationed and when I'm to report to that station. I only hope and pray that it's on or near the West Coast.

How's everyone making out? You know those bookends that you sent me? I could sell them to anyone in the barracks for 3-5 dollars! That's how much notice they have drawn!

You know that there is a lot more to being a Lieutenant than one sees on the surface. He has the lives of 50 men in his hands, and he's responsible for their well-being. It's also a rather cold-blooded affair. In combat, he's allowed to lose just so many men for a given period of time. I hope that I get the chance to keep my 'allotment' below that amount of casualties allowed.

You know, I can say that I've learned a lot here. I only wish I'd studied harder in High School. But we never realize our mistakes until it is too late.

How's Dad? OK, I hope. I still don't think he can beat me in bowling. Tell Clint I'll write to him later. And give my love to Addie and Essie.

Well, mom, I guess that's about all for now.

Love from your son,

Frank

Thoughts for "OCS Training"
December 1942—March 1943

The Americans continued to prepare for war, joined forces with the Allies, and went into battle in North Africa in May of 1942. Overnight, the United States' vast industrial machine began to produce everything from soup to nuts for the war effort. Everyone who was not in the service worked to support the troops in any way they could, and Rosie the Riveter was born. It was a welcome duty for most Americans coming out of the Great Depression, as many were grateful to have steady work and a paycheck.

At this point in time, the United States was prepared for war to some degree. At the same time, there was a handful of ardent isolationists in Congress who knew that the war was inevitable, but they strongly opposed any US involvement in either the European or Pacific theater. The America First Committee was one of the leading factions spearheading the resistance to our participation. Charles Lindbergh was a spokesman for this committee and spoke out against our involvement before the bombing at Pearl Harbor. However, it is worth noting that, after that attack, he did fly numerous missions in the Pacific for the US Army Air Corps.

It was important to Roosevelt to find a way to come alongside the Allies with several concrete measures of substantial support, and it has been well documented that he forced many war preparations through Congress in spite of objections from the isolationists. One of the first actions the United States took was the Lend-Lease Act, enacted in March of 1941. This program offered our ships and some weapons of war to England in a lend/lease arrangement, as well as food, oil, and fuel. (The ships and weapons were ones that we had used during WWI.) The agreement was that England was to return the ships to the US when the war was over ... if there were any left.

There was also a resolution that the US promised to come to the aid of the South American countries if they were attacked by any Axis countries. Roosevelt had already started the peacetime draft, which drafted 1.2 million men and 800,000 reservists in 1940 alone. Then, once we were officially conjoined with the Allies, he ordered the US Navy to attack any German submarine that came too close to the East Coast of the United States. In addition, FDR doubled the size of the Navy. However, much of this newly strengthened Navy was lost in the attack on Pearl Harbor.

Meanwhile, Frank was very confident that he would pass OCS. He had purchased the uniform he would need for graduation, which would serve him thereafter in his position as a lieutenant. Frank's mother had been a little confused when she heard that he was wearing "Pink" trousers (the slang for a dress uniform), and she was in a tither for a while. But it seems that Clinton had been able to set his mother straight on the meaning of the term "Pinks." They all knew that Frank was a man who liked nice clothes. He was a class act, dashingly handsome in uniform during his time in the Army.

At this point in Frank's Army career, he was on his way to becoming an officer. He had done well in Officer Candidate School, reaching the rank of Second Lieutenant. He was just what the commander ordered, and his personality fit military life to a tee. He was honest, hardworking, and smart. He was organized, knew how to take orders, and knew how to give them. Now, he was off to worlds unknown to fight the "ugly foe," as he put it. This enemy threatened to change the American way of life, and there was no choice but to "sally forth" and win this war.

Having completed this chapter in his training, Second Lieutenant Francis Royal Ward received his second lieutenant bars on March 19, 1943. His OCS graduation ceremonies were held at Fort Benning, Georgia, and unfortunately, his family was unable to attend.

The boy-man had just become a man. But here's hoping the boy was not lost forever. He was just 21 years old, and Frank loved being a boy. He went home on leave to visit his family in Los Angeles, California, as a second lieutenant before he was assigned to a post.

While typing the letters for this book, I decided to leave spelling, punctuation, and grammar in the original form in the letters.

Camp Mackall, North Carolina

The 17th Airborne
April–March 1943

Frank graduated from Officer Candidate School on March 19, 1943, and received his lieutenant bars. Shortly after graduation, he was able to go home to California to see his family—as a second lieutenant! As you can imagine, the Wards were very proud of their younger son—not only because he had met with success and recognition in the Army but also because he had grown into quite the officer and gentleman.

They were proud, yes—but they were also deeply concerned about Frank's future. It was wartime, and they knew that lieutenants led their men into battle. They knew that when he returned to North Carolina, he would report to a new assignment and that he could be deployed at any time. And this left them sad beyond words.

This same story was being lived by so many American families at that time: families who were proud of the young sons who had proven themselves as sterling young men during the course of their military training. These were families who fought back the tears and kept a stiff upper lip as they took their boys to the airport or saw them off at the station. These same families resolutely set their own feelings aside as they courageously held down the home front and supported the war effort in any way they could "back home." There are no words to describe the dark cloud of uncertainty that hung over the whole nation at that time, nor are there words for the fears that they fought every day.

Up until the day that Frank and his unit stepped off the train in Rockingham, North Carolina, he did not know where he would be stationed. He was one of 7,970 enlisted men, including 509 officers and 29 warrant officers who had been assigned to a new Army base. This new base was originally established in February 1943 for the training of paratroop regiments and glider Infantry units. It was named Camp Mackall after Private John Thomas Mackall. Private Mackall was a paratrooper who had been fatally wounded during Operation Torch, the Airborne segment of the Allied invasion of North Africa in 1942. The day he was wounded was the day that construction had begun on this camp, and because he was the first paratrooper to die in WWII, they named the camp in his honor. "Thunder from Heaven" was their motto, and the Eagle Talon Claw was their insignia. To this day, Camp Mackall is used to train Army Special Forces.

When Second Lieutenant Frank R. Ward and his unit arrived at this brand new Airborne command training center on April 1, 1943, the camp had not even officially opened as a training facility. Still under construction when he arrived, the camp was still a vast expanse of North Carolina wilderness. In his letters, Frank spoke about the forest of Southern pines and the sand dunes where the 17th Airborne would train for the battles in foreign lands—a task they would take on with a vengeance.

The 17th Airborne was made up of two groups: the Paratroopers and the Glider Air Troopers. History tells us that the two did not get along at first because the paratroopers were volunteers and the glider troopers were draftees. However, the hard feeling soon thawed when the paratroopers rode in gliders for the first time and experienced the uncontrolled landing that comes with a vehicle that has no engine. Because the gliders were towed to the point of deployment and then released to land without engines behind enemy lines, they were often referred to as the air troopers' "flying coffins." Yes, Frank got his wish to fly and be in the air ... *but in a glider?*

*****

March 30, 1945
Co. A., 193rd Glider Infantry 17th Airborne
Camp Mackall, North Carolina

Dear Folks,

I'm sorry I was so late letting you know of my safe arrival. Communications have been poor here, and I wasn't able to wire until Saturday.

The trip to get here was pleasant and uneventful. I was able to get a good coach in El Paso, and I had a very pleasant trip from there to New Orleans. I met a cadet and an officer on the train, and we had a very nice time getting to know each other. When we pulled into New Orleans, we had just missed our connection by 15 minutes—boy, was I mad! The next train wouldn't pull out for another 6 hours, so the three of us decided to see the town. We walked around in the French Quarter, Bourbon Street, and a few other parts of the city. Then we got the train at 5:00 p.m. As luck would have it, I got on one of those coaches that make a soldier want to go over the hill—but I managed. Then we arrived in Atlanta. So, to while away the time I went shopping, had supper, and went to the show. I managed the time along with the bankroll. I arrived at Hoffman not at 4:35, but at 7:35.

The name of our camp is actually Camp Mackall, formerly Camp Hoffman. It was recently renamed after the 1st parachutist killed in action, Private John Thomas Mackall.

The nearest towns of any size are Southern Pines and Rockingham (more about Rockingham later). We get our recruits on or about the 15th and start training about then. Right now we are training the Cadre and getting company areas in shape.

Boy, I thought Benning was tough—but that was *kindergarten* next to this! The cadence is stepped up to just a little below double time. Our first day we went on an orientation "walk"—it was really a *run*. I only had my dress shoes, and by the time I got back my feet were very, very sore. We have a saying around here, "Don't be as tough as the paratroopers—make them be as tough as we are." Today we went on a hike. The ultimate objective is to be able to double time it for a full half hour and still be able to be on the scene to fight. This is a really tough camp.

You know, this business about being a Lieutenant isn't a cinch, but I'll manage.

We had a very interesting experience last Sunday. We were in Rockingham, about 10 miles from camp. We had gone to church and were walking around wondering what to do. We noticed 2 girls, 2 paratroopers, and a middle-aged woman walking down the other side of the street. They threw a high ball salute to us, and we returned it. As we passed, one of the Lieutenants made the remark, "Those parachutists are doing better than we are." Then 30 seconds later the lady asked us if we would like to come home for dinner with her. We accepted and had a very interesting time. We also have an open invitation to return.

There's a town about 10 miles from here that is very beautiful and also very ritzy. Last Saturday night we got stuck there; we couldn't get home, and we couldn't get a hotel room. In the end, it cost $8.00 to get out of the damn town! So we're looking into getting a car—an inexpensive one!

Folks, I'm sorry I wasn't able to wire sooner, but as I previously stated, the communications are in an uproar. Hereafter my letters will be regular. It's just this business of getting moved around and settled down that keeps you on the run—to say nothing of the "old man."

Well folks, with all of this double time, I had better get a little rest. So I am bed bound.

Adios,

Frank

*****

To Clinton from Frank:
April 1943
Camp Mackall

Dear Clint,

The day is Sunday, the hour 1600, and the weather, damned hot. My activities have been confined to going to a show and writing a couple of letters. I am recuperating from my week's work. We had the most enjoyable time. There was only one thing wrong, and that was the washing facilities. Have you ever tried to wash out a canteen cup? Well, try it some time. What is even *worse* is *shaving* out of it.

Not long ago our formation officer Colonel Stubbs called a meeting of all the officers in the 193rd Glider Infantry and proceeded to give us a little speech. He stated that in a recent conversation with General Miley, the General had hinted that our basic training would be cut short on this side. Yesterday we got steel helmets. Our division is pretty close to the top of the priority list—put two and two together. Of course, it may not mean anything, but who knows other than Franklin and Winston. I can just hear Franklin saying to Winny ... "Well Winny, old boy, I've got 3 or 4 Airborne Divisions that I'm sure would be more than glad to help take Cologne." And then Winny says, "Franklin, how soon can they arrive in England?" Franklin: "Well, give me 3 more months, and they will be ready." And so the 17th Division is ready. Of course, other than the rumors and steel helmets, all of this is just supposition. This is information for your ears only. I don't even want mom to know. I will let her know when the time comes for us to move.

Clint, I'm darned glad that you've taken up Civil Defense work. I think you will enjoy it very much.

Clint, I wish you could find a nice place to move to. I think that if mom had a place of our own, where she could do as she pleased, that there would be a great change for the better.

Yes, you can send my tripod. Once in a while, I'm able to get films at the P.X.

The Airborne personnel and the parachutists mix it up quite a bit around here. But outside of that, things are quiet. One of my boys is still over the hill. It's really going to be bad on him when they catch up with him. If he's termed as a deserter in time of war, it's punishable by death.

They sure are giving us enough firing practice with the M1 Rifle. Tomorrow we go to the landscape target range and fire some more. The next day we went to the anti-aircraft range, and from there to the moving target range. So when we do hit combat, the men ought to know pretty well what their rifles will do, also pretty well what they can do with them.

Well, Clint, I guess that is about the limit of it. Write soon and be good.

Adios amigo,

Frank

("Loose lips sink ships" was printed on his stationery.)

Thoughts for "Camp Mackall, North Carolina"
April to September 1943

March and April of 1943 seemed to be a starting point for Frank to get settled in a unit. In the months to come, the Camp would develop into a marvel of wartime construction. Formerly an area covering 62,000 acres of North Carolina wilderness, it would shortly become a bustling training ground with 65 miles of paved roads, a 1,200-bed hospital, five movie theaters, six huge beer gardens, a complete all-weather airfield with three 5,000-foot runways, and 1,750 buildings. But when Frank and his unit settled in for their training, the camp was very simple in design. Most of his time was spent in the great North Carolina outdoors and felt like one big campout—but with guns and rifles. As a kid and as a young man, Frank had loved to camp in the beautiful mountains of Utah with his family, so his life at Camp Mackall was right down his alley.

It was the intense training that made it all so grueling. This 17th Airborne unit was an elite group that would be dropped behind enemy lines in gliders and land in the roughest of terrain. In the meantime, they knew they were being trained to become killing machines. In their night maneuvers, they routinely captured villages and destroyed them.

After all the running in double-time up and down hills during their maneuvers, they were in remarkable physical shape. Beyond all the physical exercises, there was a great deal of mental, emotional, and practical training as well.

Much of their regimen was concentrated on becoming proficient with the guns of this war: the M1 rifle, the M1897 Shotgun, the M1A1 Thompson and M3 "Grease Gun" (both submachine guns), the M1 rocket launcher (nicknamed the "bazooka"), and M2 flamethrower, to list a few. It was critically important that each man knew how to disassemble his weapons, clean them, reassemble them, shoot them, and then disassemble, clean, reassemble, and shoot them again—*and* in record time. The men practiced this until they could almost do it in their sleep. They knew that in the weeks to come, they would have to depend on their weapons as much as they did on each other.

In addition to becoming expert marksman, they learned to be excellent map readers. With this kind of comprehensive training, the men knew that the Army was saving their unit for a special assignment. In one letter to his brother, Frank speaks of the possibility of his unit going into Europe to help with the liberation of France, adding, "Believe me, this Lieutenant has big plans for Hitler!"

In one of his letters to Clint, Frank talks about how he would like to help clean up those "Zoot Suiters." This is a term that referred to a particular group who were vilified as being unpatriotic—which was difficult to tolerate during wartime. Zoot suits were considered luxurious apparel in the 1940s and were especially popular among young Latino men. Unfortunately, those who wore them incited anger among those who were doing their best to support the war effort by, among other things, complying with rationing and leading a frugal lifestyle. At a time when the tension in racial and ethnic relations was at an all-time high in California, there was an incident nicknamed the "Sleepy Lagoon" in which a young Latino had been killed in a Los Angeles barrio. This incident fed local tensions and led to the Zoot Suit Riots in the streets of Los Angeles between the Mexican-Americans and the European-American sailors and marines. The soldiers stationed in Southern California at the time were especially incensed at the sight of those wearing zoot suits because they had pledged their lives in service to their country, and they saw this as a flagrant disregard for the spirit of the times. This explains Frank's anger at the Zoot Suiters—and his support of those who participated in the riots against them.

Frank was stationed at Camp Mackall from April until September 19, 1943, when he left to go to war. He learned to love North Carolina, the people, and the towns. He and his friends attended church in Rockingham, often followed by dinner and a show. They ventured to Myrtle Beach and discovered Charlotte. However, apart from a ten-day leave in August to visit his family in California before his deployment overseas, this six-month period had meant a tremendous amount of physical and mental work for Frank and his fellow young soldiers. Even so, I believe that Camp Mackall was a positive experience for Frank and that he left with nothing but good memories of his time there.

It was during his time at Camp Mackall he met the "little southern gal" whom he talked about in his letters to his family. Little did he know back then that this little Southern gal would go on to be an important part of his future.

MARCH WAR NEWS:

- Devastating Allied convoy losses in the Atlantic due to increased German U-boat activity. The middle of the Atlantic is apparently not sufficiently covered by Allied planes or ships.

- General George S. Patton leads his tanks into Gafsa, Tunisia.

- Montgomery's forces begin a breakthrough in Tunisia, striking at the Mareth Line. (The Mareth Line was a line of fortifications built by the French to protect Tunisia from surrounding countries.)

- American tanks defeat the Germans at El Guettar, Tunisia.

Catherine with her friends at
Myrtle Beach, August 1943

Wait for Me, Mary

Myrtle Beach
Friday, August 7, 1943

It was still warm in her bedroom when Catherine popped out of bed. The August heat and humidity were stifling in Charlotte. She was excited about this day; she would be going to the beach for the weekend with two friends from work. Her friend Dump was going to drive, and Dump's roommate, Millie, who was married to a soldier overseas, was coming along for the fun.

"Now, Mama," Catherine pleaded, trying to console her mother, "I just *love* the beach, and I don't burn—I just tan! I'll be alright." Even at 24 years old, her mother, Dora May Oliver, would worry about her oldest daughter when she was away. But she knew she was a good girl.

"I just don't know ... What is so great about the old sandy beach, anyway? Lordy, Lordy! Help me, Jesus!" Mama would say, mumbling under her breath in disapproval.

Dora May Oliver was rather a homebody and had never ventured far from home. "I just don't know," she drawled in her fine Southern accent, shaking her head and mumbling to herself as she continued to fix breakfast.

Myrtle Beach was the favorite beach spot for both North and South Carolinians. Close to three Army bases, it was especially popular with local servicemen who were eager to forget the war just for a few hours.

Her friend Dump (we are not sure how she came by that name) had a car, which was useful because the Olivers did not own a car and Catherine had never learned to drive. Catherine was doing her hair when Dump arrived a bit early to pick her up for their big day. She rushed to collect all of her things and was careful not to slam the front door on her way out. Her mother hated it when the door slammed. "Bye-bye, Mama," she yelled again, just to make sure her mother knew she was leaving.

At 24, Catherine was a young woman with a lot of friends. She was happy, funny, loving, beautiful, and full of life—and believed in having a good time! And that's exactly what she had planned for this weekend. She knew that with Dump and Millie along, they were sure to have a great time.

With a sparkling smile and a carefree laugh, Catherine was exciting to her pursuers. As one expression of her support for the war effort, Catherine had been writing to three or four servicemen—and many a beau would have been happy to sweep her away—but Catherine was not smitten with any of them. When it came to her occasional dates and her wartime pen pals, she was only interested in being friends—just a friend, with no benefits. She didn't mind playing or flirting; however, she was a Southern lady at heart. One thing was sure: no one ever wanted to see her cross over from sassy to fiery. The truth is, Catherine had a temper. Lots of boys had stopped in their tracks at the first sign of that flash in her eyes, wondering what they had done to make her flare.

Catherine worked in the bookkeeping department of Associated Transport, tracing the company's lost shipments. And because it was wartime, she also volunteered at the Red Cross as a nurse's aide. She was very proud of her status as a nurse's aide and often bragged that she gave the best back rubs in town.

Catherine jumped into Dump's car with all of the eagerness of a child going to an amusement park. She just loved the beach. She never went into the water because she didn't swim. Besides, she didn't like to get wet because, well, she was just too pretty! But she did love to get "toned up," as she would say. She loved to walk down the surf line to get the back of her legs tan, and she laid in the sun for hours, sometimes putting her feet in the water once or twice, just to cool off. She preferred to wear a "sun suit" rather than a swimsuit because she could get the same results without getting wet. A sun suit consisted of a halter top and some short shorts, a short skirt, or culottes. Her dark olive tan showed off her figure, and the sun suits were flattering enough to show off just what she wanted to show. Besides, with a sun suit on, she couldn't go in the water for sure.

The girls had just passed the South Carolina border on Highway 9 to Myrtle Beach when they noticed that they were being followed by three servicemen in another car. The guys slowed down when the girls slowed down, and they sped up when the girls sped up. They felt sure that the men must be from a base close by—either Camp Mackall or Fort Bragg.

"Hey, Dump, do you know the boys in that car?" Catherine asked.

"No, Cat, do you think we *should* know them?" she smiled in her Southern drawl.

Just then, the servicemen's car pulled up alongside. "Hey there, you lovely things, where are you going this wonderful day?" the blond one yelled out the window.

Just then, Catherine noticed the boy in the front seat. He was riding shotgun and smiling as he almost hung out of the window. It was clear he was enjoying every minute of this chance encounter.

"Now, just wouldn't y'all *like* to know where we're going?" Catherine teased in reply.

"Now, come on, girls, you can tell us! We're officers in the United States Army!" said the dark one in front. "I bet you're going to Myrtle Beach," teased the blond in the back seat.

At first, the girls gave the boys the cold shoulder—as all good, proper Southern ladies should—but that didn't last long.

They were having too much fun laughing and giggling at the boys' bold attempts to get to know them on the fly.

Catherine couldn't take her eyes off the good-looking, dark-haired young man sitting in the front seat of the other car. Of course, she tried *not* to look, but somehow, she just kept turning her head his way. He was like a magnet.

"But we are officers—two lieutenants and a captain! So, you can tell us," one said the next time they pulled up beside the girls.

"Sure, that's right, and we are Betty Grable and Rita Hayworth!" (two popular pin-up actresses during the war years). Over the next few minutes, the handsome officers kept trying their luck, flirting back and forth with these Southern gals in the other car. But eventually, the girls pulled away, eager to get to the beach.

As soon as they arrived, the girls signed in at their hotel and unpacked for the weekend. Even in 1943, beach rates were high, but by splitting the bill three ways, it was affordable. Catherine was excited. She had come down with her friends and her sister many times before, and she knew Myrtle Beach well. Every summer, they would come and stay for a few days or a week. She knew the restaurants, the dance clubs, the fun spots, and all the shops. Once the girls had unpacked, they headed straight for the waterfront; the afternoon was still young.

The guys were very new to this Southern-Atlantic paradise, but they were headed for the beach too. There might be a war going on, but they wouldn't be fighting on this day in August! Heck, no! They were here for some R and R! They quickly found a hotel and took a few minutes to settle in.

"Hey, let's go down and see if we can find those girls from the highway! Whaddya say?" said Smokey, the blond lieutenant. He was the loud one and a little on the reckless side.

When they arrived at the water's edge, the men looked around. It wasn't long before they spotted the girls. "Well, gents, look who we have here! If it isn't the girls from the highway!" Smokey grinned as he came up to the three girls stretched out on the sand. The girls were secretly pleased to see that their highway pursuers had managed to find them. Now that they had met up on the beach, the girls *knew* the day was going to be filled with fun.

Catherine, Dump, and Millie had already set up for the afternoon, lounging on their beach towels and working on their tans, when the men showed up. "Hello, ladies! Isn't this just amazing, running into you like this!" the captain said as they walked up to the spot where the girls were sunning themselves. "It must be fate," Frank said with a little devil in his smile. Before they knew it, they were all in a lively conversation. From the moment this little dating game started, it seemed that Frank and Catherine were an instant and natural pair.

"My name is Frank—what's yours?" he asked with a beguiling smile.

"My name is Catherine, but most people call me Cathy." The game went on from there. "Where are you from, soldier?"

"I'm from the land of sunshine—Los Angeles, California," Frank replied. Catherine noticed the way he talked. She just loved his "Yankee accent."

Minutes turned into hours as they walked on the beach, taking pictures in the surf. Before they knew it, the August sun was sinking low in the sky. Frank was fascinated with Catherine's Southern drawl, her laugh, and her Southern sweetness. He liked her petite figure and her style. She was different from all of the other girls he had met or dated before. She sure was a pretty, pretty girl, this Southern gal.

Frank noticed another thing. After talking for hours, he could tell that they shared the same values, and that impressed him. She was wholesome. He liked the way she talked about her family, and she had a strong faith. But best of all, he liked the way she flirted and teased with that sugar-sweet Southern drawl.

As Catherine listened to Frank, she couldn't get enough of his "Yankee accent." His deep blue eyes beamed with mischief, and she loved his smile. On top of that, he was charming and drop-dead gorgeous! Even with those white legs that turned bright pink before the day was over! It had only been a few hours, but she felt an undeniable attraction to this handsome officer.

It had been a lovely day, and none of them wanted it to end. So even as the sun headed steadily for the horizon, they knew they should make plans for the evening. The girls stopped back at the hotel just long enough to change into some lively colored dresses for the evening. Catherine's red-and-white sleeveless sundress had a tiny floral pattern, a square neck, and a fitted bodice. Red was a good color for her, and she loved that dress. It showed off her tiny waist, and because it was hemmed just above the knee, she could show off the tan of which she was so proud.

The group had decided to go to the Ships Ahoy restaurant for supper, only a short way down the boardwalk from the girls' hotel. When the officers picked them up at their hotel, Catherine was stunned to see Frank in his uniform. She had been captivated by his good looks when they first met, but now he was movie star handsome: Robert Taylor, Tyrone Power-kind of handsome. Did he have any idea how good-looking he was, she wondered? He certainly didn't act like it, she thought to herself. She felt herself blushing at the sight of this tall, handsome officer, but she tried not to let it show. As much as she wanted to be a lady, she just couldn't help but stare.

The Ships Ahoy did not fail to delight. Frank and Catherine ordered a delicious steak with all of the trimmings and topped it off with a Coca-Cola. Catherine was not a drinker and didn't care to spend time with those who were. Frank was 22, and even though he might drink with his friends at the Officers' Club, he wouldn't drink around the ladies, and certainly not with a date.

After supper, they walked down the boardwalk to the dance club at Myrtle Beach Pavilion. Catherine was so pleased to be on his arm as they walked. As they passed other servicemen from the base, the non-commissioned and enlisted men would stand and salute Frank when they saw his gold bars.

At the dance club, they danced to "Wait for Me, Mary," "Sunday, Monday, or Always," and "Close to You." It was such a lovely evening; they danced and danced and danced some more. Both Catherine and Frank enjoyed dancing, and they found a natural fit in each other's arms. When the band played "Irene (Goodnight Irene)," Catherine knew it was the last dance, but she didn't want the night to be over.

They strolled down the boardwalk and found a diner where they could grab a midnight snack. Frank ordered a hamburger and bought Catherine a bacon-and-tomato sandwich with a Coca-Cola. As they walked back to her hotel, they were both thinking that this was the perfect ending to a perfect day. They had so much fun.

The next day, the officers found the girls on the beach again, working on their tans under the South Carolina sun. Catherine was the first to comment on Frank's pink sunburned legs. He brushed it off as if it were nothing, even though it hurt like hell. Some idle chatter followed: conversation about the music of the night before, the people that the girls worked with back in Charlotte, and more. Then suddenly, Frank said that he was trying to arrange for leave to California for two weeks. Catherine listened intently.

Frank mused idly about how he wanted to take the train home to Los Angeles to see the country, even if he did have to stand up halfway across the country to do it. As he spoke, Catherine could tell how anxious he was to see his family and friends.

"Well, Lieutenant, just who *else* are you going to see when you get there?" she asked with a teasing smile in her voice. "How many girlfriends do you have waiting for you back home?"

"I have some friends at home," Frank replied, noticing the spark in her eyes.

"What are their names?" Catherine pushed the subject.

"Well ... I have a few friends: Don, Alma, Vern, Carol, and Wilma."

"So, who is the sweetest of them all?" she asked, pushing even more.

"Well, before I went away, Carol was pretty sweet—but I don't know about now." He paused. "Let's go for a walk and forget about my friends in California," Frank said, eager to change the subject. He was feeling a little uncomfortable with the conversation.

They strolled for a while in the sand near the surf when suddenly, Frank said enthusiastically, "Hey, let's go into the water!" It was almost as if he were proud of himself. He may have been a lieutenant in the US Army, but he was at the beach to have a great time. The boy in this boy-man was there to play and have fun with this "little southern gal."

"Uh ... I don't swim," she said quietly.

"Oh, don't worry—I'll save you!" he grinned. "Come on! It's not cold at all!" The warm Atlantic water was not at all like his beloved Pacific. "The water here is almost like bath water," he said, trying once more to coax her to come in.

"No! I don't like that old water," she declared emphatically, with a lot more determination in her Southern drawl.

"So why do you come to the beach?" he laughed playfully. Then, in an instant, before she knew what was happening, he had pulled her into a small wave. Shocked and drenched, she pulled away, but he just kept pulling her back into the water again. What he didn't know was there was a large rock hiding under the water where they were playing.

What a picture it was to see this six-foot, handsome, strong man pulling this 5'4" petite young woman into the water. Genuinely annoyed at the thought that her Prince Charming kept pulling her into the water, she continued to fight to get back to the warm, dry sand. But the more she protested, the more he had a ball, just laughing and giggling and enjoying the entire episode. He just loved to tease.

"Ouch!" she screamed loudly, now completely out of sorts. "I told you I didn't want to go in that old water, and now you've hurt my foot!" She fought back the tears as she limped back down the beach to her blanket. Thoroughly annoyed, she let him know in no uncertain terms that she was in pain—and a lot of it. Stricken at the thought that she might really be hurt—but confused about whether or not it was partly an act—he spent much of the rest of the weekend apologizing, over and over again. He saw that she was walking and not limping too much, so he couldn't tell—was she really hurt or not? He really didn't know *what* to think.

Well, that was a great way to impress this beautiful Southern gal! Frank knew he had caught her eye, but now he had also managed to annoy her. Not only had she hurt her foot, he had also pulled her into the water, which she clearly hated. Not a great way to start off if he wanted to win this girl's heart ...

Catherine could have gone home with her sore foot; nevertheless, she didn't go home. In spite of the fact that she really was in pain, there was no denying that she was taken with this handsome soldier and eager to spend more time with him. So, she stayed for the rest of that Sunday. On the other hand, she didn't miss an opportunity to play the convincing part of the damsel in distress who had been injured at the hands of this "Yankee."

With most of the afternoon's drama behind her, they spent the remainder of their time together eating, taking pictures, and dancing. Late that afternoon, they went on a tour through Brook Green Gardens, a well-known Myrtle Beach landmark whose romantic paths were strewn with beautifully manicured flowers and shrubs, statues, and captivating water features. Spending their last few moments together at this iconic site was the perfect way to end this perfect weekend at Myrtle Beach.

The hour was late, and the time had come to get back to the base or go AWOL. But Catherine was taken by this lieutenant, and so she accepted a ride home to Charlotte with him and his fellow officers. They arrived in Charlotte about 3:00 a.m. after a long and perfect day.

As they were saying their goodbyes, Frank told Catherine that he would call her when he got back from California, adding that he would show her the pictures that they had taken at the beach together. It was late, they were both tired, and at this point, he was unsure about the girl from Charlotte with the smile that sparkled and teased. This girl with such a sweet, sweet Southern accent ... Had he lost her when he tossed her into the ocean, or would he one day have a chance to dance those dreamy slow dances with her again? Oh, he hoped so! She was like no one he had ever met before, and it would be a shame to lose her after such a special weekend together ...

The very next day, Frank's two-week furlough came through. Two days later, he was on the Southern Pacific train headed for El Paso and then Los Angeles. It would be a long trip, but it would be worth it to finally get to see his family and friends at home after the arduous weeks of training at Camp Mackall.

In the meantime, Catherine was limping around, her foot swollen and in pain, and she was not enjoying the tail end of her summer at all.

Over the next few weeks, they both thought of each other often. They thought back on the great weekend they had had, the fun times they had shared, and, of course, the dances they had danced—especially to "Wait for Me, Mary." It was with these memories that they first began to dance their way into each other's hearts ...

The Officers and the "Souther Gals" from Charlotte
at Myrtle Beach

Frank & Cath
August 1942

Catherine's Boyfriends before her Lieutenant

Dear Jack

On August 12, 1943, three days after she returned from vacation at Myrtle Beach, Catherine was still in a lot of pain, and her whole foot had turned black and blue. After taking a few X-rays, the doctor assured her that nothing was broken. However, her foot was severely swollen, and two toes were badly sprained. Truth be told, she had a talent for making things sound a little more dramatic than they actually were. If this was one of those times when she was guilty of a little grandstanding, we will never know.

In a surprise letter, Catherine wrote to "Jack" to remind him that he was responsible for her sprained foot with all the swelling and bruising. She addressed the letter to Lieutenant "Jack" Ward. Did she know that Frank's name was not Jack? She was writing to four or five servicemen at that time, so was she confusing her lieutenant with another young man named Jack? We will never know; we can only guess, and of course, in the years that followed, she would never say one way or the other. Still, the letter was a sure-fire way to get "Jack's" attention!

In the days that followed their wonderful weekend together, Catherine was a little miffed that a certain lieutenant had not checked in to ask about her injured foot. The story goes that it was hot in Charlotte that summer and her evenings were spent at home, soaking her injured foot in hot, salted water without the tiniest bit of sympathy from that lieutenant. Yes, the same lieutenant who had pulled her into the water and laughed when she didn't want to go in. No dancing for her now, while "Jack" was off on leave. Meanwhile, he was probably dancing with "who-knows-who" in Los Angeles, California ... (Was it Carol? Or Willie?) Anyway, he was thousands of miles away, dancing with other girls, a whole world away from Charlotte. And here she was, soaking her foot every night, not even able to get her foot into a shoe! Time to drop "Jack" a line and get his attention.

This was the first letter she ever wrote to Frank—the first of hundreds.

*****

To Jack (Frank) from Catherine:
August 12, 1943

Dear Jack,

Surprised? Go ahead! How did I get your address? Oh! *That's a military secret!*

First of all, we got home OK—about 3:30 Monday morning. It was 4:00 am before we got to bed. We were a dopey gang Monday, don't let anybody fool you!

Now, as for my foot—well, I am still a crip. That is all I have heard all week. It wasn't getting any better, so I went to the doctor today. He was fairly alarmed when he saw that it was swollen twice the size of my other foot, and blue all over. He reassured me that it wasn't broken, but did tell me that I had a bad sprain in two toes.

Funny, ain't it? Not really ... I have to stay off it as much as possible, which is hard! Even as I am sitting here writing to you, I am soaking it in hot salt water: something I have to do for two hours every night! Oh! And the *bad* part is, I can't even wear any shoes for two or three weeks! Oh yes, I have two broken blood vessels—that's what made it look so blue. Oh well, that's enough about the old crip.

Now for you—how have you been? Those little pink legs of yours, are they any better? I bet they felt good on Monday. Was the Captain good to you? If he wasn't, just let me know—I will fix him!

How is the furlough? Are you going home? Jack, if you do, I hope you have a wonderful trip. I hope Carol is just as sweet

as ever. I bought a new record today, "Wait for me, Mary"—
Have you heard it? Ha! Ha! It is a new one. Ha! Ha!

No kidding, Jack, I hope you enjoy your little trip home
because there is no place like home ... Ain't that right?

Now, do you want to try for the $64.00 question?

Bye for now—don't forget the picture.

Remember,

"Katie" (Crip)

PS: Excuse the handwriting—I am writing on my knees!
Tell the Captain hello—and Smokey, too!

*****

To Catherine from Frank:
August 25, 1943
Los Angeles, California

Dear Katie,

Well, the vacation is fast drawing to a close, darn it. But
they say that all good things must come to an end. One thing
I'm not looking forward to is the trip back "home" (Camp
Mackall).

Oh, yes—how's the foot by now? OK, I hope. I still thought
you were kidding me when you told me you had hurt it.

This old home town of mine looks pretty good, but also
so very dark and dreary. There are no neon signs visible on
the streets, and very few street lights left that haven't been
dimmed out. Despite the fact that the town is dark and dreary,
it still has the inner spark which keeps it going. I paid a visit
to the beach a few days ago, and nearly got another bad case
of sunburn.

As yet I haven't received those pictures, but as soon as I
do, I'll bring them around.

Did you see Smokey when he was in Charlotte a couple of
weeks ago? His hair has really turned blond.

Well, I'll be back at Camp on Tuesday, or I'll be in the guardhouse—one or the other. Then I'll be up to Charlotte to see you as soon as possible after I get back to Camp.

Well, Katie, this letter has been in a glider with motors (an airplane), and I don't know if I trust that kind of transportation.

Adios amigo,
Frank

*****

To Catherine from Frank:
August 31, 1943
Camp Mackall, North Carolina

Dear Katie,

Boy, what a trip. If I ever take one like that again, it will only be because I'm going for good. The trip out wasn't half bad, but oh, coming back it was murder! I daresay I stood up halfway across the continent! But live and learn.

I received a slight shock when I got back to Camp and found the barracks all nailed up and not a soul in sight. I was beginning to think that maybe they had all moved to California. But no such luck. They were only on bivouacs, running platoon problems.

I called you up last night (or rather it was around eight this evening), but to my disappointment, there was nobody home. I told you that when I got the pictures of Myrtle Beach, I'd bring them up and show them to you. Well, it's even better than could be expected. The Captain has also received his movie film and says that they are very good pictures. So the Captain and I were able to duck our few details for this coming weekend, and have decided that now would be a good time to give you a preview of some of our handiwork with cameras. We will not be able to get away from here before 1800 (6:00

pm to you civilians) Saturday. So we won't be in Charlotte before 8:00 p.m. (2000 my time.)

I hope your foot is better. Let's see—it was two sprained toes and two broken blood vessels? Well, according to Army medical specifications, you should now be ready for action. The medical officers told me that sort of injury was good for two weeks of "goldbricking." All kidding aside, I hope it is better.

Well, we've got a night problem to run yet, so I guess that I'll have to go out and get myself lost. Until Saturday night,

Adios, Frank

*****

To Frank from Catherine:
Tuesday night, August 31, 1943

Dear (Jack) Frank,

Better known as Frank, you didn't forget to write, DID YOU? How was the trip back? It was a long trip, but it was worth it. There is no place like home ... ain't that right, soldier?

Well, Crip is about to recover. I am in shoes this week for the first time. No, Frank—I wasn't kidding you when I told you I hurt my foot. It's been terrible. I went to the doctor twice, and have been off it as much as possible for the past three weeks. The hard part was I had to stay home and soak it every night for two hours. That wasn't much fun, as hot as it has been, to soak my foot in *hot water* for two hours.

That is enough of that—it is all well now.

Frank, as soon as you get the pictures, send them to me. You said you might be in the guardhouse. It is not nice to keep people waiting. So bring them or send them... I can hardly wait to see them!

By the way, when you come up, bring Smokey with you or

one of your friends for Dump. We will have fun, OK? Don't get me wrong—I would like for you to come up by yourself, but we can get around better in a car.

I know you had loads of fun while you were home. Was your family glad to see you? (Katie, what a silly question!)

How was C_______?? Ha! Ha! You know who I mean, don't you? Just as sweet as ever? Just kidding.

Yes, I saw Smokey when he was up. I went riding with them when he was up. He is a crazy boy!

Frank, I need to hurry because I think we are going to have a black out, and I don't want it to catch me.

Hasta Mañana,

'Katie'

The Date
September 4–5, 1943

This "Yankee" lieutenant was very fascinating to Catherine, and you could say she was already taken with him. She had never dated a "Yankee" before. He was charming. She liked his height, his black hair and blue eyes, and the way he looked in his uniform. She liked the way the non-commissioned servicemen stood at attention and saluted when she entered a restaurant on his arm or when they walked together down the streets of Myrtle Beach. He was fun, and when they were together, they laughed a lot. He danced like a dream. And she still liked him, even if he *had* dragged her into the water.

On the other hand, she was a little upset that he had left for California and hadn't even inquired about her hurt foot— the injury he was responsible for! In one of his letters, he made fun of it, joking that she was a "goldbricker." And why did he have to talk about those girls in California—that "sweet

Carol" person—or was it "Wilma"? Or both? Well, a man this charming was sure to be swimming in the attention of a lot of pretty girls back home. It made her a little uneasy, but even with all of the strikes against him, she was definitely charmed, and she *liked* being charmed.

Once he was back in North Carolina, they set a date for Saturday, September 4, 1943, at 8:00 p.m. civilian time. Dump and Catherine waited at Catherine's home until the men were due to arrive. But 8:00 p.m. came and went. Then 9:00 p.m. came, then 10:00 ... Finally, at 11:00 p.m., the two lieutenants, Frank and Smokey, arrived at her door. It *was* wartime, and they had been detained at the Camp.

Now Catherine had a temper, and patience was not her forte. She listened as they offered their excuses, stories, and apologies and then quietly told the lieutenant she understood—WOW!

"Why, of course, I understand. It's wartime, right, Lieutenant? It would be almost un-American not to understand, ain't that right, Lieutenant? You're only three hours late. We'll just have to make up those old hours some other time." For a moment, Frank wondered if she really did understand or if she was just doing a great job of covering up how annoyed she really felt. But either way, her words were in the sweetest little Southern drawl he had ever heard and came from the sweetest "little southern gal" he had ever seen.

Once he was convinced that she really didn't mind his being late, Frank was pretty well floored at her patience and understanding. Where did this perfect little Southern gal come from? *And*, he thought to himself, *even after I pulled her into the water and hurt her foot, too!*

"That is very nice of you, Cathy, not to be mad at Smokey and me. Most girls would be pretty darn upset. Let's find a place to get something to eat and look at some of the pictures we took that day."

They found an all-night diner in town and settled in for

a late dinner together—probably of eggs, knowing Frank. He showed her the pictures he had taken the day they were at Myrtle Beach and followed those with some he had taken during his recent trip home to California. It was a late night, and once the lieutenants had taken the girls home, they got a hotel room for themselves. That's the way it was done in 1943. These Southern gals who taught Sunday school every Sunday morning would not have had it any other way.

Frank and Catherine met early the next morning to go to her church, the First Reform Church of Charlotte. Normally, she would have been singing in the choir, but this Sunday, she wanted to sit with him in the sanctuary. At the end of the service, she proudly introduced her lieutenant to everyone she knew. He looked very handsome in his Army-issue cottons, and she knew that the whole congregation was checking him out. He met her sister Rebecca (Becky) and Becky's husband, David Kelly. Already, it was clear that Frank fit right in and that he felt right at home with this North Carolina family.

After the service, Pastor Nolan was at the door greeting his flock by name. It was a perfect opportunity to introduce the pastor to her lieutenant. "Why, Catherine, I see you have a fine young officer here. Now be sure to bring him back to visit us again, y'hear now?"

"Oh, I will be sure to do that, Pastor Nolan," Catherine assured him with a beaming smile.

Dinner is the main meal in the South, especially during the summer months. It was customary to prepare it during the early morning hours before the heat of the day had had a chance to set in. There was no air conditioning in the Oliver home in 1943, and summer was always as hot as the hinges! Dinner was served at noon or shortly thereafter, and there would be a light snack served at suppertime.

The Olivers loved Frank instantly—even before Catherine did! Mama Oliver would say, "That Frank has such sweet ways about him. He is a good man." Oh yes, the Olivers loved Frank Ward.

That first Sunday dinner together, Mama Oliver put on quite a spread. There was baked ham, fried chicken, succotash made with homegrown lima beans, sweet corn, sliced tomatoes and fried okra straight out of the garden, mashed potatoes with pan gravy from the chicken, homemade biscuits, sweet iced tea, coffee, and coconut white layer cake for dessert—topped with strawberries and fresh, grated coconut!

"Dinner's ready!" Mama called. They all gathered around the old oak table to say grace. Frank felt instantly at home. The conversation was easy, and all of these Southerners loved to hear Frank talk with his "Yankee accent."

"Well, Frank, where are you from in California?" David asked him.

"Los Angeles," Frank replied. "My family lives in West L.A., close to the ocean."

"How far is that from Hollywood?" asked Betty Jean, Catherine's sister.

"Oh, just a few miles away."

Betty smiled shyly. "Have you seen any movie stars?"

"No, but I have seen Hollywood," Frank replied with a broad grin and a laugh in his voice, "No, Betty Jean, movie stars don't come over to my neighborhood."

"Now, Betty, don't you pester Frank! Let him eat his dinner in peace, y'hear?" Mama scolded in her sweet Southern drawl.

Frank smiled at her and said, "That's alright, Mrs. Oliver; Betty is not bothering me."

Wow, this Southern cooking is the greatest! Frank thought to himself.

He was very comfortable here. After dinner, he helped with the dishes and enjoyed visiting with Catherine's Family. After the KP, he and Catherine walked for a while, rode the bus downtown, took in a movie, and walked some more. Then they had a light supper and danced once more until Frank had to go back to the base.

With most of the day behind him, Frank was happy to have the chance to dance again with this "little southern Gal," especially after the foot incident at the beach. It was hard to see the day come to an end, but they had already made plans for him to come down again the following weekend. As they danced their last dance, Frank knew that he would spend his nights dreaming about the next dance and the next and the next—with his special Southern Gal.

*****

To Catherine from Frank:
September 6, 1943
Camp Mackall, North Carolina

Dear Cath,

For the next three days, I'm going to be lost. By that, I mean that my platoon and I are going out in the woods to do a little snooping patrol work on our own. Our only means of getting food will be C-rations, which I'll tell you about the next time I see you. The next time you see me you will probably wonder what has happened to me. It'll be because of the bivouac. I'll probably be as thin as a pole. We leave tonight and walk all night—no sleep again tonight, but I'll try to get some sleep tomorrow during the day. This will be our schedule for the three days and nights. (Oh, boy! no shaving for three days!) Well, enough details for the sordid Army.

I keep kidding the Captain about getting off for Friday night, but it seems that all of my attempts are in vain. I'm keeping my fingers crossed for next weekend. If I'm not the on-duty officer, it looks like I'll be getting off early Saturday. If I get an early ride to Concord, I'll be getting into Charlotte by seven. Don't quote me ... verification by phone Thursday or Friday. While you have my camera, you might as well take some pictures—mostly of yourself! Don't forget to adjust the footage.

I sure had a good time Saturday and Sunday. In fact, that's the best time I have had in many moons. Only there is one thing that I'm still mad about. It seems that we lost three hours that night. We are going to have to make them up somewhere!

You were sure sweet about that too. Most girls would have gone off the handle half-cocked before they'd had an explanation.

Well, when it was time for our departure from Charlotte, Lieutenant Forbes (Damn Yankee) and I (foreigner) left together. Imagine being on patrol with a damn Yankee for three days! The Captain is in a good humor for some unaccountable reason. We made him drive all the way from Charlotte. We combined our ranks and pulled it on him. After the Captain got on Tryon Street, I don't remember a thing until we pulled into Camp.

Well, Cathy, I guess that will be all for the time being, seeing as how our zero hour is here.

Write soon,

Adios, Señorita,

Frank

The Dance
September 12–13, 1943

The next date had been set for Charlotte. However, Frank and Smokey were, in fact, appointed as officers of the day, and they would have to work until 7:00. It was a two-to-three-hour drive from Camp Mackall to Charlotte, so if they kept the date in Charlotte, it would mean another very late date.

As an alternative, Frank and Catherine made arrangements by phone for the girls to drive out to meet them at Camp. This would work out well because the Red Cross Officers' Club had planned a dance for that weekend on the base. Well, that was just fine with Catherine and Dump! They packed what they needed for the weekend, and Dump was all set to drive. When she arrived at Catherine's house, Catherine jumped in the car, laughing, "Well, this sure beats waiting until 11:00 p.m.!" Dump laughed as she agreed, and they drove off.

Frank thought about Catherine more and more those days and was delighted that he was going to see her again. He loved to hold her, even if it was simply while they were dancing.

The days had begun to get busier and busier on base, with rumblings and rumors about the 17th Airborne going overseas. During the last few frenetic weeks of training, he and his men had taken villages and lost villages. He had blown up villages and saved villages. He knew this training wasn't just because Uncle Sam had a thing for villages; something was definitely coming down the pike. He just couldn't quite put his finger on it. The truth is that even if he had known what was coming, he wouldn't have been able to talk about what he knew.

On the evening of the dance, Catherine wore a sleeveless navy dress with a scooped neck and a waist-length jacket of white linen. The navy dress was trimmed with two white casings around the bottom of the dress, and the white jacket was trimmed in navy. It was appropriately dressy for the evening and yet casual at the same time. She looked beautiful.

Once Smokey and Frank had arrived, they greeted the girls warmly, and Catherine scooted into the back seat with Frank.

"You look lovely tonight," he said. She *did* enjoy dressing in the chic fashions of the day, and she was always right up with the times.

"Thank you," she smiled.

"How hungry are you girls?" Smokey asked. "We've got a place called Scotty's lined up for dinner. They've got the best steaks and brew in all of North Carolina." They all agreed that that sounded good—with one concern from Catherine:

"Is beer all they have to drink?" she asked sheepishly in her small Southern voice. Frank smiled and reassured her that Scotty's had plenty of soft drinks and sweet tea along with the homebrew. So off they went to Aberdeen for the best steaks in North Carolina.

Aberdeen is a town not far outside of Camp Mackall, and Scotty's was a great choice. Steak was Frank's favorite dinner in the whole world, and he was happy to introduce Catherine to his favorite hang-out.

After dinner, they headed to the dance at the Red Cross Officers' Club. The hours seemed like minutes as Frank and Catherine danced, talked, and laughed, and the evening went flying by. It is easy to visualize this attractive couple on the dance floor in 1943. The live band was more than happy to play all of their favorite songs, including several requests for "Wait for Me, Mary." Everyone was having a great time, but Frank couldn't help but notice that they had quickly become the center of attention. Other couples were a little jealous as they watched this handsome pair dance as if they had danced together for years, not days.

This was the time of their lives, and Frank knew it. They both embraced every minute.

Frank was still amazed at how he felt when he was with Catherine. He had had many girlfriends before, and some of them he thought he truly liked. But this was different ... *way different*. There were moments when she was naïve, but make no mistake! She was also smart, well-dressed, sweet, funny, and altogether good for him. He already knew that he was crazy about this "little southern Gal." He especially loved that she was a city girl with a country soul.

Smokey and Dump finally showed up after the dance was over. As the four of them drove back to Aberdeen, Catherine and Frank were snuggled in the back seat together. She loved the warm feeling that filled her when she had her head on his shoulder. Knowing that they were only minutes away from the hotel, she stole a quiet moment to look up at him one last time. He kissed her lightly and said, "Catherine, I love you."

His words caught her off guard. She didn't know what to say. She knew that she cared—she would even admit that she was smitten with this handsome lieutenant—but *love*? It just seemed way too soon. Did Frank know something that no one else did? Did he know his time in North Carolina was limited?

The whole thing was happening so fast for her! But things *do* happen fast in wartime. Her head was swirling. She could not think of a response to this confession of love. Has she been hurt before? Or was she just afraid of these feelings? Suddenly, she realized she was terribly confused. It was true that she had been rather sheltered during her young years and that she had always had pretty high expectations for herself. But these words of love seemed to come out of nowhere, and in some way, they almost seemed to issue a challenge—one she wasn't sure how to meet! In another way, they almost pressed her to question what she knew about herself, about the person she knew herself to be. What did this confession of love really mean? Did she feel the same way? What were these feelings she felt now? All she knew was that on the day that she finally told someone that she loved him, it would be for certain—and forever. Dizzied with all these unexpected thoughts and feelings dueling in her head, and with only a few minutes left on their drive, Catherine fell asleep on Frank's shoulder. Precious last moments together until they reached the hotel.

That Sunday, they spent the day and the evening together in Aberdeen. Catherine was relieved to see that the serious mention of love the night before was not going to hinder any of the day's activities. They went for breakfast, saw a movie, had dinner, walked around Aberdeen, and went dancing again at the Officers' Club. Every minute was precious. But before they knew it, it was time for the girls to head back home.

Frank and Catherine both knew that it would be a long time before their memories of this perfect weekend would even begin to fade ...

*****

To Frank from Catherine:
September 23, 1943

Dear Frank,

First of all, Frank, I want to thank you for the lovely week-end. I enjoyed every minute of it. Hope you did the same. You were so sweet to find us such a nice place to stay, etc. (We did have fun, didn't we?)

Dump and I drove straight home and arrived at 1:15. How is that for a record? Pretty good, I'd say. We didn't even slow up until we got to my house. Once I was back in the house, I didn't even unpack my bag. I just brushed my teeth, washed my face, and dropped into bed. I tell you, I was so sleepy this morning, I didn't think I'd be able to make it to work, but I did. This afternoon about four o'clock, I thought I would fall asleep right there on the job, in spite of all I was doing to stay awake. In the end, I did manage to keep one eye open until 5:10, but then I came home and slept until 7:30! Ha! Ha! My mother woke me up for supper, and now I feel fine. In fact, I'm so wide awake now, I think I could stay up until 3:00 am! Ha! Ha! But don't worry, I will be in bed by 10:00.

I bet you could never guess what I had to do tonight for K.P. I was a bad girl. I went AWOL! No, I'm just kidding—you know me better than that. I just helped my mother with the dishes.

How did the Nazi village go today? Pretty rough, I would think.

Is that Damn Yankee still your commanding officer? I hope you don't have to put up with him much longer. I just don't like him.

Well, Royal, if I am going to make it to bed by ten, I had better hurry. (Catherine did not know it at the time, but Frank hated his middle name, Royal.) I must unpack my bag, and I have lots of things to get to before I can go to bed.

Be good, and thanks again for giving us such a wonderful weekend. I am speaking for both Dump and myself.

Love,

Katie

The Porch
September 18–19, 1943

Frank pulled into Charlotte just before noon on Saturday, September eighteenth. A little thrill ran through Catherine when she heard the ring of the doorbell. She had been waiting all week for this moment when she could open the door and see her handsome soldier standing there.

"Hey there, soldier," she smiled, giving him a big hug. He hugged her tight and then flashed a big grin as he took a good look at his Southern Gal.

"Come in," she said invitingly.

He hesitated. Something mysterious flickered across his face—and then it was gone. He grinned again, saying, "It's so beautiful out today—could we just sit out on the porch for a while?" He studied her face to make sure he wasn't disappointing her with the request.

It was true—it was an unusually lovely afternoon. September days can be so fickle in North Carolina, sweeping wildly between sticky hot and chilly cold. But that day, the sun was pleasantly warm with a hint of fall in the air. A light breeze surprised them now and again with little whiffs of honeysuckle from a nearby creeping vine.

"Yes, let's!" she agreed quickly.

He was relieved that she liked the idea—and eager to steal a few moments alone with her before greeting the rest of the family.

The house was an old Craftsman-style home from the early part of the century. The classic, roomy Carolina porch was a full twelve feet deep and spanned the entire width of the front of the house. Array chairs and rockers were arranged side by side: some in a small group so that folks could sit in a comfortable circle, and some facing the street so that the family could spend their evenings greeting neighbors as they strolled by. On one end, a large swing hung from the porch ceiling, beckoning all first-time visitors with a welcome. *"Hey y'all!.*

Frank took her hand and led her to the swing, which was gently swaying in the breeze of a honeysuckle.

It had only been a couple of minutes since he had arrived, and Catherine was still tingling all over just to hold his hand in hers. But something was off. Frank's smile was warm and sincere, and she knew he was happy to see her—so what was it? He looked so serious—almost sad. What was on his mind?

"Cath, there's something I have to tell you." He looked down, choking a little on the words. Finally, he said almost mechanically, "We've received our orders, and I'm going over-seas. I leave tomorrow night on the 11:01 train. First, we go to Fort Meade, but from there, I have no idea."

The swing slowed to a stop.

Frank hardly dared to look at her face after delivering the news, afraid of what he might see there. On the one hand, he was anxious to read all her thoughts and emotions in an instant. On the other, he was carefully guarding his own feelings, where quite a battle was raging. He wasn't sure how she would take this news. He knew it would be a shock, but beyond that, what would she think? How would she feel? As for his own emotions, he knew that he loved her, even though they had only known each other a very short time. He was sure of his love. But when he had declared his love for her a few nights before, she had said nothing.

*****

Maybe she won't really care if I get called away. Will she write to me after I've been deployed? Or will she just find another soldier to take her to the next dance?

For several minutes, he just held her hands tight and choked back his fears.

Catherine looked at him in disbelief. His words fairly pounded in her head. *This is why he spoke of love so soon,* she thought. *He is leaving ... He is leaving, he is leaving, he is leaving,* she repeated silently to herself—as if the repetition would either make it real or make it go away. For a moment, she could not catch her breath. It was like a punch in her stomach. She had never met anyone like him before, and they were having such fun together—what was she going to do on the weekends without him?

Frank was still staring at her hands, unable to look up. The words had finally stopped pounding in her head, and the sound of the soft summer breezes wishing through the trees had restored her composure. She gathered a wary smile and smiled into his eyes, begging it wasn't so.

Frank broke the silence, looking down again. "Catherine, I will be gone for at least eighteen months. It is a long time, and last Saturday night, I told you that I loved you, and I mean it, Cath. I can't ask you not to go out and not to have fun, but I will ask you to wait for me. I cannot expect you or even myself not to date or have some kind of entertainment, but I have a job to do." He stopped for a quick breath, then continued, in a more resolute tone: "This war won't last forever, and this lieutenant is coming home." His eyes were on his lap again, and he held her hands so tightly she could feel them going numb.

"Catherine," he said in a softer, hushed tone, "I know that we have not had much time together, but I do know that I love you. Please wait for me."

He blurted it all out so quickly; it was as if he were afraid the words would escape him if he didn't string them all together in one long breath. But then he fell silent.

Now it was Catherine's time to spend a moment studying the white buttons on her white piqué dress, afraid to look up. Her turn to blurt out a string of words before she could catch herself. Even so, she spoke them softly, in a more measured, deliberate tone: "Frank, I care for you deeply, I love to be with you, and we have such fun together. I have never had such fun, but I am afraid to say it is love. I can't say it unless it is true, and we have known each other for such a short time." She looked up at the crepe myrtles and magnolias that lined the street. Then she added cheerily, "Meanwhile, if we keep our chins up and work real hard, the time will fly by, and you will be back here with me in no time flat."

He looked up at her, grateful for the warmth of her hands and the confidence of her words. He loved that she could endorse this new phase with such cheery optimism. If he could hold on to that, he knew he would have the strength he needed to face the dark and lonely days that were sure to come.

She looked up. Tears were floating in her amber-green eyes. Then his heart jumped a beat as she spoke softly.

"But even if you are gone for a long time, Frank, I will still be here. I will wait for you."

The Train: "Never Say Goodbye"

Later that afternoon, they went to a football game at Central High, Catherine's high school. Frank did love Catherine, but he had to admit football was his first love. It was such a great afternoon: he yelled for the good passes as well as the bad, and in the end, Central won. After the game, they rounded out the outing with a stop at Catherine's favorite coffee shop, where they had a couple of great hamburgers, BLT sandwiches, and a "Coke-Cola."

Early on Sunday, Frank met Catherine at her church. Pastor Nolan looked pleased to see Catherine with her young man again, two Sundays in a row. Rebecca and David came over, and they all had dinner as a family at the Olivers.

This was the second time Frank had Sunday dinner with the family in this lovely, large Southern dining room. . With windows on three sides of the room, sunlight streamed in from every direction, on all the old dining room furnishings. In the far corner of the room was a china cabinet displaying dozens of dishes nestled in amongst the family's china, crystal, and serving dishes, adding a touch of interest and character to the room. The deep tones of the solid oak dining table was covered with a lace tablecloth. The olivers did not have much, however they were proud of what they had.

The Olivers were always very welcoming, and the food was just too good to describe. Mama Oliver always started making her Sunday dinner early in the morning and then went to church. Once they had returned home from Sunday services, Catherine and Becky would join in, helping her to wrap up the finishing details of this Sabbath feast. Even Catherine's baby sister, Betty Jean, joined in the act by setting the table for dinner. Frank could tell that the Oliver women enjoyed this Sunday routine, especially on the weekends when Papa Oliver managed to join them, home from his job in Tennessee. It was clear that they enjoyed having him here, because their time together was so rare. Now they had a new special someone to enjoy as well! And Frank loved it.

He felt comfortable every moment of this time with Catherine's family. He prayed there would be more Sunday dinners in his future with this Southern Gal in Charlotte.

The Sunday menu usually consisted of either baked or fried chicken and included quite a number of sides: mashed potatoes or rice, pan gravy, ham, green beans, creamed peas and baby potatoes, sliced tomatoes, and homemade biscuits. Iced tea was the daily beverage, and the meal was always topped with a mouth watering dessert: a homemade cake or pie, served with coffee or Sweet tea. Yum!

Catherine's parents liked this lieutenant, and they were totally at ease with Frank now that he was dating their daughter. He was genuinely kind to all, a true officer and a gentleman, and it showed. He was a lot of fun, and his contagious laugh was usually with a mischievous twinkle in his eye—especially when he was teasing little Betty Jean!

Frank never talked just to hear himself talk. But when he did have something to say, people listened. And that weekend, they *all* listened. He had news. They were stunned to hear that he would be leaving tonight for Fort Meade and that soon thereafter, his unit would be deployed overseas (destinations unknown) to fight in this evil war. Would he be off to the South Pacific? Italy? England? Or North Africa? So many countries in so many parts of the world had been roped into this war; it was scary just thinking about the grim assignments that lay before him.

After dinner, the dishes had to be done. "I will be more than happy to help with these dishes, Mrs. Oliver. How about you, Betty Jean? Isn't it your turn to dry?" Frank said with a playful smile, teasing her a bit. With that, Betty Jean got up and vaulted straight out the door. What she didn't know was that Frank ran about five miles every morning before breakfast at the base. So, as soon as she tried her best to escape KP (kitchen patrol), he ran out the door like a shot, chased her down the block, and hauled her back home. Then they laughed their way through doing the dishes together. Even little Betty Jean.

Before Frank left Camp Mackall, he had called his family in Los Angeles to give them the news. They knew he would be going, but when they heard him say the words, it still came as a shock. Needless to say, he now had family on both coasts who were sad and anxious at this turn of events. But he also knew that both families would be praying extra hard tonight and for weeks to come.

After all of the KP was over at the Olivers', Frank and Catherine made their way to the Kellys' small home. The couple wanted to spend the last few hours with Becky and David before Frank had to leave on the 11:01 train back to Fort Meade. Both Becky and David had really enjoyed getting to know Frank and had already remarked to Catherine how much they liked him. David mentioned to Frank that he had considered joining the North Carolina National Guard, adding that he was working with his draft board in order to stay home with his family. Frank encouraged David, telling him his story about how the National Guard had given him a jump start and great training for the Army and OSC (Officer Candidate School). At this time in our country's history, Uncle Sam did not draft married men with children. David did not want to leave his wife and son to go to war, but he knew he would do his duty if he was called.

Before they arrived at the Kelly home, it started to rain. Becky opened the windows and doors, welcoming the fresh air. It was about 7:00 when Catherine and Becky fixed a light supper of cold cuts, ham, chicken with potato salad, late sliced tomatoes from the garden, cheese biscuits, and iced tea, with cookies for dessert. Frank loved every minute was a warm, almost sticky evening, but the rain brought a refreshing breeze through the screen windows, open on all sides of the room. *How* different this was from the summer evenings Frank knew well in Southern California! would follow o Yes, the memory of this moment would be with him forever.

*****

The hours spent with the Olivers had just flown by. It seemed as though he had just arrived, and now it was time for him to leave. The 11:01 train for Fort Meade would be leaving in a few short hours.

The rain was coming down harder—much harder! It was pouring outside! They called several times for a cab to take Frank to the train station, but when it became evident that no cab would come, David offered to drive Frank and Catherine to the station. "I would sure appreciate it, David," Frank said, thanking him. The epitome of a Southern gentleman, David grinned and said, "Why, I don't mind at all."

In spite of the rain, the station was a hub of busyness that evening, with many servicemen going off to war—even at this late hour. The image was way too familiar in 1943: the handsome young serviceman saying goodbye to a beautiful young woman. Frank and Catherine stood on the platform saying all the things they needed to say—but being careful to say everything *but* goodbye.

"If we just work hard and keep our chins up, time will fly, and soon you will be home," Catherine said with half a smile on her face. "You will be home soon, and then we can make up for those three hours." She really smiled at those words, laughing at the thought of the late-night date they had shared only a few weeks earlier. But even though she was laughing, it was clear that it was just her way of choking back the tears.

"This war won't last forever, Catherine, and this lieutenant is coming home," Frank reassured her. "Wait for me! Wait for me, Cath. I miss you already," Frank told her over and over again.

"Frank, I will wait for you, I promise," Catherine said with a crack in her voice.

"All aboard!"

Catherine pushed back the tears. "It *can't* be 11:00 already!" she said, almost begging for it not to be so.

"*Love you, so long for now, never, ever say goodbye*—never! I love you." He held her close, and for a moment, it felt as if he wouldn't let go. But they both knew the time had come for him to leave. He kissed her again—an embrace that would have to carry him through eighteen months or more of war.

"I will wait, Frank. It's only 'so long': *so long for now, so long for now*," she said over and over, waving and waving in the rain, never saying goodbye.

He climbed on the train, rain pouring off his Army-issued raincoat. He rushed to his seat just long enough to put down his gear and then returned to the doorway of the train car for one last farewell before they chugged away. There he was, hanging on to the safety bar with one hand and waving wildly with the other. As the train pulled out of the station, he could see Catherine fading into the night, but he still strained to see her, eager for one more glimpse of her dark curls.

The train rounded a bend just outside the station, and then he was gone. Even though he was out of sight, Catherine kept waving, as if somehow it could bring him back. But she knew he was gone. Finally, she let the tears come. Her eyes were stinging, and she was soaked to the skin. She stood there, miserable, wanting him to be OK, but unable to swallow the irrepressible anxiety about where he would end up next. She knew that Fort Meade was a major deployment base for all the Armed Services on the East Coast during WWII and that he could really end up anywhere.

She was soaked to the skin as she hailed a cab to take her home. Suddenly, she was stricken with the thought that she may never see him again. But she was careful to dismiss the thought rapidly. She couldn't let herself think like that. "*He will be back! He promised me!*" she told herself. "*No Germans or Japanese out there can hurt my lieutenant!*"

Catherine was grateful at that moment that she had such a positive side. Or was she just part of that generation of Americans who won WWII with positive thinking, a lot of hard work, dogged determination, and courage? "*That's it,*" she told herself from a place of deep conviction. "*We will work hard and keep our chins up, and before we know it, Frank will be home.*"

What followed in the next few minutes was a rush of con-flicting thoughts. *Why didn't I tell him that I loved him? What are these feelings? And why am I feeling this way? I hardly know him, this Yankee. I can't say those types of things unless I mean them,* she argued with herself. *It has just been five short weeks since I met him, and he was in California with his family for ten days at that time. No, it is way too soon to say those words. But now he's gone. Will he be back? What if we don't get a chance to finish what we've started?*

*****

To Frank from Catherine:
September 27, 1943

Darling,

Just a note at lunch time. I want to mail the pictures so you could (maybe) receive them before you leave. Here's hoping!

Frank, it was wonderful talking to you this morning. The only thing is we didn't get to talk long enough! I could have talked all day—but you know how it is. There were so many things I wanted to ask you. First: did you have a chance to have my pictures developed? Second: if not, why not? Third, I wanted to tell you how much I missed you last weekend. I was lost—really, I'm not kidding. I'm so used to seeing you every weekend—I guess you've just spoiled me. No kidding Frank, I do miss you. But it won't be long until you are back. Then we'll have a chance to make up for all the lost time. We will have to "keep our chins up" and "work hard and the time will fly by."

Frank Darling, wherever you go, here is wishing you the best of luck. My thoughts will be there with you.

My time is up—I must run.

All my love, Cathy

*****

To Frank from Catherine:
Wednesday night, September 27, 1943

My Dearest Frank,

Honey, I am sending you the rest of the pictures. They're not that good. I'm annoyed because I asked them to enlarge them for me—but they didn't.

Thanks again for calling this morning. I kept humming happy tunes at work, and had such a productive day all day after talking to you! I guess you will have to call me every morning. Ha! Ha!

By the way, we have been tracing a shipment all day for Fort Meade. I told Charlie I could do a much better job if he let me take care of it in person. For some reason, he didn't quite see it my way. I think he's just an old meanie, don't you?

Darling, I was a good girl Sunday. (Aren't I always?) I went to Sunday school in the morning, and to church on Sunday night. If I keep this up I will be a real good girl by the time you get back. Oh, yes—and I am going to Wednesday night church tonight.

It's almost time for choir practice, so I must hurry along.
So long, Darling, and good luck!
Love always, Cathy

Thoughts for "Wait for Me, Mary"

At this point in their story, Catherine was 24 and Frank was 22. She knew that he was very special and that they had a bond that was worth cherishing and preserving, but she couldn't see what the future might hold. What would she have said if someone had told her that Frank was going to be the love of her life? Would she have believed them? And what was it about Frank? Was it his smile that got to her? Or that mischievous little glimmer in his eye? Maybe it was his kindness, his gentle ways, or his drop-in-your-tracks good looks. She wasn't sure. Well, whatever it was, she knew she was in love with this lieutenant, even if she wasn't quite ready to admit it out loud.

Frank knew that he loved her, and he had told her so. But they had known each other such a short time—did she really believe him? Were there other servicemen who had kissed her goodbye at the train station, he wondered, or was he the first and only one? Had she dated other servicemen who were not as honorable as Frank, leaving her wary of any man?

Both Catherine and Frank had a lot of unanswered questions on that lovely Sunday in September 1943. But *we* know that this lieutenant was about to change her life forever!

The Crossing

The First Month of Deployment
October 1943

Catherine was a firm believer that busy hands were happy hands and idle hands were the devil's playground. Idle hands also gave her too much time to feel and think. She often kept herself so busy that she would fall asleep the minute she sat down. Her letters repeated what she told Frank the last days in Charlotte: "We have to work hard and keep our chins up." Her positive attitude always prevailed because she would not let a negative thought enter her mind. She always reminded me a bit of another Southern heroine we know, Miss Scarlett O'Hara, when she said, "I will think about that tomorrow." Maybe if she pushed it way, way down, it would go away. That way, she could ignore any of those feelings that made her unhappy.

It had only been eight short weeks since she had met Frank, and now her happiness depended entirely on this war and the return of this second lieutenant. It only took a few days in August and September 1943 to know for sure that they belonged together. She had really started something when she wrote the "Dear Jack" letter on August 12, 1943.

She often wrote to Frank about her church and what a good girl she was because she went to church three to four times a week. Catherine and Frank were glad that they shared the same faith; the church was important to both of them. In her letters, she was always talking about the music in her choir. She especially loved to tell him what they were singing that week. Her parents were Methodists; however, when Catherine and Becky were teenagers, they joined the First Reform Church of Charlotte because it was a younger church and more progressive. For Catherine, her many church activities were the highlights of her week. Whether she was facing stress at work or worrying about Frank at home, going to church was like pushing the refresh button or having a day at the spa.

In her letter to Frank of October 5, 1943, Catherine sounds off about something that had gotten under her skin. Smokey and Dump had started seeing each other on a regular basis, which would have been fine—except that Frank had discovered that Smokey was already married! When he first found out, he spoke to Smokey and insisted, in no uncertain terms, that he tell Dump the truth about his marriage. But Smokey was having too much fun, and as far as Frank could tell, he had never quite gotten around to talking to Dump about it. This infuriated Frank, as he had no time in his life for cheats and liars. At that point, he decided that if Smokey wasn't going to fess up, he would spill the beans for him! So, he told both the girls about Smokey's situation. This made Catherine angry too because in "the world of Catherine," everything was either right or wrong—and this situation was definitely wrong! This letter shows her temper, and it may be the first time Frank had a chance to witness what she was like when she was angry.

*****

To Frank from Catherine:
October 5, 1943

Darling Frank,

How is my little old soldier tonight? OK, I hope. I am fine—just got home from the hospital. I'm telling you, I haven't stopped since seven! I have never seen so many people wanting things all at the same time. When I started to leave, all the lights were on, and that hall looked like Broadway!

*****

Honey, they moved my desk up beside Millie yesterday. We have laughed all day. Except this afternoon I got mad. I have never been any madder in my life than I was today. I talked to Dump at lunch time. She told me she had a letter from Smokey. He said he sure did not appreciate you not looking out for him. Doesn't that sound like the old sot? I won't tell you the other things he said, or that she said. Dump told me today that on the Saturday that we were at the Camp, Smokey told her that he was married. That he didn't love his wife. He was getting a divorce. But the day I told her he was married she played like she didn't know it. So I believe that even though he is married, she was going to keep on dating him. I really let her have it. Enough of that. I just would like for someone to tell me if I was going with a married man. Frank, please excuse the ugly words, but that brought out the bad in me.

Frank Darling, it doesn't make any difference to me if she goes with a married man. *As long as my Frank is not married.* I don't believe he is. In fact, I know he's not. It doesn't matter what Smokey says about you. It doesn't change the way I feel. Let us, you and me, forget the whole thing. We did what we thought was right. They didn't have enough sense to appreciate it, so to hell with them.

I guess that's enough for tonight. I will write a good letter tomorrow night. But I thought you might like to know about this little episode.

Please excuse my writing. I got cold, so I crawled into bed to get warm, and I am writing in bed.

Good night, Darling.
Love Always,
Cath

*****

To Frank from Catherine:
Saturday night, October 9, 1943

Hello Darling,

How is my little old soldier tonight? O.K, I hope. Well, I am fine. Except I miss you this Saturday night. I miss you more on weekends than I do through the week. Oh! I miss you all of the time, but even when you were here in North Carolina, I didn't get to see you during the week.

They are playing our song, "Wait for me, Mary," on the Maxwell House program tonight. Honey, your song, "Sunday, Monday, or Always," was just on the hit parade! Oh yes, I heard another song that you like so well: "Pistol Packin Mama." It was fifth in the line-up. Ha! Ha! I told my mother I wish you could hear that because you hate that song so.

I kept David this afternoon. We went for a walk to the drug store. When we got there, he said "Coca-Cola." I just *had* to buy him one! He drank about half of it. That's all he could take. He is so cute. When Becky came after him, I said, "Kiss me goodbye, David." He just smacked his little old lips so cute. And said "bye-bye."

We went to the show last night. We saw Bud Abbott and Lou Costello in "It Ain't Hay." I laughed until I hurt—they are so crazy!

Have you heard from your mother since you left Mackall? Honey, I guess she was just as surprised to hear that you were going overseas as I was. I bet she hated to hear that. I hated it too, but we will just have to be brave soldiers and keep our chins up, won't we, Frank? Just as I have told you before, with

God's help, you will be coming back soon. That will be the happy day—when Frankie comes marching home again!

My mother said to tell you 'hello,' and so did my sister.

Good night, Sweetheart! I wishing you best of luck and I will be thinking of you.

So long for now,
Love always, Cathy

*****

To Frank from Catherine:
October 14, 1943, Thursday night

My Dearest Frank,

Honey, this has been one of those lazy days for me. It has rained all day. I am always lazy when it rains. I didn't go to the hospital tonight. I called, and they said they wouldn't be very busy, so I told her I would not come then. I had lots of things to do at home. Believe me; I have been working like a little beaver.

By the way, I just heard that old train go by—the one you left on. Darn it, I hear it every night! I just don't like that old train.

I heard the Mackall band tonight on the radio. I started to cut them off, but they played our favorite songs, "Wait for me, Mary" and "Sunday, Monday, or Always."

Oh yeah, two girls from the office are going to Mackall this weekend. They were telling me about it, and I said, "Don't tell me about it. I am jealous because my Frank's gone." One of the girls goes with Captain Clark. Do you know him? I told her I would take a second Lieutenant.

How are those bars? Has the gold come off yet? Have they turned yet? Or is that pretty good gold on those? Ha! Ha!

How is the ocean tonight? Is it rough? I should think it would be. *Are you having fun with the nurses? Is it a luxury liner? How*

are the nurses??? Oh yes, don't forget your nurse's aide!
Good night, Darling.
Keep your chin up.
Love always, Cathy

*****

To Frank from Catherine:
Saturday night, October 16, 1943

My Dearest Frank,

How is my little old soldier tonight? I am fine. I just got home from the movies. I bet you can't guess who I went to the show with! My little old mean sister, Betty Jean. She was having a fit to go, so I felt sorry for her and took her.

Honey, I have really been working today. My mother was sick, and our colored girl did not come today. I had to clean all the house and cook. Oh, boy, did I have fun! Well, I like to cook anyway. I am going to try to make my mother stay in bed for a few days. She will be OK.

I went to the fair again last night with a crowd of girls: Becky, Dump, Millie, myself, and two more girls that you don't know. You know me—I will never grow up. Frank, you would have thought we were kids, the way we acted. You should have seen us eating popcorn and hot dogs! Oh, it was fun! The only bad thing was that you couldn't be alone. We rode the fast Ferris wheel. I thought I was going to die before I got off! We kept telling the man to let us off, but he just rode us that much longer. My favorite is the Merry-Go-Round. It doesn't go so fast. No kidding, we did have fun. But I missed you.

Frank, your song was number 1 for the fifth time on the Hit Parade tonight, "Sunday, Monday, or Always." I never hear the song without thinking of you. I don't know why, do you?

Darling, I will have to say good night. My mother wants me to rub her back.

Good night, Darling. Keep your chin up.
Love Always,
Cathy

*****

To Frank from Catherine:
October 17, 1943

My Dearest Frank,

Yes, another Sunday. I was a good girl this morning—I went to Sunday school and church, and sang in the choir, too. Do you remember the anthem the choir sang the last time you went to church with me? That's the one we sang this morning. But it was much better this morning than it was that Sunday morning when you were here because I was in the choir today. Frank, I did miss you going to church with me today.

Oh, yes—I must tell you what else I did today. I cooked dinner! We had a good dinner, even if I did cook it. Do you want the menu? Baked chicken, dressing, green peas, candied yams, creamed carrots, tomato salad, ice cream, hot rolls, cake, and coffee. You didn't know I could cook, did you? Ha! Ha! This is the first time I have cooked in a long time. Becky and David ate with us. They seemed to enjoy it, so it must have been O.K. Honey, we took some pictures this afternoon with the film you gave me. If they are good of me, I will send them to you. That is if you want them. We made some cute pictures of David Junior. I hope they are good. He gets cuter every day. He is beginning to put words together now. He will get up in the rocking chair and say, "Rocky a bye Baby goes to sleepy." That is what Becky sings to him when she rocks him to sleep. I could eat him up. He is almost as sweet as you!

Gosh, Frank! It has turned cold here. I think old winter is here. I slept under three blankets last night and hated to get up this morning. I wish I could take my other weeks' vacation next week so I could catch up with my sleep. I think I would sleep all week. I won't take it until the last week of this month since I did take the first week of the month to go to Baltimore. Darling, I wish you could have stayed there just a little while longer. We could have had a lot of fun. But you will be back, and we will have a lot of time to make up for—including three lost hours one Saturday night.

I guess by now you have reached your destination safely. I hope. I am waiting patiently to hear from you about your trip over. I want you to tell me all about it.

Dump apologized for the way she acted and told me she sees now that she was wrong. She said she hoped that I hadn't told you about it and that she wasn't going to see Smokey anymore. I told her that I had told you, but that you wouldn't be angry with her. That you were man enough to overlook such childish behavior. Ain't that right, Darling?

Well, Darling, I guess it is "good night" again. Be good, and keep your chin up. I will be thinking of you,

Love Always, Cathy

*****

To Frank from Catherine:
October 24, 1943

My Dearest Frank,

Did you go to church today? I went to Sunday School and church. I was a few minutes late this morning to Sunday School. They thought I wasn't coming, so when I walked in they said, "*Oh, Boy!*" They like me.

I bet you can't guess where we spent this afternoon. We went to a concert at the Mint Museum. You didn't know we had a museum in Charlotte, did you? You never did see it. They only have concerts down there in the fall and winter; it is too hot in the summer. It's a beautiful place—I wish you could have seen it—and the concert was very good. Do you like concerts?

Frank, I stayed with Becky tonight while David went to church. It was raining like nobody's business. I remember another night when David took us to the train station when we could not get a cab because of the rain. Do you remember? David was so nice to take us to the train. I can see you standing on that train in the raincoat ... waving 'so long,' not 'goodbye.' That seems like a long time ago. It has only been a month.

Did you get the other pictures I sent you? The ones we took on Sunday before you left? I hope you like them. I think some of them are good.

Becky and David said to tell you hello. Hope you had a safe journey over. I told them you would have plenty of company, darn it. I hope those nurses were not too cute. You must remember me. Not Carol or Willie—that is just too many to remember—just me. Just kidding, you know me!

My preacher was asking about you today. He said, "Where is that good-looking Lieutenant?" I told him you were tired of them playing around over there and wanted to get this war over with. I said, "Did you see that Italy has surrendered since he left?" David is afraid he is going to have to go to the Army soon. I wish he would be in your outfit. You all could have a good time. He likes you.

Good night, Darling, write soon,

Love always,

Cathy

*****

To Catherine from Frank
Postmarked Oct 1, 1943:
September 30, 1943
Somewhere on US soil

99

Dearest Cath,

Time is growing short fast and will have to write in a big hurry. First I want to tell you how much I miss you, and how swell it was to talk to you yesterday. The only thing that was wrong is that it didn't last long enough. It was like everything that has happened lately—not enough time, not enough time—especially in Charlotte and especially with you. As yet I haven't received your letter and the pictures. There's still a chance it'll come, though. How do you like the Camp Mackall stationery I am writing on? How I wish I were still there.

My new address is:

Lt Francis R. Ward 01313830
A.P.O. #15005
c/o Postmaster New York, New York

Every station I have gone to has always been worse than the previous one, and it doesn't look like there's going to be any improvement on my next stop. Every time we turn around here, they make us have an inspection of all the equipment and clothing we're to take with us. Yesterday we had no less than three full inspections and the day before that we had two or three. Incidentally, the letter I sent to you was returned to me and (of all the reasons!) for insufficient address! It seems I left off the city in North Carolina. Yes, I know, I'm a case for Section VIII. (Army code for mentally ill.)

Well Cath, I guess I've made my time and papers come out right, so it's time for me to go. I miss you, Cath, and I'll keep on missing you ... but this war isn't going to last forever, and this is one Lieutenant who is coming back.

Love, Frank

p.s. I used my old address in hopes that they won't hold it up.

Regards to everyone,
Frank

Thoughts for "The Crossing"

In March of 1942, Frank joined the California National Guard. From there, he was drafted into the Army. It was during his time in basic training at Camp Roberts in California that the Army took note of his leadership abilities. In December of 1942, he went on to Fort Benning, Georgia, where he received his second lieutenant bars in March of 1943. In 1943, they called these second lieutenants "ninety-day wonders." From there, he was stationed at Camp Mackall. Now, almost twenty months later, in October 1943, he was about to board a Henry J. Kaiser Liberty ship, a massive luxury cruise ship, to unknown destinations.

He knew that he was going to war, and the 17th Airborne had been trained to be the best of the best. This unit of air troopers was trained to fly their gliders over front lines, after which they would crash-land their motorless gliders and infiltrate villages and towns behind enemy lines. Frank's unit was determined not to rest until they saw Berlin. It was their *esprit de corps*, loyalty, and honor that eventually helped them cross the Rhine to Berlin.

Frank was 22 years old when he sailed away to war. In the letter below, he gives Catherine a moment-by-moment account of the departure. We can almost feel his irritation with the contrast between the Army's "hurry-up-and-wait" attitude and his own sense of urgency: he was eager to get over there and "get this over with."

*****

To Catherine from Frank
No date or location:

Dearest Cath,

I'm still on good old US soil, although I can't say where. Where we are going and when still remains a secret—although I will tell you that today is D. Day (Departure day) and H. hour is about an hour away. Does that mean anything? I received your letter just shortly before I left Meade. I liked the pictures, and I agree with you as to the quality ... kidding aside, Cath, wherever I go, I'll try to have one made.

It was wonderful to talk to you the other day and, like you, I could have talked all day. I used Millie's name because I still do not trust the old battle-axe you have got for a telephone operator. But again the sinister villain, "time," had to interfere.

The order of the day: full field pack, belts, canteens, carry a bag and prepare to load the ship. In a very few minutes, those words will be coming over the loudspeaker. So I guess I sort of got in a hurry. Cath, did you get my new address? I'm pretty sure, but just in case I didn't, it's as follows:

Lt. Francis R. Ward 01313830
APO #15005
c/o Postmaster
New York, New York

Speaking of being spoiled, Cath, I think it was you who spoiled me. I miss you very much and think of you often, Cathy. I wish I were able to talk to you again and tell you these things, but __ ______ ___ _ _ and Cath, don't forget that time we'll have to make up for. There'll probably be a lot of time to make up for it. Did we ever make up those three hours on that Saturday night, or should I say 1 lost?

Well, Cath, I guess this is it. I can see the officer in the control booth—so write soon.

Love, Frank

*****

To Catherine from Frank:
October 20, 1943
North Africa (Morocco)

Darling,

Well, another couple of days and I'll be able to turn native. At least it seems that way. It's a good thing that letters don't wear out from reading because I'm afraid your last letter would be done for. We won't get any mail at this camp, and it will be a good little while more before we get any mail—let alone replies to our letters. I told you, Cath, that I'd try and get a portrait made. Well, it doesn't look any too hopeful, although I haven't given up yet. I have that do-or-die spirit.

I have only been into town twice, and the more I see it, the more I dislike it—although it is quaint and picturesque. I intend on getting some pictures of it before I leave. The main language is French, and it wouldn't take too long to learn it. How is everyone doing—Dave, Becky, Millie and your friend Amarah? Have you seen any of my gang? Give my regards to all.

The other night we were at the theater, and just before the show, they had a recorded interlude. The tunes (one tune in particular) made me want to be back in Charlotte. I'm sure you can name it: "Wait for me, Mary." It is funny how pleasant tunes will remind you of different places and people.

Well, Cath, my candle is about at its wick end. I miss you, Cath, and Darling, write soon.

With my love,
Frank

*****

To Catherine from Frank
October 1943 (no date included):
North Africa

Darling Cath,

Did you ever write a letter by candlelight? That's how I'm writing this one. We get one candle to last three days. After that, we have to revert to our flashlight, and batteries are far too precious to use. We had a very pleasant crossing—in fact, it was more of a pleasure cruise.

The officers had no duties at all. Except for me: I was given seven second Lieutenants to look after, and that was a full-time job if I wanted to make it one. But I decided to be a man of leisure, and I was. We had a very unexciting crossing: no wolf packs to threaten us and no bombers to bomb us. The only excitement we had was a couple of bad storms which threatened to make us all sick. That was the worst that happened. That storm though was a sight to behold; you can see them in the movies, but it's nothing like experiencing the real thing. Our time was taken up mostly by eating and sleeping. At least it seemed that way. We did get in quite a bit of reading. Our special ship wasn't the Queen Mary or the S.S. America; it was a more popular ship: the Henry J. Kaiser Liberty Ship. The crew was jovial, and our men were carefree, so it all made for a happy crossing.

Tomorrow I'm going into town and trying to fulfill my promise and find a portrait studio because I'm sure that even with six rolls of film I wouldn't be able to get a good picture.

My address remains the same. Have you heard from any of my "associates"? If I thought Camp Mackall was bad, I'm sorry, and I take back everything bad I said about it. The camp I am in now doesn't even have hot water. It doesn't have half of the facilities that Mackall had. (The above is known as G.I. griping.)

Gee, Cath, but I've sure missed you. Remembering you and the fun we've had together has made the time go faster. In fact, it's shortened my stay here already. It's just a little over a month ago that fateful short Sunday at exactly 11:01 that I left. Darn it. That was the shortest Sunday ever recorded.

There were a hundred and one things I wanted to say, but I didn't know where to start. I guess, Cath, we can talk about them when I get back.

Well, Darling, I guess that's all for tonight. I miss you very much.

Adios,
Love always,
Frank

Catherine's letters to Frank were like a diary—an open book to her heart. Her trivial day-to-day letters reminded him why he was fighting this war. Her letters would give him a reason to live and to come home. They were more than love letters. Her letters were honest, simple, open, funny, angry, corny, loving, and by today's standards, redundant and occasionally insecure; she would always have a heavy dose of 'just kidding' humor concerning Frank's old girlfriends, the foreign gals, and those cute-cute nurses. Her letters were like the DNA of her soul. She didn't hide a thing. He could always tell if she had had a good day or a bad one. If Frank didn't know Catherine before he left, he did by the time he came home—just through her letters.

In October 1943, Frank spent most of the month crossing the Atlantic. His destination was North Africa, and the date he left is unclear. However, we do know that it was sometime during the first week of October 1943. In World War II, luxury ships such as the *Queen Mary* and military vessels like the USS *America* were used to carry the troops to the war zone. Frank's unit went on a Henry J. Kaiser Liberty ship. He enjoyed the trip. He ate extremely well, slept a lot, had a lot of time to read, and appreciated the luxury of being carried on a Kaiser Liberty ship across the Atlantic, which must have felt like the extreme of a trans-Atlantic cruise in the 1930s–40s during peacetime. He tells his family he hated to see the crossing come to an end.

He writes to Catherine that the crossing was peaceful except for a storm that threatened to make everyone seasick. In a letter to his brother, Clint, he tells of a sighting of a German sub, saying that the Navy escorts went wild with depth charges going "thither and yon" after the submarine. In the end, "... the sub took off, never hearing from Arian friends again."

Frank was not impressed with North Africa. We believe that he was in Morocco and CasaBlanca, but he couldn't mention specific towns or countries because of the censors who made sure communications didn't jeopardize operational safety.

North Africa

The Second Month of Deployment
November 1943

Yes, Catherine loved to do good things and to help people. She volunteered with the Red Cross, and she gave time to her church in many, many ways. In addition, she wrote to Frank almost every night. She had a genuinely good heart, but I believe that, in part, she needed to keep busy with these activities because she enjoyed the recognition and the appreciation that she received in the process.

The truth was that she needed this recognition because, for weeks on end, she wasn't getting any affirmation from Frank. In fact, she hadn't heard from him since his deployment six weeks before, so I can understand how she felt. She had known him such a short time—could she trust him with all of the cute and smart nurses on that transatlantic voyage? Her personal anguish, tinged with jealousy, was thinly veiled by her "just kidding" humor. In reality, she was still trying to figure out exactly what she felt for this lieutenant. It didn't help that she hadn't heard from Frank for almost six weeks.

In her letter of November 1, 1943, she became a bit more demanding with her "just kidding" humor, saying, "If you don't write to me, then I won't write to you." However, in the very next breath, she pledged, "I promise to write as often as I can." What in the world was a lieutenant to do?

Catherine often said or wrote hurtful things without thinking about how the other person might feel. When she realized how unkind her words sounded, she would try to take them back. However, it was often too late.

*****

To Frank from Catherine:
Monday night
November 1, 1943

My Dearest Frank,

I just got home from work. I wanted to write you a note before I eat because this will be the only chance I will have to write tonight. Some friends of ours are coming over later. One of the girls, Emilie Newel, used to live with me. Her husband is home for the first time since going into the Army. We are going to have a little get-together. Becky and David are coming over, too. I don't think you know the rest of the people, so I won't write all of them down.

This has been a busy day for me. I always have a lot of mail on Mondays. Millie and I have worked hard. But we have played a little too. In fact, we have laughed most all day. This old man who works out there thinks Millie is the cutest girl in that office. He is about sixty. He doesn't have any hair, and his head is as slick as a dime. I have teased her about him all day.

By the way, Dump told me today that Smokey has gone to Benning. She hasn't heard from him since he left Mackall. So she says. But I doubt it.

Well honey, how have you been doing since I last saw and heard from you? I bet you have been a busy little boy, Ha! Ha! Just don't get so busy that you don't have time to write to me. Frank Darling, I do miss you so much. If you don't write to me, I just won't write to you. No, Frank, I don't expect you to write to me every day—that is too much—but twice or three times a week. Ha! Ha! Or, should I say, as often as you can. Sometimes I write every night. I promise I will write as often as I can.

So until next time, so long. I will have to hurry to get ready.

Love, Cathy

*****

To Frank from Catherine:
November 5, 1943

My Dearest Frank,

I received my first letter from you today. You have no idea how glad I was to hear from my Frank! I know that you had a nice cruise over, but what? No nurses? Ha! Ha! I bet you did enjoy just eating and sleeping—that must be a wonderful life, but I've never had a chance to do that. You couldn't help but have a safe cruise with a Navy escort. After all, there is an Oliver in the Navy.

Darling, there is one thing I want to know. Can you tell me where you are? It took your letter ten days to come. If you could tell me, I wish you would. I won't tell anybody if you don't want me to. I just want to know where my Frank is. I have been waiting all of these weeks, and I don't even know where you are. It must be an awful old camp not to have the things you need. This is war. When you come home, Darling, you can have all the hot water you want. I hate for you to shave with cold water because I have heard my dad fuss about that.

Just don't be looking too good, because those foreign gals are after the Yanks. I read a letter today that an English girl wrote to one of the boys' sisters. I am telling you she was after that boy! He had only dated her once. So you see, you better be careful and remember me (not Wilma Ha! Ha!) No! Just me. I am selfish.

By the way, have you gotten the pictures we took last Sunday when you were here? I sent you three pictures of me last week in one of my letters.

Honey, you didn't say anything about receiving my letters. Have you received any of them? You must have received them. It's November. I know at least, I hope you have. Because I have written every chance I get.

Frank, I think you are so sweet to write to me by candlelight. That must be a terrible camp you are in. Is it in the war zone? I will always love you for that. I know it is hard to write when you have good light much less candlelight. Ha! Ha!

Frank, you said that you miss me, but not half as much as I miss you. Yes, I remember that Sunday—every minute of it. We did have fun, didn't we? That old train had to be on time for once. It was raining cats and dogs. I got soaked running to the cab. But I didn't even care. My thoughts were with you. There were so many things I wanted to tell you. Someday soon you will be back. Until then, we will just have to keep writing. That is the next best thing.

I was so happy to hear from you today, I could not even eat my lunch! What about that? That is not like me. Everything was funny this afternoon. I laughed all afternoon. Charlie said I wish you could hear from Frank every day if it makes you feel that good. So see what your letters mean to me? Don't let me down, Darling. Well, Frank, I guess this will be enough of this scratching for one night. Good night, sweet.

Love always, Cathy

Notes from Frank

On the envelope of this letter, dated November fifth from Catherine, Frank wrote a list of things to answer from her letter in his own handwriting: Where am I? How long did it take? Concerning foreign gals, Willie, and I'm Selfish too.

*****

To Frank from Catherine:
Tuesday night
November 9, 1943

Darling Frank,

Gosh, it is cold here. After the rain, old winter is here. This time, I'm afraid I will have to wear my heavy coat tomorrow. I hate old coats. I just got home from the office. We had to work until ten tonight. I tell you, I am a tired little girl. But not too tired to write a note to my Frank. If you look forward to my letters as much as I look forward to yours, then it is worth all of the time I spend writing them.

I bet you can't guess what they are singing over the radio: a new song, "Wait for Me, Mary." What does that make you think of? The dear old beach. Darn it.

Frank, I think I told you that Millie's husband is coming home. He is on his way but won't get here until Saturday. Dump is going to stay with me while he is here. She and Millie have the apartment that Millie and Vance had before he went to the Army. Three in one bed is kind of crowded. So I told Dump that she could stay with me while he is here.

Some of the girls at the office are going to dear old Camp Mackall this weekend to an officers dance. Darn it. I wish you were still here, and I was going. Wouldn't that be fun? We did have fun when we were there, didn't we?

I will never forget that Saturday night. We had a good time at Scottie's, even if Smokey and Dump did lose us. What I liked most was when we were going to Aberdeen from Camp Mackall. Do you remember what you told me that night? I have not forgotten and I never will. I couldn't say a word. But I can say it now. What I should have said then. Frank, I love you from the bottom of my heart. I miss you more than you will ever know. Just like I told you before, I don't say these things unless I mean it. You know yourself. I never told you these things when you were here because I was not sure. Darling, I am sure now. I hope it does not make any difference to you. These are my feelings. I had to write them. This is the second letter I have written tonight. I tried not to write them because I was afraid that you wouldn't like it. So I tore it up. Frank, I hope you won't think I am silly. I guess all people in love are silly to other people. But who cares? I don't, do you?

I am getting cold, so I will have to hurry. I am sitting in my bed writing this. I will go to sleep in about two minutes. Good night, Darling.

Write soon!
Love always,
Cathy

Thoughts for "North Africa"
November 1943

It took Catherine two months to decide that she was in love with her lieutenant. Nevertheless, after November 9, 1943, there was no other man or love for Catherine. She loved her lieutenant for the next 55 years.

There is something to be said for this love of theirs. It was real, and it was lasting. It was not always good, but it was not always bad, either.

And as far as I know, they are still in love—somewhere.

*****

To Frank from Catherine:
November 11, 1943

Darling Frank,

I received your letter of Oct 25th today. So you don't like Africa—but Frank, please do not turn native on me! Ha! Ha! I guess I would love you just the same. But I believe I love you better like you. I guess you do feel like that at times. You know the old saying "Don't let your feelings run away with you." There is more truth in that than poetry. If I know Frank, he can take __ ______.

Darling, I am so sorry to hear that you have not gotten any mail. I have written almost every night since I got your address. I wrote you five or six letters and sent them to Fort Meade. When they do catch up to you, you will have to take a day off to read them. Not to mention the letters from your family—and yes, don't forget Willie—darn it. Oh well, you will have a good time. It makes me mad you have to wait so long to get mail. Did you only receive one letter from me while you were at Meade? The one with the pictures in it? Frank, I wouldn't take anything for those pictures. I like those of you so much. I look at them every day and remember how much fun we had that weekend. Darn it! It all had to come to an end too soon. But this old war will be over one of these days, and then you will be coming home. Hooray! Hooray!

Honey, I do appreciate you trying to have a big picture made for me. It would help the looks of my bedroom. More than anything I know.

Darling, they would have to play my song, "Thinking of You," wouldn't they? It is a pretty thing, isn't it?

I went to the hospital tonight. I am telling you, I have not stopped since 5:10 p.m. I went to the hospital at seven and worked until ten. It takes me about an hour to come home. I have already had my bath, and I'm ready for bed. So it is getting late—past my bedtime. But Darling, if you were here, I would not get sleepy. I would stay awake all night. I wouldn't do like I did, and fall asleep. I would be so glad to see you, I would not even think about sleep.

Gosh, it is cold here tonight. The moon is so pretty tonight. It makes me think of the pretty moon we had the night we came home from the beach. Remember?

Darling, my candle has not burned down to the wick, but my eyes are almost closed. I will keep on writing, hoping you will receive the letters soon. You do the same. I miss you more every day.

I love you,
Cathy

*****

To Frank from Catherine:
Friday night
November 14, 1943

Darling Frank,

How is my Frank tonight? OK, I hope. I am fine. Just a little tired, but that don't count. With a few hours of sleep, I will be good as new. Ha! Ha!

I went to dinner with Dump and Millie tonight, and then to the movies. We saw a good picture: Sweet Rosie O'Brady, with Betty Grable. She is so pretty. Do you like her? Frank, I bought a couple of new records today—"Only a Rose" and "Close to You." Here are the words for "Close to You":

Close to you, I will always stay,
Close to you, though you're far away.
You'll always be near, as though you were here,
By my side, no matter where
In my dreams, I'll find you there ...
Close to me, sharing your caress
Can't you see you're my happiness,
Wherever you go, my heart will go, too
What can I do?
I only want to stay close to you.

Don't you think that is pretty? If you get a chance to hear it, you can pick up the tune. That is the way I feel about you—I just could not word it like that. I mean it, Frank—I guess you are wondering what happened to me. It is just one of those things that you can't help.

Well, Darling, it is late, so I will say goodnight. Write soon,
Love always, Cathy

*****

To Frank from Catherine:
Sunday night November 14, 1943

Darling Frank,

Yes, another Sunday has almost gone. I have been a busy little girl all day. I don't miss you as much when I am busy. Otherwise, I would have too much time on my hands to think.

I worked at the hospital from seven o'clock this morning until two o'clock this afternoon. That is a long time! I did lots of work. I bathed seven people and changed their beds and rubbed their backs. That's lots of hard work. But I like it. Sometimes I wish I had gone into training. I guess I will just be a Red Cross nurse's aide for the duration.

This afternoon I went to a concert down at the Mint Museum. It was very good.

Frank, I am sending you a little old picture of myself that was made the week before I met you. This was made in the mountains. See how brown I am—I look like a "high yellow" Ha! Ha!

Oh, yes—I meant to tell you that one of my patients told me this morning that I was the best nurse's aide in that hall. That he looks forward to my nights on duty. He said it would be nice if all of the nurses had a smile on their faces like me. If they smiled more, he would get well faster. Wasn't that nice? He is an old man—don't get jealous. He is as old as my dad. But he is a good patient. *Aren't you proud of your Nurse's Aide?*

I am proud of my Frank—gosh! I sure would like to see you now. Almost two months out of the eighteen are gone! Goodie! Goodie!

Mrs. Smith was asking about you today. You remember her, don't you? She lives next door to me. I told her that you were called overseas. She couldn't believe it. I told her you had gone to win this war, and that it would soon be over, now that you are over there.

Darling, I am afraid I'm spoiling you, writing to you every night, right or wrong, but I don't mind spoiling you. They are singing my song "Close to You."

Write soon, love always, Cathy

*****

To Frank from Catherine:
Saturday night
November 20, 1943

Darling Frank,

I had the most wonderful surprise today when I came home and found the cute little package from my Frank! Darling, the little pin is lovely! I appreciate it more than you will ever know because you are so thoughtful. And it came from Africa! I shall always keep it. How did you know that I liked pins, etc.? You are so sweet. I had to call my good friend Amarah to tell her. You remember her, don't you? She got a bracelet, but it couldn't be half as cute as my pin.

Darling, did you know it was just two months ago yesterday that I saw you last? darn. That night I went with you to the train. I didn't know until yesterday that the city you went to from Charlotte was a P.O.E. (Point of Entry). Is that where you sailed from?

Have you had any mail yet? I hope you have. Because it

must be hard to keep up the old chin when you can't get mail. But Darling, I know your chin is up, mail or no mail.

Guess what I am doing tonight, and where I am. I am over at Becky's. I am keeping little David while she and David have gone to the show. I have been on the go all week. So I told her I would keep him for her tonight. Don't get me wrong—I have been working most of the time—two nights at the hospital. I went to the show and to an officers dance out at Morris Field. But there was one Lieutenant missing, and his first name is Frank ... I do miss you. Really, Frank, I do miss you. All of the time I was dancing I wished you were here. But someday soon you will be back, and we will go dancing. We will have all of these dances to make up for, gosh! Won't we have fun? It is something to look forward to.

Poor old Dump has tough luck. The boy she went to the dance with is married. I think she is going to date him tomorrow night even if he is married. I can't understand her.

Well, I couldn't date a man if I knew he was married. I did date one last summer. He was a Captain out at Morris Field. That night when he took me home, he told me he was married and asked to see me again. I said no, and I meant no. I told him I couldn't date a married man. I was afraid he might like me Ha! Ha! I didn't want to break up a happy home. He said he admired me for that and said just stick to it. That is one thing I hate is married men dating. That is what made Dump mad because she could not keep dating Smokey.

Sweetheart, I hear little David. I will have to run and see what is the matter with my boy. He is so sweet. Good night, Darling. Thanks again for the pretty little pin. I can't wait to wear it and show Millie and Dump what my Frank sent me from North Africa.

Bye for now,
love always,
Cathy

*****

To Frank from Catherine:
Thursday night, Thanksgiving Day
November 25, 1943

My Darling Frank,

Happy Thanksgiving! I hope you had a nice Thanksgiving. I was thinking about you all day, wishing you could be here with me ... maybe next time.

I went home with Dump. We had a good time. Didn't do much—just went to a dance Wednesday night. It wasn't very good. The old boys stepped all over my feet. Today we had turkey and all of the trimmings. I ate so much. I know I gained five pounds today when you come home you won't even like me anymore, I will be so fat. No, I was just kidding—I haven't gained any. We went to Dump's sister's this afternoon. She has the cutest little girl about little David's size. When we got home, it was freezing cold and there was no fire in the house. We had to make a fire and fix ourselves a bite to eat. Darling, I wore my pin to Dump's home, and all of the girls had a fit over it. I like it so much. I thought one of the girls was going to take it from me. She would have had a hard time getting it! I am not kidding—I wouldn't take anything for it.

Darling, it is late. I must get my beauty sleep so that I can get up in the morning. My dad is not here to wake me up.

Good luck and good night,

Love, Cathy

*****

To Frank from Catherine:
Friday night
November 26, 1943

Darling Frank,

Gosh! It has been a hard day for me. I sure hated to go back to work after being off and lazy all day yesterday. I made it OK., but it was a tough fight.

I received your letter of Oct. 29 today. I am telling you—I was glad to get it. What I want to know is why are you not getting my mail?

Frank, you wanted to know how I liked the pin. I have it. It is beautiful on my brown suit. You are so sweet. Gosh! I would like to see you right now.

Darling, you said that it looks like you are going to be in the center of the action. Wherever you go, Darling, I wish you the best of luck. I will be pulling for you, and with God's help you will come through OK. I know it is tough, Darling, but we will have to face it like brave soldiers and keep our chins up. (Ain't that right, Darling?) I know you are the bravest soldier in North Africa or Italy or wherever they send you.

The war news sounds good today, thank goodness.

Frank, you said the Red Cross was doing good work. I am glad to hear that. I know they are doing good work here because I work for them! I am one of their "little angels of mercy" Ha! Ha! You know your Red Cross nurse's aide. I know you have my picture, remember? Or do you still have it?

My family has gone off and left Dump and me by our sweet little selves. We had to cook our own dinner and make a fire when we came home. We didn't have time this morning—we overslept—forty minutes late! Charlie has teased me all day. He is so crazy. He said to tell you "hello." He thinks you are a swell fellow.

Darling, we are going to the show, so I will have to hurry. So long for now, wherever you are.

Love, Cathy

*****

To Catherine from Frank:
November 16, 1943
North Africa

Darling Cath,

I now have a few more hundred miles of North Africa dust under my belt, and when I say dust, I really mean just that. We have more or less now settled in our semi-permanent homes on the rock bound coast of the Dark Continent. Our homes are pyramidal tents that come completely equipped with such modern facilities as running water (when it rains), good solid hard floors (good earth), canned lights, candles, tin chinaware, and constant air conditioning. It never rains but what it pours, and as yet it hasn't stopped raining.

My old outfit was tough, but over here they want us tougher. Instead of running four miles in 50 minutes over here, they want it done in 40 minutes. We do have quite a bit of free time. The American Red Cross is sure to make things a lot nicer for us. In fact, they furnish just about all our amusement and recreation, and there's one here on the base and one in town. Every night they serve ice cream and believe me, it's about the best that I've ever had. They sponsor American films that the G.I. wouldn't ordinarily get to see. And some of the stage shows that they put on are really very good. The first show I saw over here was the last show I saw in the States—"So Proudly We Hail"—remember it?

Darn it, the mailman has forgotten where I have gone to because as yet I have not received any mail from the States. None of the officers that I serve with have received mail either.

I have my camera and my film, and I have taken some good ones, too. But that is as far as it goes. I can't send any in the mail because of the censors. I can't get them censored until I can get them developed and printed, and that I can't do. I hope they will keep until after the duration.

Enclosed is a five-franc note. In American cash, it is worth less than one dime. But it is aggravating when we get a pocket full of cents. A centime is 1/100 of a franc, and it's not worth the bother to carry them around. Have you received the small package yet? How long is it taking my letters to get to you? Say hello to all of you. How is Central making out in football? The closest I get to a football game is listening to them. The last two games were Notre Dame games. Well, Darling, that brings this chapter to a close. I miss you always, Cath,

Adios,

Love, Frank

*****

To Catherine from Frank:
November 21, 1943
North Africa

Darling,

I just received my first letter from the States. It was from a sweet girl somewhere in the vicinity of Charlotte. And by the way, where I long to be. I never knew how much a letter meant to a man overseas until now. I've seen majors and Colonels stand in line for an hour waiting for a letter, only to leave with a long face when they didn't score, and most of them don't. I'm the only one in our tent who has scored so far, and I'm looking on with envy. I am cussed and even congratulated. Letters are not just read once or twice, but many times. It was sure swell to get your letter. I wish you knew how swell.

In one of your letters, you said we would have to work hard. Gee! I wish they would give us some work. We have our first formation at 0800 and at 1015 we're through for the morning. We have an afternoon formation at 1400 and in an hour and a half, we are through for the afternoon. Three uniform work hours in a day. I wish they'd work the devil out of me so time would fly. The officers are practically begging for something to do.

Cath, please send me the pictures of you that we took. You are always too critical as to the quality of a picture.

I was just looking at the calendar, and it has been just eight weeks today that we took those pictures. It was just eight weeks that I took that train also.

Darling, did you get that little package? I hope that you are getting my letters OK. Where are you going on your vacation? Say hello to Charlie for me and tell him his position is saving the records. And as you go out the door tomorrow night, give "Poison Ivy" the telephone operator a good swift kick.

Darling, someday that train I caught eight weeks ago is going to pick up a Colonel or a major and the first stop is going to be Charlotte. Or wait—was it Major? Major sounds better with Ward. I miss you, Cath, ever so much. I think about you ever so much. I think about you all of the time. And the good times we had. But I think too about the good times we're going to have just as soon as I get back. Remember me to Becky and Dave and your Mom and Dad. Cath, please send those pictures.

Love always, Frank

*****

To Catherine from Frank:
November 25, 1943
North Africa

Darling,

Today is Thanksgiving Day, and I ask myself ... What have I to be thankful for? Well, for a young Lieutenant who is on foreign soil, who has few friends, and who is away from home on Thanksgiving for the first time—to him or anyone else like him things might look a bit on the gloomy side. But then I remember those boys on the front lines who aren't even having cranberry sauce, who are eating cold C-rations and drinking cold lemonade, sleeping in wet clothing and sleeping in a fox hole half filled with water. Then I think of something even more enlightening—I think of the girl I have left in the States who loves me and whom I love ever so much. Yes, I have so much to be thankful for.

I do love you, Cath. I told you that one night in Aberdeen … remember? I missed you so much when I was going to see you next weekend. But now I miss you ever so much more, Cath. I wish that I were there looking at you as I was in that picture we took. But in time, Cath, I will be there—what a swell difference!

Time sure goes slow. They haven't given us a good day's work since I got here. They give us some physical drills to keep us physically fit, but the only exercise our minds get are ways to beat the other fellow to the mail line or the chow line. First, we wait in the mail line then we sweat out the chow line. Then we wait in line to wash our mess gear. Then if we are going to town, we have to wait in line for both coming and going. The old Army game of hurry-up-and-wait.

Darling, I've received three letters from you dated October 23, 14, 4. The mail system over here is really messed up. Some fellows haven't even received a scratch of the pen from the States. Your three letters are the only ones I have received. I wish I had a dozen more. Have you received any of my letters yet or that small package?

Well Cath, that's all for now. I'll write very often. Say hello to all of you.

Love always, Frank

*****

To Catherine from Frank:
November 27, 1943
North Africa

Darling Cath,

Time still goes by slowly. There are hopes that there'll be something to do coming next week. I hope so.

Well, it's Saturday at the Red Cross Club as usual. It's becoming my favorite haunt. Right at this moment, it's only 4:00 p.m. in Charlotte, but here it's nearing that hour when Taps calls.

Yesterday, I was in town giving it the once-over again. About the only reason that we go there is for a change in scenery, and, as usual, I was looking for a place to have a picture taken. Well, I found it but—and here's the only trouble—they make four small ones and one picture a large one. It is not a portrait picture. It's a copy of the small picture, done in crayon—and it is really good work! Portraits are very hard to obtain here because of the material. Gee, Cath, I hope you like it. Please do not judge it too quickly. These French are not good at photography but are very good at drawing and copies. They make them in color crayon, and they are hard to tell the difference from a real portrait.

I just had my handwriting analyzed, and he fit me right to the tee. He told me a lot of things that after I thought about it seemed right on.

I finally got a letter from home today. But darn it, honey, I did not get a letter from you—maybe next week.

All of us are pinning our hopes on next week. Regardless of what it is. Some got assigned this week but the rest of us maybe next week. So it goes. Despite the lack of something to do (work), this bunch is still in high spirits. If this is moral, those Hinnies (jackasses) had better start to run. From where we sit, things are looking good.

Cath, honey, I will write as often as I can. Only remember

there may be some times when I won't be able to write. But even when I can't write, I will be thinking of you all of the time.

Well, Mary, those Taps I told you about are blowing. Good night, Darling. I love you.

Love Always, Frank

*****

Letters from Home
To Frank Junior from Frank Senior:
November 17, 1943
Los Angeles, California

Dear Frank:

It is surely surprising how quickly these Wednesdays roll around. Seems like every day is either Sunday or Wednesday. I guess it's because everybody is keeping busy. I hope that by this time at least some of your mail has caught up with you. But if not, please do not think you have been forgotten, because there are plenty of letters on the way. To begin with, there seemed to be a slight misunderstanding as to the proper way to address them. However, that difficulty has now been straightened out, I think. We were certainly glad to receive your letter a few days ago. I believe it was about fifteen days on the way, as we got it about the 11th.

*****

Well, Frank, everything is all good at home. We are certainly learning to live the simple life nowadays. If it were not for going to work, no one would be farther away from the place than Allen and Hick's Groceries. Clint is still driving the Plymouth, as he has not been able to get the Chrysler suffi-ciently loosened up to run it to work. So mother and I walk to

Fifty-Fourth Street, and that's about as far away as we get. We see our Maize cat every day over there. She is everyone's pet, and I have seen several customers stand in line waiting their turns to pet her. They say she has cleaned out all of the mice and rats in the place. She seems perfectly contented, although she remembers mother and me. Or do I just imagine so?

Yes, it is almost Thanksgiving, and the weather is more like September in Utah. Warm and sunny days, and nights that make one reach down for the old extra blanket. I am afraid that I have now become a confirmed Californian. I dislike even to think of ice and snow and twenty below zero and all that sort of thing.

Well, Thanksgiving is just around the corner, but it seems that the usual spirit of the occasion is sadly lacking. I guess everybody has put the holiday spirit away in the moth balls until all the boys get back home again. Here's hoping that will be before the next season comes along. We are going to try to have Ernest up for dinner if he can come. We still have not heard from him.

So I will stop for now and continue in my next letter which will be soon. I wish you the best of luck, my boy, and convey to you the love and best wishes of all of us. Also, hope to hear from you again soon.

Cheerio from Dad, (FR Ward)

To Him Over There

May the tie that binds the heart of home
To loved ones over there,
Draw closely 'round you as you roam
Afar from the home heart's care.
And we who tread the old, loved way
While you tread the new,
We can but watch and wait and pray
Our days apart be few.
So may each long and dreary day

From hope some brightness borrow
To help us on our lonely way
'Til you come home tomorrow.

Written by: Francis Royal Ward Senior, November 1943. Papa Ward wrote beautiful poetry. He never said much except in poetry; that was the way he expressed his feelings.

*****

To Frank from Anna Ethelda (Mama Ward):
November 9, 1943
Los Angeles, California

Dearest Son,

I do hope you have received some of the letters we each write at least once a week. I'm afraid our letters are not very newsy, but I trust you are glad to get them anyway.

Well, how are you, son? Are you well and do you have all you need? I will be so happy when I can hear from you. This has been the longest six weeks I have ever spent. I hope that we will hear from you soon. Tell us as much about yourself as you can.

Everyone is just fine here at home, although Clint did sprain his ankle—he fell off the back step. I think you did the same thing once or twice, didn't you? He really did have a bad foot. He stayed home from the office for three days. He had to borrow Mrs. Wolfe's crutches. You can imagine how he liked that! Dad is just the same dear Dad. I think he is feeling pretty good. Poor Essie has been having trouble with her legs, and she has not been able to do any walking. I want her to go to the doctor, but she thinks she will get better. Addie is about the same. I am feeling fine. The Crockett family seems to be alright. Virginia took the bus and came in and spent Sunday afternoon with us. George and David go fishing every Sunday.

They really have good luck.

Essie had a long letter from Janice. Seems as though there is a little blonde nurse who feels quite bad because she has not heard from a certain Lieutenant. Would you know anything about it? Or is the gal in North Carolina taking all of your time? I talked with Wilma the other day—she is also waiting for that letter—my, how you do get around!

I feel so bad that you are not getting all of our letters. You know we do write. I don't understand why you get letters from your "little Southern Gal," and not ours. Do you suppose she has a pull?

In one of your letters you ask what I thought of your "little Southern Gal." Well, I think she is a nice looking girl, and I am sure she is as nice as she looks or you wouldn't want her. I also like her name. Did you know that Catherine was my mother's name? That was the name I had picked out for you if you had been a girl. So maybe we might have a Catherine in the family after all.

It sure seems good to see some of the lights on again, although they are not going to take the shades off the street lights. But the cross on the church is on again, and it seems to promise that everything will be alright again.

Well dear, I guess this is just about all I can think of tonight. Dad has gone to work. Clint went over to the movies to see "Wallace Berry in Salute to the Marines." You saw it, didn't you? I went out to the Chinese Theater in Hollywood to see it. It is surely a good picture. Addie and Essie have gone to bed, and I think I will do likewise. I have been listening to the Bob Hope and Red Skelton programs. Do you ever hear them? So if my letter is rather jumbled, you will understand. All the neighbors send their love. So until next time, I will say bye for now, and God bless you.

With all of my love, Mom

*****

To Frank's family:
November 17, 1943
North Africa

Dear Folks,

Cause for celebration! I received my first letter from home today! It was one from Dad which was written on the 20th of October. The mail system is really messed up over here. I received three from Cath (North Carolina), I received one from Wilma dated the 12th of October. It was V-mail, as was Dad's.

Well, it's Saturday night, and I'm at my usual haunt—the Red Cross Officers Club. It's our only source of amusement and recreation. I still don't know if you are receiving my mail. I'm afraid that Santa Claus is going to be late this year—real late—and I'm afraid that he won't be able to send much, either.

Has Don got the car back in working order yet? Tell the big lug "hello" for me, and tell him to write. Did Clint get my letter?

These francs over here sure make you forget how much you have got. You spend them like they were pennies and pretty soon you have got no more francs.

I just had my handwriting analyzed. Boy, he sure pinned me on the ground. He also pinned someone else to the point. Mom, you would sure enjoy him. He is the best I have heard yet.

Well, tomorrow I'm going in and giving the town a real once-over. I met up with one of my classmates from OCS, and we decided to find out what makes the town tick.

How is everything? Someday I hope to get another letter from home. So far my total for two months away from home is six letters.

Well, another week is in the offing. I wonder what strange experience awaits me. Well, it won't be long.

The war situation looks good from where we sit—but don't think too optimistic of the future—it's still a rocky road to victory. They have been going pretty good in the Far East.

Well, folks, those long mournful notes of Taps are sounding, and they're making me sleepy. So, 1 guess that I'd better sign off for now.

Love to all, Frank

The "nothingness" was getting to Frank. His whole unit was suffering from the same ailment: boredom, where their days moved by in slow motion. On the other hand, the snail's pace of the 17th Airborne didn't affect their morale. In fact, Frank even said that "Those 'Hinnies' (jackasses) had better watch out when we get there to the front lines."

Somewhere around the first week of October, Frank sailed the Atlantic and ended up in North Africa. He did not receive any mail from the States until November 21, 1943—a letter from Catherine. It was approximately six weeks without a word from home. Letters from home lightened the soldiers' hearts and nourished their souls. It was the oxygen to their very spirit—oxygen that they needed to fight this horrid war.

Frank received two letters dated November 9, 1943. The first one was from Catherine. In it, she told him for the first time that she loved him from the bottom of her heart. The other letter was from his mother, in which she questioned his intentions regarding this "Southern Gal." In response to his mother's letter of November ninth, Frank writes, "Dear Mom, do you think I am the type of guy who has a girl in every port? That is not quite my policy. Cath (the girl in North Carolina) has brown hair and brown eyes, and I wish you could know her."

It sounds like this "little Southern Gal" is very troubling to Mama Ward and the family at this point. In the years to come, the Wards would face a number of challenges as Catherine established her place in the family.

Frank was still in North Africa and was not fond of the country where they were stationed. He never specifically says it in his letters, but it appeared to be a primitive, backward country. His quarters were primitive, to say the least. He mentioned that the running water in his pyramidal tent was water that ran right down the middle when it rained. He calls the Red Cross Officers' Club his haunt; it seems to be a refuge for him in this primitive situation. He spent much of his time writing letters, going to dances, listening to music, and watching the movies of the day. The Club was the only place that sounded, looked, and sometimes even smelled like home. I hope that he danced at least a few dances with those "cute-cute" nurses Catherine was so concerned about. Maybe a *lot* of dances with those "cute-cute" nurses.

According to the history and the maps of WWII, it appears that Frank was in CasaBlanca, Morocco. He mentions that French is the primary language spoken in town, and says he feels it would be easy to learn. In a cool GI manner, he speaks of replacement troops on the front lines, which leads the reader to think that he felt the replacement policy was harsh but perhaps an evil that was necessary for victory. He writes many times, "Our Uncle Sam knows best."

The replacement policy was the brainchild of General McDonald, designed to keep the troops on the front lines. Contrary to Army policy in the past, he suggested that when soldiers were killed or wounded, they would send individual servicemen as replacements rather than wait for a full replacement unit. These replacements often found themselves on the front lines and received their on-the-job training in the foxholes and at the hands of the Nazi war machine. Some of these soldiers were rotating between the front lines and Frank's unit; however, as Frank says, "Uncle Sam knows best."

Frank learns from his mother that after months of blackouts, some of the lights were coming back on again in Los Angeles. In one letter, Mama Ward mentions the cross on the church has been lit once more. It was a big morale booster for all Californians to be able to go out at night and resume a few of their normal routines.

WAR NEWS

- November 18, 1943, Allied leaders meet in Tehran, the capital of Iran, for a conference and a show of unity.

- The "Big Three" (the US, Great Britain, and Russia) agreed on an allied approach / mutual support policy of "One for All, and All for One."

- France was still occupied by the Nazis.

- The main topic of the Tehran Conference was the how, when, and where of the upcoming Western European invasion: the historic D-Day invasion of June 6, 1944.

Christmas in North Africa

The Third Month of Deployment
December 1943

To Catherine from Frank:
December 1, 1943
North Africa

My Darling,

Well, another month has been marked off and another month starts its inevitable march. There has been quite a bit of argument as to what great event this month will bring. Some say peace by the end of December, and they'll go so far as to give odds. That's one bet that I'd like to lose some money on. But I string along with the great majority who believe that it will be quite a few months before things are peaceful in this theater. Cath, there are a lot of things going to happen over here, and I'd like not to be in the center of activity. Boy, I am going to have some tall tales to tell when I get back. What bothers me is how I am going to remember them all. I've finally got something to do (I think). I was given an assignment today, but that's all I can say about it. Have you seen any of my old insignias lately?

I agree with you, Cath, when you say that it's hard to express yourself when you're writing. It's hard for me sometimes to express myself, always just missing what you want to say and mean by just one or two words. I don't know, Cath, maybe my letters are blunt sometimes, but Darling, they are not meant to be.

Yes, Cath, my chin is up, but sometimes it's a little low—not down, but just a little low. But then I get a letter from you and boy! You ought to see how my morale goes up! Every one of us usually gets out of bed on the wrong side once in a while, but what keeps us all boiling and in good spirits are the arguments we have. There are two boys in my tent from the Deep South: Georgia, and Old Miss. Another two westerners, the northerners, and two Californians will gang up on the two southern boys. But then the North and the South gang up on us. We have one neutral in our tent. When we start arguing, he throws up his hands in disgust and beats a hasty retreat.

Boy, it is 40 degrees here, and I'm sitting here eating ice cream. Oh yes, a new address: instead of 7th Battalion, make it 13th Battalion: Company A 13th Battalion 1st Replacement Depot.

Darn it. That tune is a curse on mankind. It's a black mark on human intelligence! In other words, "Pistol Packing Mama."

The Christmas spirit is starting to prevail. They're playing Christmas Carols, and everyone is talking about what they'd like to get for mom, dad, sis, etc.—and then end up getting the best they can, which, over here, isn't very much. Tomorrow I'm going to town to pass judgment on a picture I had taken the other day. I hope it is good.

Well Cath, it's early to bed and early to rise. So I guess I'd better hit the hay, and I mean hay, too. We have hay mattresses.

I love you, Cath. Believe me, Darling, and I'll see you soon. This war won't last forever.

Good night, Mary,
Love always, Frank

*****

Saturday, December 4, 1943
North Africa

Darling Cath,

I'm one happy Lieutenant today. I hit the jackpot in the mail line to the tune of 10 letters! Five of them were from you, and the rest were from home.

Well, it's Saturday, and I'm at my usual haunt—the Red Cross Officers Club. I'm just sitting here before the fireplace, taking it all in. The Club is still quite empty. It's still early in the evening, and it's also payday for quite a few. I was in town Thursday to see how the picture was coming along—so far so good.

Darling, I hope by now that you have my little package and that my letters are coming though.

Cath, when I was at my other African station, I had some pictures taken. They weren't so hot, as you can plainly see. Darling, any picture that you take of yourself, how about sending me a print? I'm still up against censorship troubles on my prints, but as soon as I get around the censors, I'll send you some pictures.

You know we sure had some good-looking nurses on the way over; they were sure jovial and a lot of fun. But here's the rub. They were male nurses! Anyway, I prefer my nurse's aide to anything the Army has.

No, Cath, your letters aren't censored by anyone other than the Lieutenant that censors mine. Incidentally, that Lieutenant who censors mine hasn't cut anything out yet. If it has been cut, then it means that someone else is censoring my mail.

I sure wish you could see this country, Cath. It is quaint and picturesque, crazy and dangerous. More than one GI has had his head bashed in by these "friendly Arabs." But as long as one steers clear of the native quarter, there's not much to worry about. Anyway, the "Buddy System" is employed a great deal.

Darling, they've finally given me something to do.

I met up with some of my old classmates over here—infantry school chums from Camp Roberts. In fact, there are almost enough of us over here to have a reunion.

Remember me to everyone. Cath, Tell Dump I'm sorry if I caused her any hurt, but she's too nice a kid for anyone like Smokey.

Darling, another of those weekends is at hand. Yes, Cathy, I'm afraid you did spoil me. But it's nice, and I enjoy it. It's a lot of time we'll have to be making up for (plus 3 hours). I've got to say "au revoir" for now. I love you, Cath.

Love Always, Frank

*****

Frank had knee surgery in December 1943. In the letter below, he informs Catherine of his surgery and updates her on his recovery.

*****

To Catherine from Frank:
December 12, 1943
North Africa

My Darling,

Another weekend is rolling by. They seem to roll by so slowly, and I can't do too much about it. Maybe it is because I want them to go fast when they go slow.

Cathy, I got the picture the other day, and I'm sending it just as soon as I can get it wrapped suitable for overseas ship-ment. I enclosed one of the small ones that they made. Not bad, if I do say so myself. I hope you like it, Darling.

My surroundings are entirely different from my usual weekend haunts. Instead of the 8-man pyramidal tent, my liv-ing quarters are now a long low white building with a double row of white beds with a nice white sheet showing at the head of each bed. In the middle of the room is a portion separat-ing the officers from the ER. This in all gives you a bird's-eye view of Ward #30 at one of the Army's hospitals. My quarters have been temporarily removed from my tent to this immaculate place. I've sure got a better picture of the Army Medical Corps since I arrived five days ago. The third day I was here they operated for what the doctor termed a mouse joint. I had it over in the States, but it took an ocean trip and what they threw at us over here to bring it up. But it won't be long before I'm up and at it again. And I'm not anxious to be inside of this ward (or any other, as far as that goes) for a long time—in fact, never.

I sort of feel as though I shouldn't be here when I look across the aisle and see a Lieutenant who has been on his back for over three weeks. Two legs filled with shell fragments and one arm broken. When I first saw him, my first thought was (as it still is now), *I should be up there carrying on where he left off.* Maybe that sounds crazy or silly. But that's the way I feel. He and I have done quite enough conversing and found that we were born not but a few blocks apart and that we have a mutual friend. Funny we didn't know one another. Strange the way "Fate" will throw people together.

Darling, I've got to go now. I miss you and love you always. Remember this, Darling, and I'll see you soon.

Love always, Frank

*****

December 19, 1943
North Africa

My Darling,

Well, today I tried out my new leg. Boy, it was like walking on a rubber one. It was quite a sight to see me holding on from bed to bed, steadying myself as I went. But as the day wore on, the rubbery-ness of my leg wore off, and at the present time,

I'm able to get around with just a slight limp. I hope to be discharged the first part of this week.

I went to church this morning and enjoyed it. The Christmas season is prevailing, and Christmas carols are heard everywhere. I wish that I could be in the States for Christmas. But I'm not the only one with that wish. The Red Cross sure is doing a bang-up job over here. They make things very nice for the men here, bringing in reading material and giving the men chocolate. That's a treat because chocolate is really scarce—although we really don't starve for candy.

This 19th day of December is the anniversary of my going away. Cath, you spoiled me. By the way, I like it. Darling, I've told you before that I love you but Darling, I wish you knew just how much you mean to me. Anything I say doesn't sum up or quite express the way I feel. But Cath, I love you, believe me. Someday I'll be back, and then I will be able to tell you just how much I love you. Yep! Cath, you've spoiled me, but I like it that way.

Give my regards to everyone. I am still trying to get some film developed but no luck. I'm sending the picture tomorrow as today is Sunday.

I had a surprise arranged for you, but my plans went haywire. The certain letter I sent that contained the surprise came back by the request of the US censor. It was marked "You are making a reference to a geographical location more specific than 'North Africa.'" Boy, was I ever mad, as this letter was mailed over a month ago!

I am hoping for some mail today. One of the Lieutenants went over to the A.P.O. and I'm hoping that he brings some back.

I just missed committing murder yesterday when those musicians were here. One Georgian asked them to play "Pistol Packing Mama" but much to my pleasure they did not know it. I am afraid I would not be responsible if they had. Remember that night at Dump's? Boy, if only I would have got to that record!

Well, Darling, I guess that's all for now. C-rations (darn it) are calling.

Love, Frank

*****

December 21, 1943
North Africa

Hello Darling,

How's my nurse's aide tonight? I'm up and around now, and I'm hoping to get out of here in a couple of days.

I received some mail the other day. Darling, you know you are spoiling me. Eighteen letters altogether. Gee! Cath, those pictures are sure swell. They make me feel like a million dollars every time I look at them. Those of you are almost as lovely as you really are. I'm going to try and have a crayon drawing made of us two together. I got the crayon drawing of the small picture that you now have. I'll send it as soon as I can pack it properly. Cath, honey, your letters mean so darn much to me, and I'm constantly looking forward to each one. Today was my reading day. I read my mail which amounted to a good hour's reading.

I read a book today called the "Magnificent Obsession" by Lloyd C. Douglas. It's entirely different from the movie. It's really very good. I wish there were more of his books around.

I bet Millie was happy when her husband came home. Say hello to Dump and Millie for me.

They've sure decorated our ward to correspond with the season. Now if we'd have a little snow, it would give us a White Christmas. That song is enjoying much popularity over here.

Well, Cath, I guess that's all for now. Except I miss you ever so much.

Love Always, Frank

*****

To Catherine from Frank:
December 25, 1943
North Africa

Darling Cath,

I'll bet it's a beautiful day in Charlotte. It's very nice here for a change. The sun is shining, etc. This weather isn't suggestive of the season. I was hoping for a bit of snow to make it a white Christmas. But I'll be satisfied with the warmth and the sun. The Red Cross has surely decorated the town! It is decorated to look like the main street of my hometown. Cath, they are doing wonders for everyone over here. They more or less made the fellows enter into the spirit of everything. This afternoon they put on a show in the different wards of the hospital so the bed patients could keep up on some of the later shows.

Boy, they've had me busy for this last week—censoring the Yuletide mail.

I am going to murder this Georgian here. He insists on singing "Pistol Packing Mama."

They have some Italian pensioners working here, and boy, we sure have fun with them. Every now and then we pick up a word of Italian in exchange for a word of English.

They put on a feed here today that was fit for a king. Turkey and all that goes with it, and it was really good.

Well, another year will soon be gone. I'm keeping my fingers crossed for this coming year. We've been listening to President Roosevelt. It's like hearing a voice from home.

Well, Darling, I'm on my way to you—that is, my picture is. Darling, if you receive as much joy and happiness out of it as I have out of your picture, then I'll be very happy. Darling, I send it with all of my love.

How's the chin, honey? Still up? That's a foolish question. Yes, mine's up, too. As long as I can crack a joke and gripe about the GI chow, my chin will be up.

How's everyone on the home front? Tell Charlie that he is a slave driver—or don't you think he is? That clipping about the bather ... We have a few more modern facilities: one is namely a shower.

Darling, I guess that is all for tonight. I miss you so much, Cath.

Love always, Frank

Interim Thoughts

Did he date some of those "foreign gals," as Catherine called them? Even if he had, we never would have known about it. She had assured him that she didn't care if he dated; she just didn't want to hear about the fun he had with other girls while he was away. As a gentleman, Frank honored that and did not kiss and tell. Here's hoping he found some sort of female companionship in addition to writing Catherine letters—just to take some of the sharp edges off his experiences in North Africa. If he did date some of those "cute nurses" Catherine writes about in her letters, he kept it close to his vest forever. He would never want to say anything that would cause Catherine to feel insecure.

Letters from Home

December 1943
To Frank from Clinton:
December 30, 1943

Dear France:

I have sent you three V-mail letters in the last six days. Each had a definite reason, and this Air Mail letter is a supplement to them. Of first importance is a V-mail being mailed the same day as this is. It is in regards to your last letter, also received today. Your letter is dated October 25th—two months and 5 days ago. In it, you enclose a money order of $10.00 for some flowers to be delivered. Specifically, I had just priced these flowers a few days ago, and was going to get some for mom, but it seems like very high prices have hit even the flower markets. A dozen of the best quality red is $8.50. So I stuck my nose in the air and sallied forth in search of dandelions. However, rest assured on my way home from the office tonight, I will tend to your request to the last detail. No, I don't think you're a sucker; if you are, it's fun to be one. I spent huge sums on flowers for little honeys and had vague conceptions of the rich dividends forthcoming but alas, they never materialized, so it's just another phase of education. Course I know your girl is different from the others, etc., etc. From the picture that we have of her, I would say sincerely, she is all you say—and more ...! I regret, however, they were so late in getting there. Still, it seems significant that she will get them on New Year's Day.

The V-mail is in regards to a letter received some time ago when you requested a pocket dictionary—you said you did not have anything to read. It seems like a strange thing for a soldier to want to read. So I presumed you were fooling—if you still want it, please remit a signed permit to send it to you. Tell me, would magazines reach you, say like if I got you a subscription to Esquire—would you get the magazine or not? Did you take your radio with you? If so, how do you get batteries? Or do you run it on camel power?

Your description of the knives and swords is very interesting, and if you don't bring or send home a trunk-full or so, I will tell Ma about your sugar expense.

It is a very gloomy, cold and stormy day in S.C. and the broad streets of L.A. are rivers. It is just 35 hours till 1944 is here, and the men of science, economics, military, and politics tell us that it will be the most momentous year in history. I think they know what they are saying. And I hope that next Christmas we can scrap over the drumsticks.

The Chrysler runs like a top now, but the cut in gas coupons has forced me to abandon it. One-half of our fair city's gas stations are closed, adorned with huge signs: No Gas. Plymouth is very tired; she folded up a week ago with a broken water pump. I am going to try to get some shop to rebuild the old crate. New motor, top upholstery, and paint job.

Dad is feeling pretty good now; he just recovered from a touch of the flu that is going around—fortunately, a light form. Essie is the same as ever. I think she worries a lot over Elwood in the Jap prison camp. Addie is just fair. She has trouble with her eyes, and it is plain to everyone that her left eye is only about 1/3rd efficient as a huge cataract is apparent in the pupil. However, she doesn't seem to realize it, and we don't tell her. But she is complaining about her impaired vision all of the time. Mom is feeling good, although as I have said before, she suffers from "war suspense" or rather she seems to be constantly wondering about you. Two months ago Dr. Mills told her that absolutely three months must not pass before she gets that other eye operated on. She wants to, Dad wants her to, and so do I. It is not a question of money; it's what in the hell can we do with Addie? I am away all day, Dad is away at night, and Essie won't have anything to do with Addie. And we cannot leave her alone. I hope to God something turns up to relieve the situation pretty soon. I mortally dread going home at night—the atmosphere is as taut as a bow string. It really has me worried and almost to the point of the jitters.

As I stated in my V-mail letter to you ... if it is possible, and you are permitted to, take a couple of bucks and buy mom a trinket or something and send it home to her. Just the fact that it is from you and adds some sort of a close contact—that will do more for her than anything else right now. You ought to have seen her when she received your telegram! And she phones me up at the office every day to see if I got a letter from you. She did today, and when I said yes, I could just hear the wires hum. Don't get the idea that she's soft or being silly—it's something too deep for us to understand, I reckon.

Well France, we are all feeling very good now, although all of us have had the light type of flu. We are living well, eating better than we ever did, and living more sensibly than before, we have plenty to wear, plenty to do. However, we don't have to wallow in a slimy foxhole or dodge lethal bullets, or even drink warm beer. We sit tight in our well-lit American homes, safe from enemy bombs and bullets. We exercise our American privilege of griping and grumbling. We are well entertained—like hell, France—but that is just a farce, and there is no sacrifice too great "to get you boys back again."

Adios Hermano,
Clinton

Letters from Catherine to Frank

December 1943
To Frank from Catherine:
December 1, 1943

Darling Frank,

Just a note to say hello because it is late. I just got home from the hospital—I worked later tonight than usual. Gosh! It was cold waiting on that bus. I am almost frozen. But I think I will make it. You have heard the old saying, "You can't keep a good man down." That's me.

Frank, do you like poetry? Here is one or part of one of Sammie Kay's poems:

Lonely without you, I have missed you in a thousand ways.
I find myself reading every letter that you send
A hundred times from beginning to end.
My heart beats faster, and I am lonesome all the more.
When I read with love to the one I adore.
But somehow at twilight, my longing seems to cease.
In the silence that comes from the quiet peace.

Don't you think that is a pretty poem? I love it. I thought you would like it because that is just like me. I do like the poem said: I read your letters over a hundred times from beginning to end. I have missed you more than you will ever know. Do you miss me???

Goodnight Darling, Best of Luck.

I love you always, Cathy

*****

December 9, 1943

Darling Frank,

I received two letters from you today. The one you wrote on Thanksgiving and the other on November 27. Boy, was I glad to hear from you! This week I am doing OK. The mail system over there must be terrible if you have only received but three letters from me. I have written one every night! Darling, you said you would write as often as you could. I don't expect you to write to me every day. After all, I know you have a war to win. No kidding, Frank, just to hear from you regularly is all I want. Although I would like to hear from you every day, that is too good to be true. After all, this is war. I was thrilled today when I got two letters. Millie was teasing me just before

I left the office and said, "He doesn't like you, and you won't get any mail from North Africa today."

Darling, you did have a lot to be thankful for. First of all, I was thankful that you were not on the front lines having to go through all of that rain and cold, etc. Darling, I have been reading all about the men on the front lines; it is heartbreaking to even think of those things, but we must be brave. I know it is easier to say than to do. It all must be done for our freedom. From the looks of the war news today, everything is going good for us. I hope and pray that it will all be over soon.

Darling, I can't wait to get the picture. I know it will be good. It couldn't help but be good if it looks like my Frank. At least it will be something different. Will it be in color? I hope so. Tell them to rush it. I can't wait to see it. I will be watching it every day. I just love to get packages and mail. Darling, I hope you received your packages OK. I hope your fruit cake will be good. I mailed them October 1st as soon as I received your A.P.O. If you are receiving my mail, you should receive your package.

Frank, I know you get tired of doing nothing, but I wish they would leave you there. I guess that is selfish, isn't it? I know you want to get in there and get it over with and come home. When you come back, I will be proud of my Colonel or Major or should I say I will be proud of my Frank. I know your mother will be too—maybe even Carol! ha-ha! I know that you could wring my neck if you could see me now after that remark. I can just see those eyes. Don't get as mad at me as you did at Smoky that time—remember? That was not fun. He was a dog.

Darling, I will say goodnight for now. I must get my beauty sleep.

Love, Cathy

*****

Sunday night
December 12, 1943

Hello Darling,

Did you go to church today? I did. The first time I have been in almost a month. My little boys in my Sunday school class were so glad to see me. We practiced our Christmas play we are going to give next week. They are so cute—I wish you could have been there with me. You came two times, remember?

I had a good time cooking today—I cooked dinner all by myself. Would you like to know what I cooked? Fried chicken, green beans, sliced tomatoes, hot biscuits, potato salad, coffee ice cream, and cake. Don't you think I am a smart little girl? David and Becky ate with me, and David ate eight biscuits—I am not kidding! I cooked chicken and noodles for my patient (my mother who is still sick). She will be OK in a day or two.

I spent the afternoon at the church. We had to practice our Christmas music. It is beautiful. Wish you could hear it. We have worked so hard on it! But it still doesn't seem like Christmas to me. I have finished my Christmas shopping, and I have wrapped all of them. They look so pretty. I like to wrap them. Now I'm going to wrap my mother's for her.

Darling, I want to tell you the news. Millie is leaving the company. She is going to Louisiana to live with her husband, Vance. He will be there for about four or five months. She is going to take her car, and she wants Dump and me to go down with her. We can come back on the train. I think it would be fun! Charlie says I can have my vacation that week.

Darling, they are playing my song over the radio, "Close to You."

Frank, one of the girls down at the office, received a pair of shoes and a pocketbook that the people wear over there. She says they are beautiful. She is going to bring them tomorrow to let us see them. I am going to take my pin in to show them.

I can't wait to get my picture. I will be looking for it every day. I know it will be good. Next time you send me a package, don't tell me—just surprise me! I like surprises. I hope you receive your packages OK.

I must write to my brother.

Good night, Darling, and good luck.

I love you, Cathy

*****

December 14, 1943

Darling Frank,

I just got home from a lovely banquet—The Memorial Hospital Volunteers Banquet for the Red Cross nurse's aides at the Charlotte Hotel. We had a delicious dinner and music—they even took our picture! There are only three hundred fifty of us at the Memorial Hospital. Oh, yes—and I received my bar, my "commission," as I call it. So I can be in almost the same rank as my Frank. But Darling, I won't make you salute when I see you. Ha-Ha! I will be *so* glad to see you. I am not kidding.

Have you received any more mail from me, or from some of your other girls? No kidding, Frank, I hope you are receiving your mail.

This doesn't seem like Christmas. I can't get in the spirit. I am not giving many gifts this year—only my family and you.

Darling, here is a poem I wrote for you:

When I think about Christmas, with you so far away
I wonder if it is Christmas, in spite of what they say.
As I sit and quietly ponder the times that used to be
I can only wish to see, the only love for me.

Darling, I wish I knew your mother's address. I would send her a Christmas card. She doesn't know me. I could tell her that I am a friend of yours. I bet she wouldn't like that—or would she? My mother would be thrilled to get a card from a friend of my brother's. I know you must have a sweet mother because she has such a sweet son.

Darling, I meant to tell you it is snowing like nobody's business. I don't know whether it will stay until Christmas or not, but it sure looks pretty while it's falling. Gosh! It is cold.

Well, sweet, I must say goodnight—it is late. I do mean late. I must get my beauty sleep. Goodnight, Darling, and good luck. I love you always, Frank.

Lots of love, Cathy

*****

Monday night
December 20, 1943

Darling Frank,

I will be in Louisiana about one thousand miles away. My mother is about to have a fit because I am going. I will only be gone for five days. Charlie is going to be good to me. He said I could be off from twenty-seconds until the third of January. That is a pretty good vacation here in the winter. He is a good egg. I like Charlie a lot. We were teasing him today—we told him he had been a bad boy and Santa wasn't coming to see him. He just died laughing. Darling, I do not have much time, and I want to catch the next bus. So goodnight, Darling, and Merry Christmas. I will be thinking about you and wishing you were here. Next year.

I love you, Cathy

*****

December 21, 1943

Darling Frank,

How is my sweetheart tonight? OK? That's good. I am

fine. I was a mean little girl today—I didn't go to church. I stayed home and cooked dinner for my mother. That was my good deed for the day.

We had to go down to the church this afternoon at four o'clock to get ready for our Cantata. They said it was beautiful. We have worked hard on it. I am glad they liked it. I just wish my Frank could have heard it.

Darling, we had a grand time at our office party Friday night, but I missed you. We had about 60 girls and twenty men—they were just the men in the office. We had fun—we would pick out one man and then give him a big hug and then go to the other. I would have been so jealous if all those girls had been hugging you. Ha- Ha!

Darling, I bet you don't know where I am right now. I am over at Becky's, decorating the Christmas tree. Gosh! It looks so pretty. I can't wait to see what David Jr. is going to say when he sees it in the morning. It is just big enough for her living room. It's beginning to look a lot like Christmas now. I like to decorate Christmas trees. I guess I will never grow up. Ha-ha!

You remember I told you about our banquet at the Hotel Charlotte Tuesday night? I am sending you our write-up and our picture. Can you see me? I know where I was seated, and that is the only reason I can find myself.

Darling, some friends of ours just came in. I will write more tomorrow night. Goodnight, Darling, I love you always.

Love always, Cathy

*****

December 26, 1943
New Orleans, Louisiana

Dear Frank,

Here I am about 1000 miles further away from you, but

my thoughts are still with you. We had a swell trip down here. We arrived in Shreveport Friday night at about seven thirty. We left there yesterday at 4:30 p.m. and got in here last night at midnight. We had a beautiful place to stay, thanks to Mr. Thompson. He is a big shot with our company. He made our reservation for us.

New Orleans is a wonderful place. So far we have seen lots of interesting places. We hope to see many more before we leave. Gosh, Darling, I just wish you could be here to see them too—maybe next time. Darling, we are having fun, but I can't help thinking about you so far away—but you will be back soon.

Darling, did you have a nice Christmas? I hope you did. How about your Christmas packages, did they arrive OK? Darling, I was thinking about you all day yesterday while we were riding the bus. By the way, while we were waiting for our bus we took our own pictures. You know, the 10-cent machines where you put in a dime and out comes a picture. I am sending you mine. Please excuse the black spot on my face. It would be good if it were not for that. It must have been in the film.

Well, Darling, we are going to eat, so I will write more later. I love you, and I miss you.

Lots of love, Cathy

*****

December 29, 1943
Charlotte, North Carolina

My Darling Frank,

Yes, I am home. I was glad to get back. First of all, I had four letters from my sweetheart. That made it worth coming home early! We had a lot of fun.

Darling, I was so worried to hear about my Frank being

laid up in a hospital at Christmas. That is tough. Frank, I remember you saying something about your leg one night while you were here. Was it the same one you had operated on? I just wish I could have been there to wait on you. I am jealous of those nurses ha-ha! I think a nurse's aide would have been much better. You said you had some good looking nurses going over there. Did you have as much fun with those nurses as you did on the crossing?

Oh! Yes, I heard about those good looking nurses in North Africa. The Captain we met on the train was telling us how much fun he had with the nurses. When he asked me if I cared if you dated the nurses, I told him no. I don't expect you to go over there and not to date. That would be silly of me. Or anybody else. After all, you must have something to do with your spare time. That is as long as you don't forget about me.

I will admit I would be jealous if I were to see you with other women. But what I don't know won't hurt me.

Frank, in one of your letters you said that I must believe you when you say you love me. Yes, Darling, I do believe you. I love you just as much as you love me if not more. But just as I have said before, for the present time we will have to put it on paper. Yes, I agree with you, it would be nice if we could tell each other all of those things.

Darling, thanks a million for the picture. I think it looks just like my Frank. You are so sweet. Gosh, I wish I could see you right now. I have received a small one. I can't wait for the big one.

What kind of surprise did you have for me? So far your letters had nothing cut out, but some of them are opened on the end and have "passed by examiner" written on the tape on the end of the letter. I don't know if you do that or not. But that is the way some of them are received.

I had a good laugh about the "Pistol Packing Mama." Every time I hear that song, I think about you and how much you hate it. I am so glad they did know our song, "Wait for me, Mary." It is a beautiful record; it brings back memories, doesn't it? Memories I would like to live over. How about you?

Darling, I hope you had a nice Christmas even though you were in the hospital. I spent my Christmas Day on the bus from Shreveport to New Orleans. We had lots of fun. Dump and I did our share to boost the morale of the lonesome soldiers. We were the only two girls on the bus; the bus was filled with soldiers that were homesick, so we started a community sing-along. We sang all of the songs we knew—mostly Christmas Carols. When we got off of the bus, the boys thanked us over and over for the songs. They said that we helped them forget, and also we made a long, dreary trip more enjoyable.

Frank, I hope you enjoyed your Christmas packages. If you don't have them by now, I will be very unhappy. Please let me know when you receive them.

Darling, I hope that you will be OK when you receive this letter. I don't like for you to be in the hospital or maybe *I just don't trust those nurses*. No, I was just kidding.

Frank, I am glad you met some of your classmates; it makes you feel good when you can see somebody you know when you are so far away.

Darling, Dump has forgotten all about Smokey. She still thinks about him now and then, but that's all.

Yes, Frank, we will have all of these weekends to make up for. Won't that be fun?

Darling, I guess this enough for now. I am sleepy anyway. So I must go to bed. Goodnight, Darling. I love you always.

Lots of love, Cathy

✶✶✶✶✶

December 30, 1943

My Darling Frank,

Today I received two letters from you. One dated December

1, and the other December 4. Gosh, the mail is mixed up. The letters I received when I got home were December 4, 19, and 20. Not bad work.

Darling, I hope that by now you are up and carrying on. I am going to find out about that operation you had when I go back to the hospital. It makes me very unhappy to think about you being in the hospital. Just to think that I could not be there to rub your back. I guess you get plenty of attention, don't you?

I took your picture to work with me today. I wasn't supposed to go back until January 3, but I am just so important, Charlie's called me to go back in. He couldn't do without me! ha-ha! Just kidding! The girl he had on my job is sick. All the girls at the office thought that you were a very good-looking boy. "He looks pretty kissable," one said. I told her you were the best. I just wish I could see you now. I had a fit over your pictures. I think my mother liked them as much as I did. She thinks you are tops, and you are. I told her she wasn't far from wrong.

Frank, I bet you do have a good time with all of those boys—especially the "Damn Yankee." I will take those California boys myself. I like them the best. I am not recalling any names, but I think it begins with Frank.

Darling, if you don't stop eating all of that ice cream you are going to get fat. Ha-ha! You will freeze while eating ice cream in this cold weather.

We took down our Christmas tree tonight and packed it away for another year.

I haven't received the big picture yet. Maybe it will come in February for my birthday. It will be a nice birthday present. Don't you think so?

Frank, we had a swell time in New Orleans. We went to all of the nightclubs, and I was the only one in those clubs that wasn't drinking. When I say the only one, I mean it. Dump drank just as much as anybody. All the boys in the club had nice things to say about your "Cathy." I couldn't get over it. Aren't you proud of your Cathy? I am proud of my Frank because he does not drink or smoke either.

Well, Darling, I want to write to my brother. Goodnight, Frank, I love you so much, and I miss you. Keep your chin up.

Lots of love, Cathy

*****

New Year's Eve
December 31, 1943

My Darling Frank,

I had a pleasant surprise today when I got home. Just as I got home, the florist truck drove up with a dozen red carnations from my sweetheart. Darling, they are so pretty! I am so glad that you were thinking of me. I was so happy I had to cry a little. I put them in a blue vase. They look very pretty on the dining room table. I can't keep my eyes off of them.

I hope you received your Christmas packages.

Darling, I was very happy to hear you received eighteen letters at one time. If you enjoy my letters half as much as I do yours, you were glad to get them. I have read all of your letters a dozen times or more. I just enjoy reading them over and over.

Frank, did you receive the two pictures of me by myself? I am glad you got them. I like yours, too. Your picture is almost as handsome as you are. I took it to work and was going to put it under the glass on my desk, but I brought it home and put it on my vanity in my bedroom. So you think they can make a drawing of us together? I think that would be cute.

Dump came by a few minutes ago. She just left. She had a fit over my flowers. She said to tell you hello.

Darling, I received a letter from you today written on Dec 21st—that's pretty good, don't you think so? You said that I was spoiling you. Well, you are spoiling me too. I have had three letters from you this week. And four that were waiting for me when I got back—that makes seven letters this week! Oh, boy! I have had a good time reading. You don't look forward to my letters any more than I look forward to yours. I love your letters. I call my mother every day and ask, "Any mail yet?" When she answers "Yes, from Frank," my face just lights up. I can work so well all afternoon. I am not kidding.

Well, Darling, just a few more hours of this old year. Then for "the Year of Victory," I hope: 1944. I hope you have a happy new year and that you will soon get home.

Honey, when you receive this letter, you will be out of the hospital, and your nurse's aide will be thinking of you. Goodnight, Frank. I love you always, and thanks again for the flowers. I wish I could hug your neck for them but I will one of these days. We will make up for all of these days. So long for now, I will write more tomorrow. I love you, Cathy

P.S. Tonight at midnight I am going to shoot the firecrackers you gave to me the night we went to the show. Remember? That is the best way I know to welcome in the New Year—with those firecrackers my sweetheart gave me.

Lots of love, Cathy

Surprise

In December 1943, Catherine received a letter from Corporal Louie Fillet, one of the men she had dated before she met Frank. Currently stationed in England, he was one of the "boys" she wrote to while he was overseas. There was a lot of interest in the little brunette from Charlotte.

*****

To Catherine from Louie Fillet:
December 1943
England

My Darling Kat,

I hardly know how to start this letter, or what to say. I would much rather say in person what I want to say—then maybe I could convince you.

I have not thought much into the future since I have been over here. Disappointments have always been rather hard for me to take, thus I haven't tried to hope too much about the time when we will all be coming home. There is one thing I *have* thought of a lot—and that's *you*. For the short time we were together, I can assure you it was probably the happiest day of my enlistment. You couldn't have been sweeter in all you have done for me. Honey, there's something about you I will never forget—nor do I want to. I have missed you very much, and it has proved one thing to me. I love you very dearly. I can assure you, you are the only girl I want.

I hope this hasn't sounded silly to you, as I mean every word of it. In your letter, you asked what I thought of the English girls. I guess some are OK in some respects, but personally, I can't see where they even come close to comparing with the American girls.

I received a very nice Christmas card from your folks. Please thank them for me, and I wish them the best of everything.

Honey, if you see me coming down the road in the near future, don't be too surprised. I am not sure as yet, but if I get the right break—well, maybe, anything can happen.

I am in the best of health and hope this letter finds you as well. Take care of yourself.

All my love, Louie

Thoughts for "Christmas in North Africa"
December 1943

During the month of December, Catherine wrote to her lieutenant every night. She was always positive, cheerful, and eager to let him know how much he was missed every day. She was careful not to talk about the war news unless it was good. She always reminded him that they both had to be brave and to keep their chins up. She talked about Dump and how she missed her at work since Dump was no longer working in Catherine's office. Catherine told him of her Christmas choir music, her Christmas shopping, wrapping, and the Christmas cards she was addressing. As she was instrumental in taking care of her nephew, she often told Frank about her time with little David and about how she "loves him to pieces."

During his deployment to North Africa, Catherine's letters were Frank's life-bread. Catherine often said things like, "Aren't you proud of your Cathy?" or "You can tell those boys, they just don't have a girl as faithful as yours." Most of the time, she wrote these things in her "just kidding" humor, but always got her point across: "I am faithful, how about you?" She occasionally asked about those "other girls," Wilma and Carol. In her mind, it was alright for her to see her boyfriends from time to time without a second thought. However, Frank never did ask her about the other "boys" in her life when he was overseas. He must have known that jealousy was a wasted emotion.

Yes, Catherine was insecure when it came to the old girlfriends Frank had known before. It is easy to understand why she felt that way. She had only known him for five weeks and then fell in love. Then he went to war. Not only did she have to worry about her lieutenant getting killed, wounded, or captured by the enemy, but she had spells of unnecessary anxiety regarding his intentions. Nevertheless, she was very much in love with him. And I believe this was the first time Catherine was in love. She worried about the "foreign gals," as she called them, and, no doubt, those "cute-cute nurses."

In spite of her insecurities, Catherine was extremely independent. She would go on vacations with friends and spend Christmas away from home. She went to dances, concerts, and parties and loved to have fun. However, in spite of the fact that she was doing well without her lieutenant in Charlotte, there is no doubt that she was in love with Frank. He was always on her mind, and she prayed for his safe and rapid return. She dreamed of the day when they could start up again where they had left off the day he was deployed.

Catherine was, however, a little naïve when she declared how proud she was of her Frank, convinced that he did not drink or smoke. The truth is that Frank just never smoked or drank around her. This lieutenant was thousands of miles from home and sometimes had only C-rations to eat. The ice cream reminded him of home, and he loved it. So, let the soldier have his ice cream, smoke his cigarettes, and have a few drinks at the officers' club. He would work it off with one of the twenty-mile hikes over the rocky hills of North Africa.

When he read the Sunday dinner menu in the letter dated December 12, 1943, that probably finalized Frank's feelings for his Southern gal. He loved everything on that table, and he longed for home-cooked meals. Did Catherine realize how those words would affect him while his normal fare was eating C-rations? The old adage about the heart and stomach was never more true!

The Crayon Drawing Frank had drawn for Catherine
in North Africa, December 1943

January 1944, North Africa

The Fourth Month of Deployment

1944 brought a turning point in the war. In retrospect, the pundits have called 1944 the "Year of Victory" as this was the year that the Allies worked to liberate France from Germany's occupation and to save England from the same fate. Of course, we could not have seen all these developments clearly at the start of that year, but Frank did have a tangible sense that victory was coming within reach, and this strengthened his resolve to play his part in seeing these things come to pass.

In January 1944, Frank was still in North Africa. He had been released from the hospital after his knee surgery and walked miles to strengthen his knee. It was also in January that Frank finally received little tasks from his commanding officers to help the time go by faster.

The Red Cross Officers' Club had become a home away from home with ice cream, music, movies, and even a Christmas tree. RCOC was his favorite "haunt," and he missed Catherine more than words can express.

*****

To Catherine from Frank:
Thursday night
December 30, 1943
North Africa

My Darling,
   Boy, this has been one busy day for me. Has Charlie been

slave driving today? Today was my first day of freedom. I've been going from one end of the camp to the other, gathering my belongings. And at last, I've got everything under control. It seems like a year ago that I left the hospital. As you say, it's OK for people who are sick—but I wasn't, and I felt like I was goldbricking. The nurses were very nice to me. They proclaimed me as a model patient. I made my own bed and started the fire. If I hadn't, no one else would have. There was one old battle-ax there that made me mad. As mad as one certain telephone operator—but the less said about that, the better. You know my temper. Enough of that!

(Frank always said he had an Irish temper, but that he kept it under control.)

I sure hope that David isn't called up. But Darling, I found out one thing: Uncle Sam's slightest wish is our command. Say hello to David and Becky for me.

I hope that Millie had a good time while her husband was home. Give her my regards and if you don't think that Dump would bite your head off, tell her hello for me also. I hope that she's not too mad at you or I. Smokey wasn't right for her. I guess that he is a buck privateer in the rear rank. From what they have on him, it's funny they didn't get him long ago.

The first stop this morning, of course, was the post office. I got your packages and a considerable number of letters. Darling, you are spoiling me. The bracelet fits just right, and I love it, Cath. The cake looks too good to eat. If you say it will last for two months, then Cath, it will last for two months. That is if I can keep it away from the hungry wolves. All kidding aside, Cath, it's really delicious.

Seeing as how you are pulling your rank on me, I'll take some pictures and do my darn best to get them developed. But don't forget Cath, I want some pictures of *you*. Darling, thanks for everything. It was swell.

I hope your mother is alright by now. Say hello to her.

Remember the tune you wanted, but couldn't think of the

title? "People will say we're in love"—remember?

Cath, I'm sure my mother would have been pleased to hear from you, and I'm pretty sure you would like her.

They are playing one of your favorites—"Paper Dolls"—it is rather cute.

I met Quinn today. It's the first time I've seen him since I left the States.

Your letters are coming through regularly, and I hope mine are arriving with some semblance of regularity. Darling, I have got to sign off for now. I miss you.

Adios,

Love always, Frank

*****

To Catherine from Frank:
Tuesday night
January 4, 1944

Darling Cathy,

How's my lovely nurse tonight? I haven't been busy today, but I've done a lot of walking. The doctor told me to do a lot of walking. I have been walking for the last 6 hours. Just walking, not knowing where to go. When I'd come to a corner I'd flip a coin, heads right and tails left. It's a lot of fun just watching people. Sometimes I'll just stand on a corner and watch the crowds go by. Beggars, there are plenty. Shoe shine boy in his clipped English, "Hey, Lieutenant, shine good 'merican polish!" And the rest of the parade—doctor, cripple, rich man, poor man, and yes, even soldiers once in a while. I'll be walking along, and I hear some song, or a tune, see some incident, a hidden voice, and my thoughts go back a few thousand miles and a couple of months ... Gosh, Cath, I miss you so darn much. Darling, believe that.

Cath, I am glad that you liked the pin. Have you received

the large picture yet? I'm having a roll of film developed and sent to you. There are a few scenic shots and about 3 or 4 of me. There's one taken with an Arab. We found out later that he was a 1st Lieutenant in his Army. There's one of the opera and one of the statues.

Your mail is coming through regularly, Darling. Boy, I sure love to get your letters. I hope, Cath, that you're getting my mail. It worries me to think that you aren't getting my mail. I keep wondering if they have died under the censors' ax. But_______.

Has David been drafted yet? How are Becky, Dave, and David? Say hello to them. Darling, I hope your mother is better by now. Remember me to her.

Well, Cath, I guess that I'll go do some more walking back to my tent. Goodnight Darling, I love you.

Adios,

Love always, Frank

*****

To Catherine from Frank:
January 12, 1944

Darling Cathy,

Wednesday Eve at the Red Cross. I'm beginning to wonder when I'm going to spend a night in camp, but there is really nothing to do in Camp except to go to bed. Boy, I am becoming the laziest guy in the Army. If they gave a medal to fellows who did the least in the war effort, I'd be at the head of the list. Darling, the above few sentences are commonly known among the soldiers as "GI griping."

There is a certain Tennessee hillbilly down here singing some native hillbilly songs. And at any moment I expect him to start singing "Pistol Packin Mama"—and you know how much I love that song! Darling, if you will pardon me, I have a neck to ring. (!@#**) My language!

Darling, I am writing as often as I can because in the near future I may not be able to write as often; if there are times when you don't get any mail, just remember I'll be thinking of you, Cath.

I met a few British officers since I've been here. They seem like pretty nice fellows.

Quinn just dropped in out of the dark. He's on military police duty—a job I do not envy him.

I've got to go, Darling.

Goodnight, Love,

Love always, Frank

*****

Tuesday evening
January 14, 1944

My Darling Cath,

Even censoring mail can be a great relief, and that it is. That's what I've been doing, and I daresay it's a pleasure to be doing something. I hope they keep me busy or otherwise I've got too much idle time on my hands, and too much time to think about the absence of a certain nurse's aide.

Have you heard of the proverbial post office pen? Well, I've got it, and I am using it right now. It screeches so much, it sends chills up and down my back. It sounds like I was dragging my fingernails across a blackboard. I hope that you can read this.

Darling, I'm happy that you got your bars—what was your commission—a Colonel or Lieutenant? You deserve a salute when I get back.

Whether Colonel or Lieutenant, let's not argue about rank! I'll be too happy about seeing you to think of rank. That will be a happy day.

How about going to the Ship Ahoy for a steak and afterward a show or dance? Well, I can dream, can't I? I saw a good show today. Edward G. Robinson in "Destroyer." It was good.

You asked about the French gals. Well, they sure can't dance as well as a nurse's aide in Charlotte.

Darling, I hope that your mother is well soon. Say hello to me. Goodnight Darling, I love you very much.

Love always, Frank

*****

Monday night
January 17, 1944

My Darling Cath,

I received two letters from you today. One written on the 22nd and the other on the 30th of December. Seems that the mail is coming through pretty good now, though still somewhat mixed up. It's really fun to do something. I was my own boss for 24 hours, and I managed not only to keep myself busy but also to keep myself out of town. Why I go to town, I do not know. There is just not as much to do in Camp.

Darling, it makes me darned happy that you liked the picture. I hope it makes you as happy as your pictures have made me. I am still trying to get some wrapping material for the crayon drawing. But it's really scarce. However, if I pester the Red Cross long enough, they might be able to find some.

Cath, don't give the hospital incident another thought. It's over with, and the knee is as good as new. There were several times when I could have used a back rub. Yes, I did get plenty of attention. That nurse was nice and cute—*mmm-mmm!* Just kidding, honey, there's only one nurse's aide in Charlotte—know her?

Fred Waring is on right now. Boy, I sure enjoy his music. I wished they'd play "Close to you." I'd like to hear it. Yesterday

I sat in the A.R.C. Club and listened to a symphony hour on the radio. Some fun!

I'm glad you had a good time on vacation. I am proud of you. I'll tell you how proud I am in about 15 months. Darling, I'm an expert at putting up Christmas trees; I even helped put up the Christmas tree in the hospital. They said it was good, too. It's funny, it never seems like Christmas without a tree, even here in North Africa. Again, thanks to the Red Cross.

Wish I could tell you where I am, but "Uncle Sam" wouldn't like it. He's funny that way. He doesn't want anyone to know where his nephews are. I guess he knows best.

Cath, Darling, I have to say good night.

Love of my love, Frank

*****

To Catherine from Frank:
Saturday night
January 22, 1944

Hello Darling,

No, Cathy, January can't possibly go fast enough. Neither can any other month to come. I wished that I could get behind each month and nudge it on, just a little faster. But time is a touchy element. If you pay it no mind, it runs away—in fact, it flies! But if you try every conceivable way to make it go faster, it becomes as stubborn as an Army mule and refuses to budge beyond a slow pace.

I went to the show this afternoon with a few of the 17th Airborne boys—Quinn, Russell, etc. Boy, rumors concerning us are flying thick everywhere from Timbuktu to the Isle of Capri, but wherever they send us, I hope it is before the 6 months of the war.

Darling, the cake didn't last two months. Russell and I just finished the last of it a while ago. Boy, it was really very delicious.

The piano just below is going as usual. I heard the song you told me about: "Close to You." Boy, I like it very much. The words and the music are very good.

I'm glad I've got a good memory. I remember you telling me your birthday was in February. But as to the date, I'm still guessing. I have a hunch it's around the 22nd, right?

It looks like the rainy season is going to set in again. It's a little colder than usual and cloudier.

No, Darling, I haven't forgotten Myrtle Beach and the girl I met there. I've got a pretty good memory. Incidentally, Crip, how's the foot? Cathy, it was so darn much fun. But Darling, good times will come again.

The retreat ceremony is a very inspiring sight. I've taken some pictures, and I hope they are not censored.

Cath, by now you should have that large picture. It was mailed last month. I hope the sharks aren't looking at it at the bottom of the ocean someplace. That's the thing that constantly keeps me amazed—the loss of mail via Davy Jones' Locker.

Well, from here to Maison De Clon for a midnight snack. What will you have? Anything but hamburgers, steaks, or bacon and tomato sandwiches. Oh well, it was a good idea!! Goodnight Darling, I love you.

Love Always, Frank

*****

Thursday night
January 27, 1944

Hello Darling,

How's my sweet tonight—ok? Boy, time is starting to take wings now that I've been assigned to a new company. It's here at the replacement depot. But it sure keeps me busy. It's a "colored outfit" and when you're able to keep track of each member, you're classified as supermen. It's like turning a hundred bees loose and trying to tell the C.O. where each bee went. But it's definitely fun.

Well, I haven't done a darn thing to earn my room and board for over two months. So it will be fun until the novelty wears off. Then it'll be work.

From now on, I am going high-hat. There are no more lines to stand in, I eat off of chinaware, but that's as far as it goes being high-hat. Otherwise, I'm a G.I. Shavetail model M-1 à la Benning.

Cath, I sure hope that you've received the pictures by now.

I was up at the Officers Allied Club last night. I think I had more fun last night than I have since I landed on these foreign shores. Quite a few of the '17th' boys just sat around and talked about the old days at Mackall. It's the only place that we can really get a decent sandwich of bacon and tomatoes on toast and a nice cup of coffee.

I just heard the news about the landing south of Rome. The war news is good in all sectors.

I've finally got some company in my tent—four 2nd Lieutenants and one 1st Lieutenant—battle casualties who are on the way home.

Darling, remember me to a certain girl in Charlotte. Her name is Catherine. Tell her I love her and miss her very much. I will see her as soon as I get through with Hitler. Goodnight Darling,

Love always, Frank

Interim Thoughts
January 1944

This is Frank's fourth month overseas in North Africa. The war effort has made it harder to buy things like meat, butter, and other items. On the other side of the ocean, Catherine's life remains almost the same. She works for the same company, Associated Transport, tracing lost shipments. She goes to the same church, spends time with her friends, and volunteers at the Red Cross as a nurse's aide. She helps her sister with her nephew David. She lives with her mother and father, and their house is still cleaned weekly by a "colored lady" by the name of Bee, whose prices are very reasonable. In December, she enjoyed a nice vacation with her friends in Louisiana and New Orleans. The only thing that has changed for Catherine is that her lieutenant is six thousand miles away.

It is cold now in January, and the red carnations Frank sent to her at New Year's have almost died in the blue vase on the family dining room table. She is dating occasionally, but her heart is in North Africa. Catherine writes long letters to Frank every night, embellishing them occasionally with sweet, homespun poetry. She writes and writes and writes some more, night after night. She writes quite candidly about her feelings in her letters, and she doesn't mind if she sounds silly. She is in love! In January, she received sixteen letters from Frank, and she wrote twice as many to him. In one letter, he lets her know that there might be a time when he won't be able to write as often because something big is coming down the pike.

Nevertheless, she feels at ease at this time in history. Her second lieutenant is in North Africa, away from the front lines and the horrors of the Nazi war machine. She has expressed several times how much she hopes that he will stay in North Africa for the duration.

Yes, while the world of her 22-year-old lieutenant has been turned upside down, where he is stationed in a strange country he doesn't like, Catherine's world has stayed the same. In the next few months, Frank will be stationed in many different countries in the European War Theater. During the last part of his deployment, ten months of Catherine's letters were lost and never recovered. We know that she continued to write to him because Frank answered those letters with on his own.

Catherine's Letters to Frank

These are the last of Catherine's letters to Frank until January 1945.

*****

January 2, 1944

Darling Frank,

How is my Lieutenant today? I hope you are out of the hospital by now. I can't stand to think of you being in the hospital. Take care of the leg, and don't get out too soon.

I was glad you received some mail from me while you were in the hospital. That helps, doesn't it? Darling, did you receive a New Year's cable from me? I sent you one. I received a Christmas cable from a friend in England. I hope you got your Christmas packages. If you don't get them, I will be very unhappy. My mother said she feels like you got them by now. I told her I hope she is right. Darling, she sure does like you. Every time I get a letter, she asks how you are. Honey, my flowers are still pretty. I love you. My mother has enjoyed them just as much as I have. Well, almost.

I went to a New Year's dance last night, down at the women's club. I had a very good time, but there was one officer missing. His first name is Frank. Do you know him? He is a sweet person. I had the orchestra play two requests for me. Guess what they were? "Wait for Me, Mary" and "Close to You." The only thing wrong was that I was dancing with the wrong person. If you could have been there, everything would have been lovely. Maybe next time. It was a good dance. It was all formal. Your girl wore a black evening dress with a black velvet top and a net skirt. It is a beautiful dress. I had lots of compliments on it.

This has been one of those old lazy days. It rained all day. I went to Sunday School and church this morning, and I have been sleeping all afternoon. I slept four hours this afternoon! Now if you could have been here, I don't believe I would have been one bit sleepy.

We are looking for Becky and David to come home today. They have been out of town all week. I can't wait to see little David. It has been so long since I have seen that little boy. It has been over two weeks. You know how much I think of that child. He is the cutest thing I have ever seen. He looked Darling in the little suit I gave him for Christmas.

Frank, how is your family? your mother, brother, etc.? What did they send you for Christmas? Frank, I hope you sent your mother one of the pictures like the one you sent me. I think it is a wonderful picture. You are even more handsome than I thought you were. Don't get me wrong; I thought you were good looking all of the time. I know your mother would like one of those pictures of her Frank and my Frank. I think her son is swell. And he rated top with this little girl in Charlotte. Can you guess her name? She looks forward to the day when Frankie comes marching home again. Won't that be a wonderful day? That day won't come soon enough for me. We will have to keep on working hard and keep our chins up. Don't let it even get low. Darling, I am doing my part to help you keep your chin up. I write every night, even if you get tired of reading this scratching, and sometimes I am half asleep.

Well, Darling, I want to write to my brother. So long for now. I will write more tomorrow. Frank, did you know that "Cathy is in love with you"?

I love you,
Cathy
P.S. Thank you again for the flowers—they are so pretty.

Every time I look at them, I want to see you, to thank you in person. I guess I will have to do that later.

Love, "Cathy"

*****

Tuesday night, January 5, 1944
Charlotte, North Carolina

Darling Frank,

How is my sweetheart tonight? I hope that by the time you receive this letter, you will have recovered. I can't stand to think of you being in the hospital. Take care of that leg and don't get out too soon. I still can't find out what you had done to your leg. I am going to find out.

I bet you can't guess what they are playing over the radio. Our song, "Wait for Me, Mary." It made me want to see you. It is a beautiful song.

Darling, I heard today from a pretty good source that your old Camp Mackall is going to be turned into a prison camp for German prisoners. That is too close for me.

Gosh, I have been working hard this week. The first of the year—oh! It is a job! The work was behind, but I will get caught up in it a little bit. Dump is working back in our office now. She started today. You remember she was across the street—but she is not in my office now. She is in a smaller office, but I see her often. Charlie was asking about you today. He thinks you are a good-looking boy. I told him he wasn't wrong—that you are downright handsome!

Darling, did you mail your picture yet? I am looking for it every day. I can't wait to see it. Just as I said before, I would get it in February for my birthday, if it takes as long as it did for your packages to get to you for Christmas. Have you received them yet?

We had a letter from my brother today—the second in two

months. He said he received all of his packages in good condition. We sent him a fruitcake just like the one I sent you. My mother said hello. She hopes that you are much better by now, and out of the hospital.

Darling, I love you more every day. I have to say goodnight. I have lots to do before I lay myself down to sleep. Don't forget to keep your chin up.

Love always, Cathy

*****

To Frank from Catherine:
Thursday night
January 9, 1944

Darling Frank,

We had a white Sunday! We got about four inches of snow last night. It snowed all morning, but the sun came out this afternoon and melted almost all of it. We took some pictures in the snow. When they are ready, I will send some. Little David was so cute. He said "cold." David tried to get him to pick it up, and he said: "No, cold!"

I didn't go to Sunday School or church today. I spent the night with Becky and David. Becky couldn't take little David out in the snow. So I stayed home with her, and they came home to dinner with me. We had baked chicken, dressing, and all of the trimmings. Wish you could have been here to eat with us. We had a good time. You should have seen little David with a chicken leg. He thinks he is just a big boy.

Darling, I went to the movies with Becky and David last night. We saw a cute picture, "Girl Crazy." It was one of the cutest I have seen in a long time. I laughed till I couldn't breathe. If you get a chance to see it, don't miss it.

I received your letter on New Year's Day on Saturday. Say, that's what I call quick service! It makes me so mad when I think of you not receiving your mail. Frank, I bet you had a good time at that football game on New Year's Day, didn't you? Well, Darling, I hope you yelled once for me. Did you? I didn't know they had football games in North Africa. Is it just like our football?

Darling, how is that leg? I guess you have been dismissed from the hospital. But you didn't say a thing about it. I have been anxious to hear how you are doing. I noticed that your letter was written at the Red Cross Club.

Frank, I appreciate you sending me your pictures. I can't wait to see them. Oh! Yes, that crayon drawing! I know it will be good. Gosh, it is taking a long time to come.

My dad said to tell you hello and to hurry and come home. He would like to see your smiling face. I told him he wasn't the only one. I would like to see you myself. It has been three months since you left on that 11:01 train. Darling, remember that rainy night? I can't forget it myself. But Darling, one of these days you will be coming back. That day cannot come too soon.

Frank, have you gone back to work yet or are you still under the doctor's care?

I think it is wonderful that you met so many of the boys that you used to know. I bet you all have a good time on your off nights and weekends. I wish I could be there. How do you like French girls? Or have you dated any of them? I hope you haven't, but I know you will. I guess I am just a little on the jealous side, or maybe I am selfish with my Frank. Darling, I have dated a couple of boys since you left, but none of them could ever take your place. Frank, I hope you believe me, Darling, because I say this from the bottom of my heart.

Good night Frank, remember I love you.

Lots of love, Cathy

*****

Monday night
Jan 10, 1944

My Darling Frank,

How are you this cold night? We have ice all over every-thing. Gosh, it is cold. You should have seen me walking this morning to work. You would have thought I was sixty. Ice is dangerous!

Frank, what have you and the other boys been doing since I heard from you last? You said something about Quinn, but I never met him. I heard of him because Smokey talked about him a lot. I didn't know he was still with you.

Darling, today was one of those busy days for me. Mondays always are. I hate them because we have so much mail.

But Charlie is a good egg. I was calling him a B.T.O. today. He turned around and said, "Catherine, what is a B.T.O.?" Didn't he know it's a "big time operator"? He just died laugh-ing. We have had more fun all day long. He was asking about you today. He said to tell you hello, and good luck.

I had a letter from Millie today. She is having a good time keeping house for Vance. He is off most of the time.

Darling, I had two letters from you last week; I hope I get two more this week. I wish I could get a letter every day. My mother tells me I am crazy. Maybe I am. That is just too much to ask of anybody. Although I do write to you every night, I can't expect you to write every day. After all, you have a war to win.

Betty Jean is playing the song I love, "Wait for Me, Mary," because it reminds me of you. Remember? She is going to play "Close to You" next. It's a beautiful record. Have you heard it yet?

Darling, not much news, so I will say goodnight. Remember I love you always. Wherever you go, my thoughts are with you, and my love will be with you, Darling.

Write when you can, and keep that chin up.

Lots of love, Cathy

*****

Thursday night
January 13, 1944

My Dearest Frank,

It is late Darling, so this will only be a note. Dump, Becky, Ruby, Billie (*Catherine's friends*) and I went to the movies tonight. We saw a grand picture, "Lassie Come Home." It is a wonderful story about a dog. That dog was beautiful.

I had two letters from a sweet Lieutenant today who is in North Africa whom I love very much. Darling, I was glad to hear that you received your Christmas packages. Just remember when you are eating that cake that your "Cathy" made it just for you. I was very happy also that the bracelet was OK. Tell me—how were the cookies and candy? I can't wait to see the picture.

One day I had your bracelet in the office (before I mailed it to you). One of the girls asked me why didn't I have "Lieutenant Ward" put on the bracelet? I told her because you are going to be a Colonel someday! Ha! Ha!

By the way, the damn Yankee didn't call Becky, so I don't know any news regarding David being drafted.

Darling, I will answer your letter tomorrow. I am so sleepy now. Goodnight, Frank.

I love you, Cathy

*****

Friday night
Jan 14, 1944

Darling Frank,

This has been one of those days that they have in London: cloudy and rainy. Sure, I wanted to sleep this morning. But I had to work pretty steady all day, so it wasn't so bad.

Darling, I received two letters from you yesterday. They were December 30th and January 4th. That's how mixed up they are. But I was glad to get them. Gosh, you have no idea how glad I was to hear that you received your packages! I hope you will enjoy the bracelet half as much as I have enjoyed the letter pin you sent me. Everybody likes it. Every time I wear it I have compliments on it.

Frank, you said that Quinn had gained weight. I hope you are not. I love you just like you were.

Yes, my mother is OK now. You can't keep a good woman down. Especially when you have a good nurse. She says I am the best.

Darling, I just wish I could be there to help you make up your mind which way to go on your walks. I can't wait to see the pictures. I wish you would send me all the pictures you make so I can see them. If you do send them, I can send them to your brother. Or Darling, I can make you a pretty little book. Don't you think that would be nice?

No, David hasn't heard from his draft board yet. So far so good. He is ready to go if Uncle Sam says the word.

Your mail is coming pretty regularly. I get about two letters a week, usually at the last of the week. I look forward to the end of the week. I have gotten mail almost every Thursday since you left.

I am still watching the mail for my big picture. Gosh! It is taking a long time—almost as long as your Christmas packages. Darling, did you get my New Year's cable? How about the Reader's Digest? I sent you a subscription. I hope you like it. I think it is a wonderful little magazine.

Darling, do you want the film? I have 12 rolls. If you will just write and ask for them, I will send them to Frank. I will send you anything else you need or want if you will just let me know. I can't mail a package without a request.

Darling, it is my bedtime. You know me, such a sleepy

head. Goodnight, Frank, and good luck.

I love you very much,
Love, Cathy

Letters from Frank to His Mother

Tuesday evening
January 19, 1944

Dear Mom,
Well, here I am again, and in a fog as to the last time I wrote. So just to put myself and my family at ease, I idly pick up one fountain pen and try to give the events of the week.

Mail this last week has not been as ample as previous weeks. But I shan't complain. I only hope that my mail is finding the speediest route to your hands. I have received letters from Clint in about 13 days, and I've received mail from Cath in about 14 days. That takes care of correspondence. This lovely North African night is being put to good advantage by the Red Cross. They are sponsoring a dance for the officers and (if they desire) civilian women (French Girls) but as yet I can't "Parley Voo" (or something like that). So until they master English, I'm afraid that French–American relationships will suffer—at least as far as I'm concerned.

Went to church Sunday morning. It was one of the nicest services that I have attended in a long while. It wasn't elaborate in any way, but it was in some unseen way big, even immense.

I had a letter from Cath today (Catherine). Maybe I've told you, but Cath is a nurse's aide for the Red Cross. The hospital where she works has given a banquet for all of the volunteers. She was one of a hundred who received the award for going over the quota of one hundred hours. I wish that you knew her. She is really swell. When I come back, I hope you won't mind if I make a slight detour by way of Charlotte. I'm enclosing a picture of her and me. This was taken just a couple of weeks before I left and also a picture of her, which is a fairly good one.

I got myself a Valpak today, which is the answer to every officer's prayer. They practically hold three times as much as a suitcase.

I saw a very good picture today—"Corvettes K-225." It was very good.

I was just speaking to my nurse, the one in the hospital I was in. She is very nice, as are most of the nurses in this area.

How is everything at home? I trust that Dad is getting his required sleep. And that Clint, in his grouchy, good-natured way, and that the rest of the family is in their usual pegs. This is "the happy-go-lucky Ward family," which I shall again soon be with.

I am glad to hear that the checks are coming through. I'd send some home this month, except I must confess that I've been a bit careless. The francs fool you as to their real value. You hear a person say 50 francs and you think of it as 50 cents. But it's just twice as much. The higher you go, the less you think in terms of francs, the better.

Well, mom, I'll write soon. There's one other letter I have to write tonight, so Bonsoir,

Your loving son, Frank

Thoughts for "January 1944, North Africa"

In a lot of these letters to Frank, the writers wish him good luck. I believe this war was so awful that luck was the only way he was going to get home.

Frank mentioned that he saw an old friend from Officer Candidate School. He told Catherine that Quinn looked like he had gained weight. Catherine answered the letter by saying, "I hope you have not gained weight, I love you just the way you were when you were here."

Catherine had zero tolerance for people who were the least little bit overweight, partly because her mother was a heavy-set woman who had many health concerns due to her weight. It was easy for Catherine to lose weight; she would almost stop eating for days. Maybe that is why she suffered from migraines all of her life. It was truly mind over body.

The New Year's celebrations are over. The Year of Victory had begun. Frank had been released from the hospital after his knee surgery, and his medical instructions were to walk in order to strengthen his knee. So, he walked miles at a time around the town, which we now believe was probably Casa Blanca. He was glad to be out of the hospital where he had been surrounded by men with wounds of war. He felt like a "goldbricker" and felt guilty that he shouldn't even be there with those war heroes. However, let's face it: he wasn't going to do the Army any good with fragments floating in his knee, causing it to lock up in pain. In those days, it was not a microscopic ten-day recovery surgery. It was a cut-open-and-stitch-up surgery, which meant weeks of recovery. So, to quote Frank, "Uncle Sam knows best."

One of Frank's main concerns at this time in history was that he would not get to do his part to stop the Nazis. He wanted to be assigned before the war came to a close. Uncle Sam had trained him to do this job, and he was eager to get on with it!

Over and over again, Frank's letters show that he was sensitive to Catherine's wishes as well as to those of each of his family members. Whenever possible, he did his best to allay their fears by always writing a happy, positive letter. Each time he did complain about something in his daily life, he shrugged it off as "G.I. griping." And because of the censor, he never spoke of the whys and wheres of the war.

Frank also mentioned a retreat ceremony in one of his letters. A "retreat ceremony" refers to the return of the US and Allied planes to the airfields in Morocco after their mission for the day was done. He was inspired by this and took many photos. In one of his letters, Frank mentioned that he was put in charge of a "colored unit"—a reminder that the Army was segregated during WWII—something unheard of in today's Army. The Black units fought every bit as hard as the White men; however, they received little recognition from this country for their bravery. Frank always taught me skin color makes no difference with the value of a person.

Frank went on about how nice and cute the nurses were in the hospital—a little jab to get back at Catherine with his own brand of "just kidding" humor. He then stole her own trick, adding, "just kidding, Darling." But we know the nurses were cute and smart, and chances are they all liked Frank a whole lot!

War News for January 1944

- The United States launches the first attack on Japanese soil.

- US bombers attack Frankfurt, Germany, with about eight hundred bombers.

- The *Luftwaffe* (the German Air Force) takes a disastrous hit over Britain, losing 57 planes.

- The US Army suffers a tremendous loss when an offensive against the Italian town of Cisterna turns into an ambush. Nearly two full battalions of US Army Rangers lose their lives.

February 1944, Letters from North Africa and Sicily

The Fifth Month of Deployment

Tuesday night
February 1, 1944

My Darling Cathy,

I received three letters from you today. And like my letters to you and yours to me, they are slightly mixed up. I received two from early in Dec.—3 & 6—and one which was a late one dated Jan 14. Darling, it makes a day perfect when I get a letter from you. I miss you so darned much.

If this weather keeps up, it's going to make me think I'm in Los Angeles. It's very foggy in the morning until around 10:00 and at 11:00 the sun breaks through and warms things up. Darling, I appreciate and enjoy very much the bracelet you sent. It fits perfectly. When I first got it, it was a little tight, but now it's just right. I must have lost some weight.

I can sure tell it's the first of the month without even looking at the calendar. The old Army games are going, and the stakes are high.

Quinn was arrested the other day for being intoxicated on duty as an M.P. He claims he is innocent and can prove it. I hope he's right because they're asking that he be reduced to private if he's guilty.

Cath, thanks very much for the Reader's Digest. It's really a swell magazine. I received the first issue today. I hope that

when I receive the last one, it will be sent to an address somewhere in the States.

Darling, I will write for more rolls of film in a couple of
weeks, as I might go sightseeing. I started another roll this
morning. There are now 4 or 5 rolls of film on the way to you.
Darling, will you send the prints to my brother? Cath, I think
a book would be nice. They have got some albums over here
that ought to go with the pictures. I'll send one.

Darling, you should have received that picture by now.
Gosh, I hope that the fish are not looking at it.

I got a letter from home today that was like 10 years to
me. My brother has been seriously ill for a month, but mother
said he's doing fine now. Gosh! I hope so.

I'm enclosing a program from the Officers' Red Cross. The
censored items are places that would give away where I am, so
as you can see, they really try to do things up right.

Cath, just to show you how mixed up the-- mail is (or
was?): one of your letters went to five different places and
camps before I got it. But that is the exception to the rule.

Well, Darling, I am a working man now. So it's off to bed
for me.

I love you Cath,
Love always,
Frank

*****

February 3, 1944
North Africa

Hello Darling,

Boy, what a day we've had! This is the first time in a long
time that I can really say I've been tired. We had a tremendous
project to undertake today. I'm afraid Uncle Sam would object
if I was to tell you about it. One of these days I'll tell you all
about these projects.

Darling, I got three more letters today. It makes me so happy when I get your letters. I've read that "Pistol Packin Mama" to some of the fellows—they sure enjoyed it. I'm sending a cartoon. It's the general opinion that everyone was more or less in a daze when they received their bars, and more than one—nearly everyone—has wished that they hadn't received them. But then, in the end, they're always glad that they've got them. I am.

Cath, it makes me happy that you like that pin. I've been trying to get something from this section of Africa. I haven't given up yet. I've been trying to get something suggestive of this and every area I visit.

Darling, my knee is all OK!

You are a poet and don't know it—or do you? Thanks, Cathy, I thought it was very nice and only too true! A lot of things can happen between now and next Christmas. I'm hoping one will be a boat trip west.

No, Darling, I haven't dated any French girls. I've danced with them, but that is all. I just don't like them. If you could see them, you'd know why. For me, the American girls are the only ones, and one in particular. That one—well, Cath, she's really swell, and I can't forget her or forget how much she means to me.

The Bing Crosby Show is on now. That's one program I like to hear.

My new job is keeping me in Camp, and I have been to town only once this week, and then, only for a couple hours.

Darling, I gotta go hit the hay. Another big day tomorrow.
Goodnight, Cath.
I love you,
Frank

*****

Sunday night
February 6, 1944

Hello Darling,

Boy, what a day this has been. No, I didn't get to church. I had to work in the Company this morning and part of the afternoon. Later in the afternoon, I started kicking the football around. It didn't have any bad effect on my leg, but boy, I found out how out of condition I am due to my idleness. Tomorrow a couple of us—another Lieutenant and I—are going to start on road runs. We're doing this voluntarily— something that is unheard of around here.

Friday night we had a big parade in honor of the commanding officer of the Foreign Legion. It was quite an impressive ceremony. It reminded me of the day that General Garand received the troops at Camp Mackall. Incidentally, I saw an article in the Stars and Stripes concerning my old outfit at Mackall. Boy, it made me homesick to be back at that place. Why, I don't know, unless it's because it's close to Charlotte. I was just wondering what I would be doing if I was back in the States. I'd give odds that I'd be with you. Then also I remember when I was D.O. (Duty Officer of the day) and you and Dump came down that weekend. Boy, what fun we had!

Since I've come into this Company, I've had my share of excitement and trouble. But that's only natural around here. I'm becoming hard as nails. Last night the D.O. took a Tommy Gun and went after a couple of boys. Some of them are pretty good boys—especially the N.C.O.'s. It's just a few of them that cause all of the trouble. Well, enough of that.

How's my Cathy tonight? OK, I hope? Every day I think, *Well, today I will take some pictures*—but by the end of the day, I have forgotten all about it. Darling, how about some more pictures of you? I received the other pictures you sent, and I like them very much.

I have not heard as yet how Quinn has come out.

I got a letter from my sweet girl today. I hope you are getting my letters regularly. For a while, almost three weeks, I was able to write every day so you should be getting a few more letters a week.

Well, Darling, I've got to say goodnight. I love you very much.

Love always, Frank

*****

Tuesday night
February ? 1944

My Darling Cath,

This interval in my letters has been Uncle Sam's fault. The question marks are exactly what I mean—I don't know the date in North Africa. Well, I'm still in North Africa—only it seems like some other place. I've been doing some sightseeing. We spent one night in a blizzard and several nights in a good rain storm. I was able to take some pictures at a couple of places. One picture shows you how we slept. And if anyone ever hands me another can of C-rations, I will throw it at them. I am still with most of the fellows that I started with. Boy, you should have seen my beard today. A couple of more days and they'd have started calling me a hermit.

Darling, I'm trying to write every chance I get, but for a while, the letters may be a little scarce. Maybe only once a week and maybe less, but I'll write when I can. I guess it'll be a good while before I hear from you. The last letter I got from you was dated about January 17. I got the one with the pictures in it. Gee, they are swell, Cath. I wish that I could have been in them with you. Darling, did you get the February surprise? I got a Valentine's card.

How's everything with you, Cath? Gee, Darling, I miss you so darned much. Sometimes I wonder if this darned war will ever end.

I've seen a lot of the spoils of war. I saw "Hill 609," a battle in which a large number of American lives were lost, but was a big victory for us. Otherwise, the countryside seems to have returned to almost normal.

Say hello to your mother and dad for me. Tell Becky and David hello. How are things at the office? Is Charlie still a kidder? Remember the picture I took of you at Myrtle Beach? I've got that and a few others. Gosh, Darling, how I wish we were there now. Cath, hereabouts we have to go to bed to get warm on some days. This is one of those nights. So goodnight, Darling. I love you very much.

Love always, Frank

Letters from Sicily

February 23, 1944
Sicily

My Darling,

It has been over a week since the last time I was able to write. After our trip through North Africa, we boarded a ship. I haven't had much time to look around the island but this much I can say: it's a 100% improvement over N.A. The people here seem more civilized. The city I am near is more like one of our own modern cities. It has streamlined public buses, and above all the people seem more human and civilized—of course, there are exceptions to the latter. For instance, a little while ago, just down the street from where I'm billeted, the following incident happened. It was about 2000, and the most awful screams commenced. It sounded more like the wail of a banshee, but it continued to grow in volume. It was one beautiful fight. 'Johnny,' as he was called, was beaten up while held by two women. Then Johnny got loose and got a tire iron, and one woman would call Johnny back. Every time he'd come back, he'd give her a tremendous whack with the back of his hand. Then he'd take out after his assailant. This went on for a good hour. Then the MPs put a stop to it. Just one chapter in the adventures in Sicily.

What makes me sore, Darling, is that it will be quite a while before I hear from you again. As yet I don't know my new return address, but I'll send it by V-mail as soon as I get it. I still remember that you don't like V-mail. Well, as a matter of fact, neither do I.

Darling, by now I hope you have received the picture. It was mailed so that you should have it by now. In fact, you should be getting the crayon drawing any day. Did you receive the flowers I sent and the perfume? Have you received any of the films?

I feel guilty not being able to write more often. Darling, I hope you understand. When Uncle Sam says move, we move, and while we are on the move, we do not write.

How's the home front? How's your mom and dad? Say hello for me. I trust that Dave is still free from the Army. Give them my regards. How's Dump making out? Have you heard any more on the Smokey episode?

Chin is still up, Darling? I am betting yours is. I'm still managing to keep my chin up, but Darling, I sure miss you.

I've got to be going, "Hon"—I'll write again as soon as I can.

Love always, Frank

*****

Sunday night
February 17, 1944
Sicily

Darling,
Go to church today? Yes, I was good today. I went and was

very surprised at the shortness of the service. It wasn't more than 35 minutes long. But what it lacked in time it made up in other ways. Good hymns, good chaplain, etc. I'd have surely given a lot to be going with you this morning. I've been thinking about you all day. About how I would go to church with you when I was able to get to Charlotte. I was thinking, too, of the last Sunday we were together. The speed with which that day went by still amazes me. And the speeds at which these days are flying by are also astounding. I guess the fact that they keep me busy is partly the reason.

Darling, I hope you get some of that film soon. I'd like to get some of myself—especially the ones of us riding on the trains. We only had three days' beard when we took that picture. As yet I haven't discovered how they handle film over here. But as soon as I get a day off, I'll look into the situation.

It'll take a couple of more days before I get settled here. By that time, someone will probably blow a whistle, and away we'll go. That's the way things happen here.

I hope I get a chance to get into town near here. It's a fairly nice town, and I'd like to browse around and see if there are any articles worth picking up.

I'm finally meeting people who have not heard "Pistol Packin Mama." Boy, how I envy them.

Darling, I got some work to do before I hit the hay. So good night.

Love always, Frank

Thoughts for "February 1944, Letters from North Africa and Sicily"

When Uncle Sam said, "Move," the 17th Airborne only asked, "When?" and "How far?" The trip required a convoy road trip over the coast of Morocco and Algiers. In his letter dated "February ? 1944," Frank explains he is not sure of the date or the country. He speaks of seeing the spoils of war in Algiers, Morocco, and mentions how some things are almost back to normal while others lay in ruin after the Allies' victory in the Dark Continent. He never writes the names of the countries, but the names have been written for us in the history books. In one letter, he writes that he had been sightseeing and "found Hill 609" in Tunisia. History tells us that Hill 609 was the site of one of the pivotal battles in the North African Campaign, after which General Rommel retreated from North Africa. He speaks about the interruption in his mail service and mentions that he has not heard from Catherine in almost three weeks.

In the letter dated February 23, 1944, Frank writes his location as "Sicily." His Company had left the North African coastline on a ship that transported the 17th Airborne across the Mediterranean Sea to Sicily. I believe he sailed from the port city of Tunis in Tunisia, which at the time was under French rule.

In Sicily, he writes, "The people are more civilized and human here." He is billeted (put in quarters) in a hotel that has all of the comforts of home and then some. He is eating well, enjoying the new scenery, and fascinated with the Italian people, who he said were more like Americans.

Frank is working a full day now, leading a platoon of 50 men. He writes that he has good sergeants, and it sounds as though he is content that he is earning his keep. It is clear in his letters to Catherine that he is eager to get on with this job for which he has been trained.

WAR NEWS

- Sicily surrenders in September 1943. Both Sicily and Italy surrender unconditionally to the Allies.

- Rome and some parts of Italy are still engaged in battle because Hitler continues to refuse to leave Italy. The Allies are not able to liberate Rome until June of 1944.

March 1944, Sicily

The Sixth Month of Deployment

Frank has been on the move once more. He remains in Sicily, enjoying the surroundings, where his unit is billeted in a posh hotel for American officers only. The most pleasurable time Frank had in the Army was in Sicily and Italy. Most of his lieutenant buddies are there, and although they are all jokingly referred to as "shavetail lieutenants" (slang for a new, young lieutenant in WWII), they share a remarkable *esprit de corps* and are proud of the role in which they serve.

The "chow" is the best he has had in the Army. His colonel has insisted that the officers eat like officers, which means that they feast on hotel food that is fit for generals. He enjoys the respect he receives as an officer, and because he has worked so hard to achieve his rank, he never abuses it. He feels more at home here than he ever did in Africa because the people of Sicily are more like Americans. He goes to quite a few of the dances at the American British Team Club and the USO, where he dances with Italian girls (or, as Catherine puts it, "those foreign gals"). This part of his deployment has many enjoyable elements, but he still feels lonely and really misses his Catherine. There is no one who dances, smiles, flirts, laughs, or talks like his "little Southern gal."

*****

To Catherine from Frank:
Saturday night

March 4, 1944
Sicily, Italy

My Darling Cath,

Boy, what a week I've had. I made another move although my Army address still remains the same. I've been billeted in a very nice hotel in the heart of one of the island's big cities. The hotel is exclusively for American officers. It's certainly a change from North Africa's pyramidal tents. They retained the hotel staff to keep things running and to serve chow. The Colonel here insists that we be treated like officers, and so far, that's the way it is. By far the best I have eaten in the Army.

When we want laundry done, we just leave it on the bed, and a couple of days later we get our laundry back, snow white and ironed. We have a barber in the building, which is very convenient. But what surprises me is the price: shave 4 cents and a haircut 5 cents. A whole month of barbering shouldn't run more than 30 cents!

Another thing that surprises me is the number of natives that speak English fluently. Upon inquiring, you find out that they lived in Brooklyn or Detroit or some such place. They all intend on going to the States when the war is over.

The variety of entertainment is very limited. We usually play cards or go to the show in the evening. Saturday night (tonight) they have a dance for officers of the ABTC (American British Team Club). Last Wednesday they had a USO show—it was a variety show. They put on an hour and a half of good entertainment. There was one girl that sang, and boy, was she good! Or maybe it was that she sang the songs the way we like to hear them.

Darling, I've finally found a place where I can get film developed and printed. This will be the first time since I left the States that I've seen any pictures that I've taken. Have you received any pictures yet? Have you received the North African slippers yet? Darling, there are so many things that I want to write, but I'm afraid I'll have to write them in another letter, now that I have arrived.

I'll be able to write more regular, Darling. I haven't received any mail for over three weeks. Gee, Cathy, I miss you. I think of you all the time—of the good times we had in the past and the good times to come. It's already been six and a half months since I left. Boy, it seems like a couple of years instead, but time is passing mighty fast right now, and I hope it keeps going this fast.

Boy, they took us on a hike this morning. It was a short one—only 12 miles. But most of it was uphill and coming down was cross country. Boy, there were sure a lot of hungry and tired fellows! After lunch and a shower, everyone went to their rooms for a nap.

I love you, Cath.

Love always, Frank

*****

Thursday night
March 16, 1944

Darling Cath,

I hit the jackpot on the mail today! This is the first time in over a month that I have received any, and believe me, it's sure a morale booster. That soldier was right when he said that mail means a lot. It means as much as pay. I've heard fellows and officers offer a month's pay for just one letter. Sometimes the enlisted men get the feeling that we're immune to such things as mail. That it doesn't bother us if we don't get any. But we're only human, and as such are susceptible to all the faults and fancies of a human. Darling, I'm just letting off steam in the form of a GI gripe.

Cath, I received the heart-shaped Valentine today. Cath, I like it very much. I wish I could tell you just *how* much.

The verse was rather clever. Darling, I'm sure glad that you've received the pictures. I had visions of them adorning Davey Jones' locker.

Cath, they've sure had me going lately. I haven't been able to turn around. I haven't been able to write as often as I like to. None of us has been able to regulate ourselves and our spare time. Sunday we thought we'd have the day off, but we found a 12-mile march staring us in the face. This afternoon we had another long march. Instead of exercises yesterday, the officers (five of us) got up a basketball team and played the enlisted men from HQ Company. Well, those are things we'd sooner not talk about; they beat us 224 to 64!

Darling, I'm sending you some photos that I took here and in North Africa. The snow scenes were taken in North Africa, and it was nice and cold. Cath, the pictures that I turned in at the P.X. in North Africa took almost two months to develop and send them. I wish that these pictures were a little bigger.

Cath, I'm not partial to V-mail either. One that you sent didn't get here any quicker than ordinary airmail.

There's not much to do around this town outside of the show. I'm still taking Italian lessons, but as yet I'm still behind the rest.

I got another letter from home today. Clint is improving, but still in bed. It never rains but what it pours. Darling, how's your mother? I hope that she's OK?

Cath, did you receive the slippers from North Africa? They are "Killer Dillers."

Have you heard anything from the old outfit?

The "old bunch" is still here. They are sure spoiling me with the food and fine quarters. I sure get a good laugh out of the Italian waiters. There is one here that is always saying, "Tomorrow I speak English."

Cath, it's nigh on to bedtime, and judging from my writing, I need some sleep.

There is a radio playing below us, and every once in a

while they get around to playing a good tune that takes me back to Myrtle Beach, like "Wait for Me, Mary." Darling, I will be back soon.

I've got to say goodnight to you Cath, and I think of you always.

Barona Notta,
Love always, Frank

*****

Monday night
March 20, 1944
Sicily

Darling Cathy,

How is my sweet tonight? They threw a nice long hike at us today, and I can still feel it. I received another couple of letters today—one dated March 4. They're starting to get here a little quicker now, and as you say, Cath, you don't seem so far away when your letters arrive quickly. I like the pictures you enclosed very much. Cathy, I am enclosing some of the negatives of the pictures in case you want a larger copy.

The officers here have gotten up a basketball team. So far we have played three games. Of those three games we've lost all three, but we are still determined to put ourselves in the winner's column. The scores speak for themselves: 1st game 14 to 24, 2nd game 21 to 25, 3rd game 31 to 36. Well, at least we are improving.

I was pleasantly surprised yesterday when I got a letter from one of my friends whom I hadn't heard from in a couple of years. He ended up in the Navy somewhere in the Pacific Theater.

Darling, I can just see you slaving over the income tax. I'm expecting one soon.

Boy, what a mad house our room is. There's four of us and

each is as batty as the next. If a couple of us come in late, and the other two are asleep, well, it becomes absolutely necessary that we wake them up. It sure wouldn't do for someone to be in with us who had a poor sense of humor. Someone wrote on our door "Joe's crazy house Enter at your own risk."

We had our usual dance Saturday—each one is becoming cornier than the last. But despite our gripes, we still continue to go. Darling, as corny as the band was, they did manage to get out "Sunday, Monday, or Always," and that's a tune that has fond and lovely memories connected with it. Cath, I wish I could—*we* could—have, as you say, a couple dances together. But, Darling, that will be soon. Time is going faster. Cath, tell that lovely Charlotte girl again that I love her very much and that I miss her.

Cath, I'm afraid that I've messed this letter up. I wrote it with one eye open. Goodnight, Cath.

With all of my love, Frank

*****

March 25, 1944
Sicily

Darling Cath,

These Saturdays are sure going fast. The faster they go, the sooner we will be together. This war that we're supposed to be fighting seems like a couple of thousand miles away. In fact, it seems like we're a thousand miles from anywhere—sort of an outpost. Well, it seems that way. Cathy, I'm not with that (censored) unit anymore. When I moved from (censored), I was moved from it.

I got a letter from home the other day. They told me Clint was up and around. That was a month ago. Darling, my brother's address is as follows: Clinton B. Ward, 916½ West 53rd Street, Los Angeles, California.

This bunch I am with is getting crazier all the time, but around here you've got to be crazy to have fun. We're crazy in a sensible way.

This evening they are having another dance, but everyone is getting disgusted with them. There are two clans over here that are invited to the dances by the AMGOT (Allied Military Government for Occupation Territories) and Special Services. If one clan is invited and the other shows up, there is immediately a hair-pulling contest. Anyway, Darling, I didn't enjoy them so much. There was one person missing that is always missing. She's just as nice as her patients say she is. But Darling, they don't appreciate or love you half as much as one Lieutenant Ward.

Cath, you should have seen the mail I got today. Everyone was complaining that "That Ward guy got all of the mail today." Some saw that nearly every one was from Catherine Oliver. Then came the remarks: "Hey Ward, what can any girl see in you?" I got quite a few letters that were written in February, and two that were addressed to this station. That is good service. Here's the topper. I got one that was addressed to APO #1500 dated December 5th—almost 4 months ago!

Darling, tomorrow I'm going to take some pictures. It will be my last roll of film. I understand they sell it on the black market for $5.00. How did you like those that I sent you?

Yesterday we did the old Camp Mackall shuffle—4 miles in fifty minutes.

Cathy, I was just talking to S-2, the intelligence and mail censor. There's a new ruling that prevents me mentioning where I was and where I am. That is why the first page is cut. They are sure clamping down on us where censorship is concerned.

How are Becky and Dave? Is he still free from the draft? So Millie is back to work. Say hello to all for me. Darling, I hope that you can read this scratching. There is no decent place to write around here. Well, Cath, I've got to get some rest, so

goodnight. I love you.
     With all of my love,
     Frank

*****

To the family from Frank:
Monday night
March 6, 1944
Sicily, Italy

Dear Mom,

     Boy, what an outfit we've got. We have been billeted in a very nice hotel in the heart of one of the island's big cities. It's certainly a big change from North Africa and pyramidal tents! We have taken over the whole hotel including the restaurant and its staff who we retained to wait on tables. The chow is about the best I've had in my entire Army career. Here we are treated like officers. I haven't yet received any mail from my previous post. I'm still wondering how Clint is making out. Boy, this weather is worse by far than California. If we see even so much as one dark cloud around, we dive for our rain-coats. The only time we are really warm is when we're in bed, taking a shower, or exercising.

     Up until now, I haven't been able to write very often, but from now on I'll be more regular. I haven't had a chance to write to Clint or Dad, but that will also change.

     It seems the closer we get to the front lines, the better the living conditions and the encounters. If you were here, you could close your eyes, hear the language, and you'd swear they were more like Americans. They dress very much like Americans, and you'd be very surprised at the great numbers who have learned to speak English in Brooklyn and Detroit. A very large number of them are set on going back to the States. The girls are all out after our fellows. But luckily very few have been snared. They have to get the commanding officer's permission (American Forces Commanding Officers), and that takes about three months. By that time the soldier involved would have been transferred to another post far, far away.

How's things on the home front? Essie? Addie? Give them my love. Are the neighbors still the same? Boy, I will be glad to get some mail so that I can get some news. Have you received the roll of film taken while I was in North Africa?

Give my regards to all, and love to you.

Your son, Frank

Thoughts for "March 1944, Sicily"

In March, it was good to hear the boy-man in Frank who still loved to play and have fun in the most mischievous of ways: basketball games and tormenting and harassing his roommates. He always was a tease. He sounds happy to be away from the North African coast, and he is enjoying his men and his fellow officers—along with "a little nonsense" now and then.

"Papa" (Frank Ward Senior) wrote a poem called "Nonsense."

NONSENSE

A little nonsense now and then
Is relished in the best of men.
But women—bless them—just can't take it.
I guess it's because the women make it.
    – Frank R. Ward, Senior (Papa Ward)

This was so true of Catherine. She took teasing very seriously and did not know what to do with it; she could dish it out, but she couldn't take it. A person might have thought that Papa Ward had written this for her—but in fact, he had written it years before.

With all of the fun and playing Frank did in March, he does mention between the lines that "We play when we are able, but Uncle Sam's work comes first." He was an officer in the US Army, and that came first; he knows this time of luxury in an "officers' hotel" won't last much longer. Where he is going, there will be no one to do the laundry, no more gourmet meals, no more five-cent haircuts, no more hot showers or warm beds made with the nicest of linens.

Frank was still 22 years old.

Frank wrote to his mother, telling her, "These Italian women are after the American enlisted men and officers." He goes on to say that "there is a system in place that takes at least three months to get permission to marry a foreign woman. By then the GI would be transferred out of the area." It is interesting that he did not mention this to Catherine; in fact, Catherine was right about those "foreign gals" who were ready to pounce on the GIs and snare them. We don't know if Frank dated any of these "foreign gals." He is just getting to know his Catherine, so why start a fire by telling her about the Italian women when he doesn't need to? He wants to keep his "little southern gal" sweet and happy, just the way he remembers her.

WAR NEWS

- Nazi Germany takes 3,800 Jewish lives at Auschwitz death camp in Poland.

- Germany occupies Hungary two days after Hitler gives the orders to march.

- "Casablanca" wins the Best Picture award at the 1943 Academy Awards in Hollywood, California.

April 1944, Sicily

The Seventh Month of Deployment

To Catherine from Frank:
Thursday night
April 1, 1944

Hello Darling,

Guess what? I'm O.D. again. How about coming down for the weekend? Gee, Cath, if that were only possible! I arose at the unearthly hour of 0500 this morning, just as the dawn was breaking. I like to be up to see the new day come in. Only this morning wasn't as pleasant as the Spring you described to me. Yet there's something pleasant about seeing the new day, regardless of the weather.

Darling, your letters have been arriving more regularly than they did in Africa, and they are arriving several days sooner. I have received several that have taken only 12 days. That is good service for this theater!

I can't imagine what has happened to the film. I turned it in at the P.X. back in Africa in January, and in February they told me that it should not take more than five to eight weeks. I would say that you should be receiving them anytime now. I'd hate to see any of that film lying around in "Davey's Locker."

This Saturday night they're planning a big dance for all of the big shots, the mayor, city officials—and it is rumored a couple of countesses thrown in for good measure! I imagine it will be one of those stiff-shirted formal affairs. I'd rather have a steak dinner and a dance with a girl named Cath at a little place called Scotty's than anything. That would be fun.

Darling, I'd almost forgotten how to drive a car until today. I had to drive some of my men to a post. But it sure felt good to sit behind a wheel again.

None of us know how Quinn made out as his trial was to come up after we left. But the fact that he hasn't arrived here yet is a silent verdict. Boy, if that isn't a coincidence—just talk about Quinn, and who walks in but Quinn! And with his usual grin of confidence. He wasn't tried after all. I guess they just dropped the case.

I bet you were glad to see Millie—say hello to her for me. Cath, how is everything? Charlie isn't making you work too hard, is he? Tell him to take it easy.

Darling, I got a call. I'm still O.D., so I've got to say good-night. I love you, Cath. This war won't last forever.

Love always, Frank

*****

Thursday night
April 7, 1944

Darling Cath,
Every week seems to go by just a little faster than the previous one. But the faster they go, the sooner I'll be able to see you. And Darling, I miss you so.

We had a day off today, and I decided to do a little shopping. I went to the Red Cross for assistance in finding some linens. They directed me to a place that had been a very exclusive antique shop and dealer in fine linens before it was bombed. The work was marvelous. One tablecloth they had, they wanted $200.00 for it. I'd say it was well worth it. They had some luncheon sets that were hand-worked that were very good. They had some scarves that were nice. They brought out about 8-10 of them, but before they could turn around, they were gone.

After the shopping tour, we went on a sightseeing tour sponsored by the Red Cross. It was a tour of the town which included the monuments and the opera houses. There was a cathedral we visited that was really marvelous. I wish, Cath, that you could have been with me to see it. It was one of the most marvelous sights I have ever seen. There is ancient history behind it. So now comes the end of our day of leisure— it's been a swell day. And soon some rest, which we all need. Quinn, Russell, Wall, and I—as you can see by the writing.

There is a song which is really a favorite of the Allied Forces: Lili Marlen. It's a German song, but that makes no difference. It's the tune we like, not the Germans. Have you heard it yet?

Darling, I hope you like the scarves.

They still continue to feed us well—sometimes almost too good! This afternoon for dessert a nice piece of cherry pie! The other evening we had cake and peaches. Nearly every morning we get grapefruit, grapefruit juice or pineapple juice. Sometimes, maybe twice a week, we get eggs any style. So they're spoiling us.

How's your mother and dad? Say hello to them and the Kelly clan. Still doing well, I trust. And Cath in particular.

I heard some news from my old outfit—Captain Lyerly is still with them. I liked him. I've got a lot to thank him for. If it hadn't been for him, I'd never have gone to Myrtle Beach one Saturday. Darling, it's eight months ago that we met on the way to Myrtle Beach. Eight months today! Darling, I love you very much.

I've got to turn in, Cath. Hard day tomorrow. Goodnight, sweet.

Love always, Frank

*****

Sunday afternoon
April 9, 1944

Darling Cath,

Easter Sunday ... Did you go to church today? I'll bet the services were nice. A year ago I was in Charlotte for Easter. This year I'm in Sicily. Yes, Cath, I'm still in Sicily. How long? No one knows.

Cath, I don't think you'll get those slippers I sent from Africa. I gave a friend of mine there several things to mail for me—some to my folks and some to you. Well here lately I received a letter from APO #761 in Africa informing me that certain packages were still there. But I think they were turned over to the quartermaster to be delivered after the war———so?

We had a delicious meal today. Spaghetti and meatballs, peas, and fresh spuds. The dessert was a cake which was made by the Italian cooks. It was very good. The special was hard boiled eggs. They were even dyed!

I had a letter from my brother the other day. It's the first I've received in over a couple of months. He's OK, and now he's going back to work right soon. In case my other letter is lost, my brother's address is:

Mr. Clint Ward
916 ½ West 53rd Street
Los Angeles, California

Darling, you hit the nail right on the head when you said I was Irish. I'm Irish as can be. Once in a while my Irish temper comes to the surface. Remember one Sunday morning in Aberdeen a certain Smokey pulled a certain trick, and my temper hit a new high.

They had a pageant here on Good Friday. It was a novel and very interesting affair. It was supposed to represent the highlights in Christ's life from the time he leaves his loved ones until he is crucified. We had a grand view of the whole affair.

Darling, I have been rather lax in writing. Last week I was only able to write once but Cath, I was doing a little sightseeing and did not have a chance.

I took these pictures a while back. They are really not very good. Darling, I hope I'll be able to send you some more soon.

How is my Cathy tonight? Gee, I wish I could see you for just a while but———I love you Cathy——Goodnight!

Buona Notta (Goodnight)

Love always, Frank

*****

Friday night
April 14, 1944
Somewhere in Sicily

Darling Cath,

Another week is gone almost. They seem to go so fast, and yet nothing seems to be accomplished. This noon I received 15 letters from you, most of which were mailed to Africa, although there were one or two later letters dated March 27. There was one letter that I wished I could have gotten earlier. It was in reference to the touchy item concerning my return. Darling, I informed my brother that if anything should happen to me that he should also let you know. It was inconsiderate of me not to let you know that I'd made such arrangements because I gave him the information last November. But Cathy, I'll be back. Neither of us should think different.

It doesn't seem like the Army is fair, does it? I worked hard (or at least I tried to) at Mackall, and then got sent overseas. Davis gets in trouble and gets a 1st Lt. out of it. Although it always was a joke there at Mackall that the only way to make promotions was to get in trouble. Then get called on the rug for it. But that's the Army, and the above is my Army gripe.

Darling, I guess the pictures are just lost. I haven't the faintest idea how to check up on them. They told me that it would take 5-8 weeks, although one roll at least ought to get through.

We've sure been ragging one of the officers here. His wife presented him with twins: a boy and a girl. But he's a good fellow and can take it.

I sure hope we change to our cotton uniforms soon. It's hotter than, or at least as hot as, it was at Mackall. So Mackall is now a P.W. Camp. As one bright fellow said, there is no change in status. I should have told you.

How's everyone there? I hope you're getting along with your new boss OK? How are they doing, anyway?

My brother is OK now. I've received several letters from him after a lull of a couple of months.

How do you like me in jump boots?

Well, Darling, I guess I will go to the show. Wish you were here to go with me. But———I love you——goodnight.

Love always, Frank

*****

Tuesday night
April 18, 1944

Hello Darling,

How's my sweet tonight? OK, I hope. I just got back from the show. Wallace Berry in "Man from Dakota." It was very good, even if it was an old show. They haven't had but very few late shows over here and I've seen most of the old ones. It's most of the old ones, but it's something to do. The evenings here are sure getting long and nice.

Darling, I wish you would keep an album for me because

the only pictures that I'm keeping are a few of my family and several of you and a couple of my friends.

I received the March and April issues of Reader's Digest and sure appreciated them.

Time still continues to fly by. I have to stop and catch up with myself on the calendar. It seems like it should only be around the 10th of April. I like time to go by this fast. It doesn't seem that we've accomplished anything, though. It seems as though the war is a couple of thousand miles away. If it weren't for the fact that we're overseas and mixed up with a bunch of Guineas, I'd swear that a war was never being fought. That's how remote the war seems. But now and again I see an officer or enlisted men with a Purple Heart and oak leaf cluster, and then I'm brought back to reality.

How are your folks? I'm sorry to hear Dave is going to get called. Maybe that's the wrong attitude; I guess our Uncle Sam knows best and knows what he is doing. I hope you get the package I mailed last week.

Darling, I've got to sign off for now. I've got to get up an hour earlier nowadays. I love you, Cath——goodnight.

Love always, Frank

*****

Thursday night
April 25, 1944

Darling Cathy,

Another week has passed. It passed so fast that I hardly realized that it was gone. Oh well, so much the better. How's my sweet tonight? OK, I hope. I'm still kicking—very much so—so I must be OK.

Sunday I went to church and spent the rest of the day cleaning our equipment and getting adjusted to our new system of quarters. I'd like to get settled once and see how it feels to live in quarters again instead of out of a barracks bag. This, Cath, is just another of my GI gripes. Sometimes I wonder whether we're supposed to be soldiers or officers or both. One thing—here we are treated in some respects like officers. That is, in regards to quarters and mess. There's no mess line like there was in Africa but our quarters, while nice, are rather crowded.

Darling, I sent a box last week. It contains a few souvenirs and a few maybe useful articles. Some native jewelry made out of coral. A pillow case with the map of Sicily on it and a few other items which I hope you'll find useful.

Quinn is still around to pester us. We were all very much surprised when he put in his appearance. But we were all pleased.

Tomorrow we might play our first softball game. We seem to have a very good team. We haven't played much together, so the team is yet not quite what we want it to be.

Darling, this scratching is because my fingers are cold. It is not quite as warm here as rumor has it.

I managed to visit Palermo one day. There's plenty to see around there. I'm pretty sure I told you about the cathedral at Monreale. I hope to get a chance to see some of the other scenic and historic spots around here.

How's everyone? Darling, news is scarce around here. So I'd better sign off and hit the hay. I love you very much, Cath. Buona Notta.

Love always, Frank

*****

Letter to Clint from Frank
April 22, 1944
Sicily

Dear Clint,
How's work? I guess it feels OK to be back at the old grind.

The news around here is very scarce. We get the same old stuff day in and day out. I did visit Palermo one day. That's where I got mom the linens that are on the way. I intend on getting her a luncheon set the next time I visit there if I get a chance. There are some mighty interesting spots around there at Monreale—there's a cathedral that was built back in around 1100. It's really a marvelous sight. Also, the catacombs and there are mummies—rather a weird sight, but interesting.

There's a lot to see on this island, and I hope to get a chance to see it. In one of your letters, you mentioned my trip to sunny Italy. Well, we *are* in Italy—now where's the sun?

Don't be surprised if one of these days you should happen to get a letter from a girl in Charlotte N.C. It will be from my girlfriend!

What is new on the home front? If you could, and you are not limited on candy, would you please send me some licorice?

The other day I received a letter from a corporal at my old A.P.O. He told me that he'd mailed my suitcase for me. So you can start watching the mail.

Do you think that you'll be able to find some of that polish I asked for?

You know, it's hard to keep from getting blue once in a while, especially when you find yourself all alone and a little blue. Especially when I think of home, mom, dad, and you, the cats, and the dogs. One measly out-of-focus snapshot is all I have. I haven't even got a decent picture of the family. Keep your eye out for some 616 film—any kind. How about looking through my album and sending some good pictures of you and the folks?

Did mom get my flowers I sent? I'd like to get her a cameo, but they're very scarce, and if I did have a chance, I don't know if she prefers a ring or a brooch.

I recently sent a picture home showing me in jump boots. I am not a paratrooper. Any reports to the contrary are false.

I'm still with my first love, the Airborne.

You suggested turning the Plymouth into a coupe. I'd sure like to do it if you could find a car of a reasonable price somewhere this side of '35.

How are the Crocketts? Every now and then I run into a Crockett over here.

Well, Clint, I guess this will be it for tonight. I'll be writing more again soon. Buona Notta

Your bro, Frank

Thoughts for "April 1944, Sicily"

Again, Frank questions the why, how, and what about how his unit, the 17th Airborne, is doing. The war seems close and yet so far away at the same time. He takes his "GI gripes" more seriously now, and the uncertainty about his part in this war effort is disturbing him. He doesn't sound quite so happy-go-lucky in these April letters. It is supposed to be the year of victory, and here it is already April. A person can almost read between the lines of his letters: *What are we doing? Why can't I help? When is D-Day? I am supposed to be part of that invasion, manning a glider behind enemy lines.*

His brother, Clinton, has recovered from a serious illness, which was a great relief to Frank. In one letter, he asks Clint if it is normal to be a little blue once in a while. He talks about missing his folks, his dog, and even the cat, Mickey. He sounds homesick and is now thousands of miles away, *not* doing what he was trained to do to win this war. The 17th has followed all of the major battles in North Africa and Sicily so far.

He does a little sightseeing and is excited about the beauty and history of Sicily. He is hooked and wants to see more. He talks of the Cathedral Monreale and the catacombs in Palermo.

He confides in Clint about some of the more difficult realities of his experience, but not Catherine. He tries to shelter her as much as possible. Catherine, of course, is always talking about "keeping your chin up," but her life hasn't changed except for falling in love with her Lieutenant. On the other side of the ocean, however, *Frank's* life is still upside down.

In his letter to Catherine written April fourteenth, Frank tells her that he had made arrangements with Clint to get in touch with her if the Army ever came knocking at the Wards' door for any reason. He had made this arrangement way back in November 1943 and had even given Clint her address in Charlotte but never mentioned it to her until she asked. It was just like Frank not to write to her about the "knock on the door." No letters from Catherine have been recovered from April 1944, but judging by his apology, it appears that she had probably asked something like, "How will I know if you are wounded or worse?" He apologizes to her for not having told her earlier. He remembers her as sweet, fun-loving, and innocent, and he is determined to keep her that way as long as he is able. No bad news for his "little southern gal"—not if he can help it! He was her protector for life.

WAR NEWS FOR APRIL 1944

- The Germans are retreating from France.

- The Japanese are forced to leave many of their stronghold islands in the Pacific.

- The war is shifting in favor of the Allies, and like Frank always said, "This war won't last forever."

May 1944, Sicily

The Eighth Month of Deployment

Frank is still in Sicily and is pretty well settled in a routine with his men and his duties as an officer. This is the eighth month of his deployment. He and his men are taking up ball games for exercise, as well as a chance for some friendly competition among the guys. But he has not forgotten for a minute about the day he will meet his "little southern gal" at the train station!

*****

Tuesday night
May 2, 1944

My Darling Cath,

The events of the last few days have come rather fast. Not that there's anything startling.

Sunday morning I went to church. It was a very nice service; several of the other officers and I were there—although I wished I could have gone with you. Sunday afternoon the officers played Co. A. It was a very interesting ball game. In the 5th inning, we were behind 13 to 4. But at the end of the game, we were ahead 20 to 19! That afternoon they also dumped a job on me. One I do not relish: mail censor.

Well, that's it for Sunday except I was thinking very much of you and wondering what you were doing. I miss you very much.

Monday morning there were exercises, etc., and after noon I went to work. Last night we played another ball game. This time, we grabbed the lead, held it, and won by 13 to 11! We've played two games and won two games.

Tuesday Ballard and I fixed up the ball diamond. I received six letters from you today—the first I've had in a week! Darling, you say you haven't received any mail. Cath, it's not because I'm not writing. I write at least twice a week and in most cases, more often. It's just that circumstances are dictating the mailing situation.

I received something very startling today. I told you the film was probably lost. Well, I received the film of the first roll I turned in. So there is a chance that you may receive it. I hope so because there were some good shots on that film. I got one shot of an Arab on his small burro.

Yesterday was payday and throughout the barracks, all that could be heard was "Come, little Joe," "I pass," "I'll open for $10.00," and then finally one or two drifted back toward their bunks—wiser by far, but very-very broke. I'd sooner have the pleasure of spending my own money than let someone take it away from me with a deck of cards. Oh, well—every man to his liking.

Tell Dave to keep it up. The training he's getting in the National Guard will be a great help to him if he has to go into the Army.

Darling, my eyes are very tired. I'd better turn in. Cath, there isn't a minute of time that I spent with you that I wouldn't like to live over. Buona Notta, I love you, Cath,

Love, Frank

*****

Wednesday night
May 10, 1944

Darling Cath,

I've just stopped for a breath and then I have to dash off again. I've been busy beyond compare these last few days. We played ball Sunday and lost. We played this same team again last night and were beat again. But this time not so bad. One of these days we'll surprise ourselves (and them too!) by beating them.

You know, Darling, it's a very lovely night. Bright moon and a nice cool breeze. It's very much like the night that we drove back from Myrtle Beach. I'm still peeved at the Captain for making me drive, but I owe him a lot because it was he who asked me to go down to Myrtle Beach with him. Yep, he was quite a boy.

I've been planning on taking a dip in the ocean one of these days. Also to do some surf and boat fishing but time is my friend and enemy—my friend because he's hurrying by, and my enemy because there is not enough of him. Strange, isn't it?

I am going to get a three-day leave soon and see a bit more of this island. Have you got your packages yet?

Mail has been treating us all pretty bad lately. We know we're not forgotten, and I know my Cath writes. In fact, Cathy, you've been swell. I love you, Cath, very much.

How's your mother—Becky—everyone? Hope all are OK— Say hello to all for me. Has Dave got his call yet?

I went in for some heavy reading this week. I started "Rebecca"—it seems pretty good. The shows of late haven't been very good. I understand that we're getting some good ones next week.

Darling, I have got to say goodnight. Duty calls for a while, and then I have to hit the hay—0630 comes early. I miss you, Cathy.

Love always, Frank

*****

Sunday night
May 14, 1944

My Darling,

Today it has been just like any other day. It's good to
get away from the other job I had, and I like the one I have
now. Did you go to church today? I would like to have gone—
especially in Charlotte. Darling, I got five letters today from
a sweet girl in Charlotte. It's the first mail I've received in
almost two weeks, and it's sure good to hear from you. I'm
glad you received the pictures from Africa. It means that the
rest should be following. And thanks for sending these pictures. Darling, the person you ask about in the picture and
Quinn are one and the same. He hails from Charleston, South
Carolina. Darling, I'm sorry, but I won't get you a date with
that Arab in the center. I was thinking about Washington in
that picture of Joan of Arc that was made outside of a temple.
It was quite a beautiful place. These aren't the pictures that
are supposed to go to Mrs. Pratt in Dallas. I think it will probably be the next roll that comes through.

Darling, please don't worry about me becoming a jumper
(paratrooper). There's a saying that you don't become a
jumper till your head rattles, and as yet my head hasn't made
any noises. And I don't expect it will. I didn't mean to worry
you. I guess it was just thoughtlessness on my part.

Cath, I received two more pictures of you—the ones that
were taken on Easter. I think they were good, but not as good
as the ones you sent me where you were sitting on the porch
and the car. I hope that the colored picture of you is finished
soon. I'm anxious to see it. Thanks, Darling, for sending the
film. I'll send the film negatives that I have as soon as I can
get them rounded up. I've lent various ones out to some of
the officers. Darling, I do appreciate those pictures you sent
me. I like that dress you're wearing in those pictures of you on

Easter. It was very nice.

Cath, tell Dump that it's the "Shavetails" that are winning this war. This is not conceit.

Say hello to Becky and Dave and everyone.

Darling, we are crazy, but we have fun. We had a treat today: Ice Cream! We used to get a lot of it back in Africa, but this is the first time we've had it since we've been in Sicily. And the Mess Sergeant promised me we'd have steak for dinner tomorrow! Will you cook me up a steak if I get the points? I wished that I was there so you could. Would you?

Cath, I have a million things to do tomorrow, so I'd better say goodnight.

Remember, Darling; I love you very much. I mean that Cath—very much.

Love always, Frank

*****

Thursday night
May 18, 1944

Darling Cath,

The mailman has been very good to me this week. I received 11 letters from early May and late April. I received one letter on the 16th that was postmarked on the 8th. Eight days!!! Darling, I know what you mean when you say it seems like you are closer.

Guess what? I proceeded to get sunburned today—but nothing like Myrtle Beach. The Captain and I were laughing at one another for a week because of our burns.

Darling, I haven't got much of an album. I, too, have a few pictures of us at Myrtle Beach, the weekend at Mackall, and when I was in Charlotte. I don't think I have all of them, though. I received the pictures of North Africa. I'm glad you liked them, Cath. I hope the rest arrive soon.

Darling, in one of your letters you said, "... my boyfriend was the catcher." Cath, your boyfriend plays first baseman! I do it rather well, so they say. I knocked out a home run, but we still lost the game.

I'm glad you liked the roses because I love to send them to you. I love you, Cath.

Darling, knowing my brother, I know he'll answer your letter, but Cathy, I think you'll note a reserve in his writing. But he writes a good letter.

We're supposed to go into cotton Saturday. I hope that's right. It's getting plenty hot.

I haven't received the package yet, but I'm looking for it any day now. Thanks a million, Cath.

The lights are getting dim so I must say goodnight. I miss you.

All my love, Frank

P.S. You asked me, Cath, "Is somebody else taking my place?" My answer: "Nobody else is taking your place, nobody else now shares my embrace."

*****

Sicily

Saturday night

May 27, 1944

My Darling,

How's my sweetheart tonight? OK, I hope. I'm doing OK. At least I can still complain, and that's a good sign. It's often said that a soldier can't complain because there's nothing to complain about.

Darling, I got the pictures of Africa yesterday. They are fairly good. That is all but the ones of me, and I don't think they're as good. In the picture of the four of us, Lt. Russell is in the center, and Lt. Beau Dion, Lt. Street (not Pratt) is the one on the right of the picture taken in front of the opera house. Mrs. Pratt is his mother. He is a swell fellow. He went through OCS with me.

I got the letter today in which you told me about receiving a letter from my brother. Darling, he's as swell a guy as his letter sounds. He does have a knack for writing. Cathy, don't be ashamed of your handwriting. It doesn't count half as much as what is written, and your letters have made me very happy. They mean very-very much.

Yes, Darling, I'm still in Sicily. Probably will be for the duration and 6 months (just kidding). I have no idea how long I'll be here. I'm more or less like a leaf in the breeze. When my master blows, I move.

I'm still working hard in the morning. I'm unable to go to church. Regardless of what you want to do, duty comes first. Believe me—they pound that in over here. I'm only hoping that after the war is over, we'll be able to slow it down.

I received an Easter card from the church, Cath. It was a very nice thought, Darling, thanks.

I had a very good lunch today. I dined with a Captain. We had spaghetti with a sauce, and the main course was fresh French fried potatoes, and the topper was the tuna fish steak. It was very good and fresh fruit for dessert. I received another letter from my long lost buddy, so maybe he isn't so lost after all. He's in the southwest Pacific.

Tomorrow I get to sleep in for another whole hour. I don't need to get up until 0715! My beauty rest? I'm beyond all hope of a beauty rest! Although sometimes I take a short nap before I go to bed.

I've got to say goodnight, Darling. I love you and think of you often. Buona Notta. All my love, Frank

Thoughts for "May 1944, Sicily"

Frank often used the word "shavetail," the slang term for second lieutenants during WWII. Catherine's friend Dump had teased her about her boyfriend being a "shavetail." This had gotten on Catherine's nerves, and she complained to Frank in a letter about it. We can hear Frank's Irish temper flaring in reply to the comment about his rank: "You can tell Dump that this war is being won by us 'Shavetail Lieutenants.'" And that was not conceit talking. He was proud of his commission and his men. He speaks of his fellow Lieutenants Quinn, Russell, Street, and others with honor and respect. These "shavetails" were his brothers in war—the ones who went straight into battle with the troops—and it was true that they were turning the tide for the Allies.

We can hear the excitement in Frank's letters when he speaks of the basketball and baseball games. He said the games were for exercise and some friendly competition. However, I think there was another more important benefit to the games. The games were like a hall pass back in time to when life was good and there were countless happy reasons to smile. It was comforting to think back on the days when life was just about winning a ball game—not a war. And it's a joy to hear the boy in Frank once more.

In one letter, he says, "It's pay day and the card games are on." He makes reference to his fellow servicemen walking back to their bunks, "a little wiser and considerably more broke." "I'd sooner have the pleasure of spending my own money than to let someone take it away from me with a deck of cards. Oh, well—every man to his liking." Frank liked to play the nickel slots sometimes, but he never gambled to any degree. He was one that never looked for the easy money. Besides, gambling was a fool's game and not worth the risk.

There was a song called "Pistol Packin' Mama," which

Frank hated with a passion, and he didn't mind telling whoever would listen. I believe he thought it was degrading to women or men—or both.

In the early days of World War II, the United States had just come out of the Great Depression, and the country often felt ill-equipped to produce the war machine needed to gear up and win this war. A rationing program was started in the States so that the troops would not lack anything they needed. Frank speaks of Catherine cooking up a steak for him when he returns "... if I have the points." Each family received a book of points and used them to buy everything from butter to gasoline to clothing. Tires and spare car parts were nonexistent; you made do with what you had or did without. The American citizens were accustomed to being asked to sacrifice for the war effort—it was just understood that this was the way to support our fighting boys overseas.

Another aspect of the war effort was that many with civilian occupations were frozen in their jobs. Clinton and Frank Ward, Senior (Papa Ward) experienced this freeze for the duration of the war. Everyone understood that it was for our men in uniform.

At the government's request, many people grew their own fresh produce in what they called "victory gardens," and in some cases, they canned their produce for the winter. This helped with both the war effort and the food shortage. Catherine and her family grew a victory garden with tomatoes, green beans, and cucumbers, along with a variety of other vegetables. In Los Angeles, the Wards shared a garden with their neighbors. From coast to coast, victory was an all-American effort.

The American citizens who remained at home during the war also stood tall as heroes. The men in uniform may have won the war, but the average "Joe and Betty US" were always working behind the scenes, doing their part to make it possible.

In one letter, Frank answers one of Catherine's questions: "Is someone else taking my place?" His answer was, "No one else is taking your place; no one else is sharing my embrace." These are the words of a man who has told her of his love for her many times before; nevertheless, she was still insecure. Her heart was invested in his love, and he was very far away.

Frank sent a photo of himself in "Jumper's Boots"—boots that the paratroopers wore. Curious, Catherine asked, "I see you are wearing 'Jumper's Boots'—are you a paratrooper now?" Frank's answer was, "In order to be a paratrooper, your head has to rattle—and as of yet, mine doesn't rattle."

THE WAR NEWS

- The Allies are bombing the Nazi locations in France, preparing for D-Day.

Frank had Catherine worried when he sent her this photo. He is wearing paratrooper boots. He apologized, saying, "To be a paratrooper, your head has to rattle—and as of yet, mine doesn't rattle."

June 1944, Sicily

The Ninth Month of Deployment

June 1944 is a big month in the history of WWII. The Germans leave Italy, and the Allies invade the shores of Normandy on D-day. Frank is still in Sicily and turns 23 years old on the fifth of June. It sounds like he is spending some time reminiscing about the time he had in Charlotte with his "little southern gal." As I read some of his letters, I wonder if Catherine sees how much he misses her and how much he truly cares.

Letters to Catherine from Frank

Wednesday night
June 7, 1944

Darling,

They're playing a tune over the radio now (or rather the P.A. system) that carries me back to the officers club at Mackall: "When the Whistle Blows Mass." It was very popular in August and September of '43. Boy, I wish I were back there about now. Come the weekends, I'd hop in the fastest thing going to Charlotte.

I received two letters from you today—May 11 and 25. Mail has been slow for this week and a half. But when it does come, I will have to take a day off to read it.

Darling, I think that there are more rolls of film, although I'm not sure. Cath, I've finished another roll, but we now have no facilities for developing them. They are working on a set-up over here. So about all I can do is wait. Did you get the pictures that were sent to my brother? Let me know.

I'm glad you like the scarves, Cath. I thought they were rather nice myself.

Fresh cherry pie and ice cream—mmmmm! Darling, that would sure hit the spot! How about now? Save me a piece of that pie!

I never did get the three-day pass, although I got something similar to it. Cath, there's no place I'd sooner spend a three-day pass than in Charlotte. Do you think we could make up a week and three hours in three days?

How's everybody there? OK, I hope. Say hello to everyone and Cath, take care of yourself and don't be getting any colds.

So David passed his exams. Well, I hope I don't run into him over here. Not that I wouldn't like to see him—but I don't want to see him on this side of the pond. Maybe he feels different. The war news looks good, and I hope it keeps up that way.

Well, now that the weather is hot, we're getting a crack at the ocean now and again.

You know those pictures of you are sure nice, and I really like them. I guess that is all for tonight, darling. I love you and miss you very much.

All my love, Frank

*****

Saturday night
June 10, 1944
2000 hours
Sicily

Hello Darling,

Nearly the middle of June already. Before we know it, this damnable war will be over with, and everyone can settle back in a nice easy chair beside a fireplace and read their paper or magazine in peace. We will not have to worry about what happened on the Russian front or how many planes we lost in yesterday's raid. But best of all, it will mean I'll be able to see you. Darling, that will be a *happy day—believe me.*

Mail is so darn slow lately. I did get a letter yesterday. A Christmas card mailed Dec. 1st 1943. Sort of a roundabout and long way to get here. I'd like to visit all of the places that letter had been.

I met one of the mess sergeants yesterday who came from Salt Lake City. That makes about three people I have met from my old home town. We get together now and then and talk about the old times. We both happen to know one certain family that lived there. We both knew them well and were able to talk on the same subjects of interest. But here is the payoff: he was in Charlotte the same time I was on leave there. Remember the game between Central and Monroe? Well, he was there approximately in that same section where we were sitting. Now we are working together. Small world!

Darling, there's sure not much news. Every once in a while, I pass the beach and boy, that water looks inviting. Oh well, one of these days I will go swimming in the blue Mediterranean.

I'm enclosing a coin that I had when I was back in Africa—50 Centimes—the equal of one American penny. How are your mother, father, and everyone? Is David still sweating out his induction? Say hello to everyone. How's Millie? Has she heard from her husband yet? I guess he is in a hot spot!

Darling, I have come to the end of the page and the end of my day. I love you and think of you often. Keep your chin up, darling. Mine is up!

Love always, Frank

*****

Sunday night
June 18, 1944
Sicily

Darling Cathy,

How's my sweet Cath tonight? OK, I hope. This soldier has been working today. One of these days I will take off and go to the beach. By the way, "Crip," how is the foot? The beach and one lieutenant sort of treated you rough last year. I sure wish that lieutenant could take you to the beach this year. But darling, I am afraid that is going to have to wait for a while. You see, he's got an appointment in Berlin.

Strictly business—and there is no beach around Berlin. How about next year? I am hoping, Cath, that it will not be that long.

You have got me all in a dither trying to figure out what you have sent me. I'm sweating this package.

Darling, do you need a good bass to sing in your choir? If so, just call on me. Of course, there will be a delay before I am able to participate. But I can sing. Do you remember the feast we had on the beach?

Cath, those cookies were delicious! That's the opinion of the fellows who had some. But I really enjoyed them, Cath. The lifesavers have saved me many thirsty afternoons. When I see I'm going to be working out in the sun, I grab a roll. These miniature portraits are what I like and really appreciate, Cath. Everyone who sees them wants to know how I rate. The mail clerk has treated me pretty well the last two or three days. It's the first time that I have not received any mail in a long time. It was swell to get some mail again. Darling, will you send me a set of those pictures that you are sending Mrs. Pratt? Lieutenant Street and Russell each want a set. Cath, I have not been able to write but twice last week. You know, you've been sweet about writing, Cath, and your letters mean so much to me.

I saw a good show last night—even if it was an old one. It was "About Suspicion." It was pretty good. Tomorrow it is "Action in the Atlantic."

Cath, there were two letters in particular that I received today: one from May 16 in which you spoke of the 'Army Nurses Aides' and the other which you wrote on D-Day (June 6, 1944). You asked me if I wanted you to join. Darling, in the letter you wrote on D-Day, you answered that question for me. If you remember what you wrote: "If you aren't in it, don't worry when you do get in it. It will be soon enough." Darling, if you aren't in it, please don't get in it. I am selfish, Cath. Darling, the Army quite often changes plans for units after they are organized. I want to meet you at the train, Cath, when this war's over. There might be a chance that you would be shipped to a foreign country and that would not be good. Cath, regardless of whether or not you enlist, it won't change my love for you. Believe me, Cath; I love you so very much. I hope you'll not hold this answer against me, but as you say, this is the way I feel.

I recall once almost nine months ago heading a letter D-Day (the day we sailed for North Africa). Remember? It seems like a long time ago. Longer than it actually is, but I'm hoping it won't be much longer.

Cath, they're playing a transcript of Kay Kyser's program. He has some good music, such as "Sunday, Monday or Always." My favorite is "Wait for Me, Mary." The fellows all want to know why I hum and sing that particular song so much.

It's getting late, Cath. I better hit the hay before my eyes fall shut.

Buona Serata, Darling.

All my love, Frank

PS: last piece of paper.

*****

Tuesday night
June 20, 1944

Darling Cath,

About nine months ago last night, remember? I sure do. I still remember you standing there in the station waving to me in the rain as the train pulled out. What I said that night still goes. Whether or not I'm a colonel doesn't enter into it, I will probably be a Second Lieutenant, but that's alright. Second Lieutenants are winning this war.

The mailman was sure good to me today. I hope that he's been treating you better. But I think that from now on, he'll be better to both of us.

I am mad. I broke my good fountain pen today. My brother gave me a Parker "51" set back in '42. I have had it ever since. Tonight I dropped it, and it landed on the point. I'm glad it's a "lifetime pen." I'll send it to Parker and let them worry about it.

How's everyone? David, and Becky, your mom and dad? And say hello to Millie for me? Does Dump ever hear from Smokey? Oh well, if she doesn't, I guess it's just as well. Quinn and I still talk about the "good old days at Mackall."

The baseball team has disintegrated in the face of hard work. We're going to try and get a game going, and this time, we're going to beat them, I hope.

The P.X. ration has been pretty good lately. We've had Coca-Cola every week for the last month. They're sure good. Today was ration day, and it was a good thing. I was out of writing paper.

I'm glad you liked the presents, Cath. I have a lot of fun trying to find things to send you. I enjoy trying to guess what you'd like. I've tried to get cameos, but there are not any good ones around here.

Darling, you know something, I love you very much.

Buone Notta, love always, Frank

*****

Saturday night
June 24, 1944

Hello Darling,

How's my sweet this evening? Ok, I hope. As for myself, I'm ok. I started reading a book last night—Without Armor—and I became so interested that I had to read on and on. I'm not finished with it yet but Cath, if you like to read, that is a book worth reading.

The mailman has been pretty good these last two days. It's funny the way mail is. From the East Coast mail comes through with regularity, but from the West Coast, it is rather slow. I'm not complaining—just wondering. Darling, I received the pictures that you sent. Cathy, I think they're very good. The coloring looks so lovely. I was surprised when I got them. I knew they were coming, but I was still surprised. Thanks, Darling, ever so much.

Cath, thanks for the prayers. They help even though we may not know it. It's very heartening to know that there is someone who is praying for you.

I guess I'm going to have to see "A Man Named Joe" and see my double. The shows haven't been good lately.

How's everyone in Charlotte? OK, I hope. Say hello to everyone for me. I hope that Millie had a good time on their vacation. My hopes for leave are still in the process of materializing—aside from the three-day rest I had a while back. Darling, I hope that you have a good time on your vacation. How's about a date to go to the beach? Then comes July and the procession of months. August holds some fond memories for me, of course—I was known as "Jack" back then, but in a short time that was straightened out. Remember?

Now for the answer to the $64.00 question—yes, Cath, I love you very much ... Goodnight, Darling.

Love always, Frank

*****

Wednesday night
June 28, 1944
2000 hours

Hello Darling,

How's my sweetheart tonight? I hope well. Here it is the middle of the week already. Last week went so fast that I'm still transacting its business this week.

I wrote a letter to you last night, laid it on my mosquito net, and was going to mail it this morning. Well, when I got up this morning the letter was gone. I've looked high and low for that letter, but couldn't find it. I don't know if the wind is doing me dirty, or if one of my friends did me a turn and mailed it. I hope someone did.

They had a fairly good show today: "Dr. Gillespie's Criminal Case." Some good laughs in it. The one tomorrow night is going to be good: "North Star."

I hope to have some pictures to send to you soon. I sure like those color pictures. They're so darned natural of you.

I guess by now Dave has gone to the Army. I wish him luck. How are Becky and Little Dave?

Say hello to everyone for me.

Quinn is still around to pester me. Every time he sees me writing to that good-looking Charlotte gal, then he goes on, "Ward, you must be in love with that gal." He is quite a card. Everyone likes him.

The Major I work for gave me a compliment. He thought I was doing a very good job. You see, your Frank is a B.T.O. (Big Time Operator). I happened to run on to some good stationery. It's nice to write on this kind for a change.

Catherine, there is a saying over here, that you don't become a jumper until your head rattles. My head doesn't rattle. That's an exaggeration, of course.

I asked my brother to send you a set of those pictures that he got. Boy, what a rugged individual. I hadn't shaved for a

week, and it shows up. And when you see that can I am holding up, that's "C-rations."

> Goodnight, Darling. I've got to roll in. I love you, Cath,
> Adios, Love always, Frank

*****

To the family from Frank:
Saturday night in Sicily
June 3, 1944
Sicily, Italy

Dear Folks,

Time is absolutely flying by. Already it's June, and it seems
that it should only be March. I've never seen a year go by so
fast. But then things are being accomplished on this side of
the pond.

Well, two more days and I'll pass another milestone. It sure
seems funny. It seems like time doesn't count anymore and
each birthday is just something that happens, but doesn't. I
guess that the milestone doesn't count. Does that make sense?
I know what I want to say, but I can't put it down right. It
seems like years have gone by since I left L.A. I guess it will be
another year before I get home, and this whole affair over here
seems like a waste of time and men. Although we all knew
that this was bound to happen, and so we have to go to work
and get rid of the infection.

Thanks for the birthday cards. I'll be looking for the packages. I received a package from Cath yesterday. She sent eleven
rolls of film, some cookies, and a couple of miniature pictures
or portraits of herself. I'm going to have a couple of copies
made and will send one home if you would like me to.

How's everything on the home front? I hope everyone is
well there. I'd like to see Tony, but maybe one day when I have
a pass.

Well, tomorrow is Sunday. I'd like to go to church, but I doubt if I can make it. I hope you can read this scribbling. The lights are bad, and the table is improvised.

After the show tonight we're going to the dance. The same old Saturday night dance with the native band and native guests. I hope you folks won't worry too much about the lack of correspondence from this end. It's just that I'm too damn busy to even go to a show, and you know how much I enjoy a show. But I'll do my darndest to keep up my writing.

We had a very lovely surprise today. The P.X. ration included a bottle of Coca-Cola! The first I've had since I got overseas, which made it even more fun.

We're now getting quite a number of magazines. American Cosmo, Saturday Evening Post, Redbook, Time, and Newsweek and Life. But we lack novels: mystery novels, etc.

Well, folks, I've written 4 pages and said practically nothing. So I guess that I'd better sign off. Adios and be good.

Adios your son, Frank

*****

Saturday, June 24, 1944
2200 hours
Sicily Somewhere

Dear Folks,

June has nearly run its course, then comes July, and the endless procession of months, and time. I've been trying to figure out how many more months would pass before I am once again to walk the streets of L.A. But I'm not a prophet, and your guess is as good as mine. But in a case like this, I think it's a little better to be pessimistic.

News is an item that is eternally scarce. News is all subject to censorship, and even personal happenings are news. How is the home front progressing? I hope that everything is going OK?

I haven't been able to write lately. I've been busy. That is my only excuse. But this coming week I hope that I will be able to improve a bit.

Mom, I trust you are going to have your eye taken care of as soon as is practical. Every letter I write from now on I am going to harp on this subject. And I am ready to carry out my threat!

So the Plymouth is on its last legs. All I can say is that it has been on them for a long time. It was on its last legs when I was there. Do you realize that was nearly one year ago? Boy, time does fly. I hope that it won't be another year.

I had a very good meal the other day. Tuna Fish steak and french fried potatoes. Both were really delicious. Potatoes—fresh potatoes, that is—are as scarce as a soldier in a W.C.T.U. convention (Women's Christian Temperance Union). We still get fresh eggs in the morning, although not as regularly as usual.

The weather hasn't become uncomfortable yet. But given time, I imagine it will be beastly.

I had a heck of a thing happen the other day. I sat down on my bed to write. One of the fellows was monkeying around, and I dropped my pen and broke (or rather bent) the point. So one of these days I'm going to send it home, and you can send it off to be repaired.

Well, folks, I guess that's all for tonight.

Adios, your son, Frank

Thoughts for "June 1944, Sicily"

Frank was extremely analytical, but not to a crippling degree. Perhaps that is why he was chosen for OCS. Nonetheless, he was a delightful romantic when it came to music, movies, and books. He enjoyed movies with a good moral theme, music with a message of love, and a book that would keep you reading until dawn. Not to mention an occasional dish of ice cream, a strong faith in God, and last but not least, Catherine's letters. All of these things gave him the heart to keep going in this WAR.

On June 5, 1944, Rome and Italy were finally liberated by the Allies with the American 5th Army in the lead, and the Germans finally withdrew. There were four major players in this battle. Number one was the Vatican. The Church was disturbed by the Russians and communism. It was widely rumored that Pope Pius XII extended grace to the Nazis. (If this is true, will history ever forgive Pope Pius Xll?) The Germans were furious with the Italian government for betraying the Third Reich, and they ended up fighting against their own partner in war. The Allied Forces comprised the fourth major player. As a result of these concerted efforts, Rome and the remaining parts of Italy were finally free of German oppression and occupation, June 5,1944. The G.I.s paid dearly for the victory.

On June 6, 1944, the Allied Forces stormed the beaches of Normandy, France. Gliders were used in that assault, and the 17th Airborne was a highly trained machine of infantrymen. I believe that Frank was beyond frustrated that the 17th was not one of the glider units chosen for this major invasion. Apart from the early days of the Sicily invasion, they had not seen any action.

Frank turned 23 years old on the fifth of June, 1944—the day that Italy was liberated. He referred to this birthday as a milestone in his letters. From the time he arrived in Sicily, he seemed to have been pleased with the accommodations which the Army provided. He mentions that it has been a year since he walked the streets of L.A. and adds that it may be another year before he walks those streets again. He is weary of this war that is dragging on, but he writes, "We all knew that the USA would have to go to war in order remove the infection so that we can go on with our lives in peace." Frank is more outspoken regarding his feelings when it comes to war—and even admits to being homesick. He does not open up so much to Catherine because of her whole "chin up" approach to life. This was in part because he wanted to protect her, but it was also because he knew that Catherine failed to understand that some people are not able to push their feelings way down until it doesn't hurt anymore. Also, she was not the person serving overseas in an Army at war, in a strange land, surrounded by foreign people who spoke a different language.

All of the soldiers' mail was censored—even personal items such as birthday cards. Frank was careful to write all of his letters with the censor in mind, leaving out any mention of the people, places, and the work he was doing for "Uncle Sam."

At this point, the 17th Airborne was still being held in reserve, but for what, Frank did not know. With the Allied invasion on D-Day behind them, the Front was being pushed back to the East.

In one of the letters that has now been lost, Catherine asked, "What would you think if I were to join the Army Nurse's Aide program?" His answer was a surprise to me but very characteristic of a GI: "Darling, if you are not in it (the war), please don't get in it. I would worry if you were shipped overseas to help with the wounded. And who knows when I would see you?" He also writes, "I hope you do not hold this answer against me, but like you say, that's the way I feel, and I cannot help it. I love you so very much, Cath." He cherished the memory of the night he had left for overseas on September 19, 1943. He remembers her standing on the platform that night, waving goodbye in the rain—a night which now "seems so long, long ago." His dream is to come back to Charlotte on the train and have her waiting for him on the platform where he left her.

Catherine loved to help people and work with people. I believe that if she had joined the Army and had received nurse's training from the Army's GI Bill, she might have gone on to become a registered nurse. It's fascinating to see how their future is already starting to take shape in 1944 and how this decision for Catherine not to go into the Army Nurse program changed their lives. Whether it was for the good or the bad, no one knows. But I do know that Catherine worked until she was more than 70 years old in high-end women's fashion clothes. Perhaps if she had become a nurse, she would not have had to work so hard.

Red Cross Nurse's Aide
Mary Catherine Oliver
1942

July 1944, Italy

The Tenth Month of Deployment

Frank was now adding Italy to the list of countries where he was stationed. The hardest part of weathering a relocation was that it meant long mail delays—sometimes weeks! This meant no letters from home or from Catherine. It is hard to express what that mail meant to him. For Frank, these letters from home and from Catherine were a lifeline, a lifeboat, a gas mask, a ray of hope. They were the one personal link Frank had to the people who meant the most to him. And those people represented the only explanation as to why he was in this foreign land, serving with thousands of other young men, trying to save their way of life and the world as they knew it.

*****

To Catherine from Frank:
July 2, 1944
2000 hours

My Darling Cath,

Another week to put down as the past. It was a week that I won't soon forget. One of the more pleasant events of this week was a visit to Rome. I was really surprised, as I have seen a lot of Italy and its beauty. I've seen about all that is possible for one person to see in a short space of time. I covered the high points of the city, the Vatican, the Coliseum, the wall of Rome which surrounds the old city, and ever so many other places. I hope that I'll be able to get back and make a more thorough trip. Fortunately, the city doesn't show any of the outward signs of war such as buildings in shambles or streets torn up. It seems to have more or less resumed its way of life. The further north you go, the more the people remind us of our own people. But not so in Sicily—in outward appearance only. Well, enough about Rome.

How's my sweetheart? OK, I hope. Did you go to church today? I did. I was able to tear myself away from work long enough to go. In fact, for nearly the whole day and this evening! I wished I'd been in Charlotte to go to church with you. We'd then proceed to town and the "Ships Ahoy." Then find something fun to do. That day's coming, Cathy. It can't be much further away. That will be a happy day when Lieutenant or Colonel Ward gets off the train in Charlotte. Will you be there to meet me? This war won't last forever.

I finished two rolls of film, and I'm trying to get them developed. I hope I can find a place soon.

Darling, is my mail coming through any better to you? Cath, I know what you mean when you say "maybe tomorrow" to get a letter. I have waited for tomorrow also, and it isn't any fun. I wish those mail lugs would get on the ball over there and get the mail delivery out.

How was the vacation, darling? I hope you had a good time. I wish I could have been with you.

How are Becky and Dave and your mother and dad? OK, I hope.

Darling, I am a sleepy guy who's going to hitch-hike to camp if I don't catch the truck. Cath, I love you, and I think of you always, and I miss you very much. Goodnight, Darling.

Love always, Frank

*****

July 4, 1944
2000 hours

My Darling Cathy,

Independence Day! It doesn't seem like it, but the calendar says it, so it must be so. I won't argue. It has been a holiday for me. Today I didn't have to go to work. I didn't have to rush to get my supplies. No. I just lay in for a while and told them not to save breakfast for me. After I got up this morning, I repacked everything the way it should be packed. This afternoon I walked around and even ventured to the beach. I only got sunburned in the face and on the hands. I remember one day I spent with a girl at a beach—I got sunburned from head to foot, and she got a sprained toe. That was a wonderful day and a very sweet girl.

Darling, when I say the mail is slow, I'm not really complaining. I know you have written so wonderfully. It is just that I have more to write back to you when I get your letters.

I managed to steal a few hours Sunday and went to church. It was a very good service aside from the fact that it was typically GI. It's funny to think of things like church service as being GI—there is going to be a strange language spoken when the GI's get back. For instance, when I get back and if you are explaining something to me and I said "No Capiche"– it means I don't understand. It's crazy the habits you fall into like that. It happens all the time here in the quarters.

It's still the same crazy bunch on a payday spree. The dice and cards, lady luck, and dame fortune—some win and some lose.

It's a lovely night, just cool enough for sleeping—but what a night! The last night like this worth remembering was spent with you. Then that Captain made me drive. Gee, Charlotte is a long way from here. I've thought so many times of moments we spent together in such a short space of time. They were grand, Cath, weren't they? There'll be more of these days soon!!!

I'm enclosing some pictures. They aren't too good. They took some of me, but as usual, they didn't turn out good. I was going to attempt to take some portrait pictures, but time is moving fast. I hope I can take some good shots for the album.

I had ice cream royal today, and boy, was it good! Chocolate and vanilla with fruit cocktail! We have been getting it quite often lately.

Darling, you know there's a lieutenant over here that loves you very much. He's constantly telling me so. One Lieutenant F.R. Ward—know him? It's getting towards bedtime Cath, and work for me tomorrow. So the Major says. This Major is a swell fellow to work for. I wish there were more like him, and this Army wouldn't be half bad.

Buona Notta darling, and remember I love you.

Love always, Frank

*****

Wednesday night
July 5, 1944
2230 hours

Hello Darling,

How's my sweetheart tonight? The Major decided not to work today and maybe not tomorrow either. I don't get it, but I guess the next day I'll get it in the neck. Oh well, I might as well take it easy as worry about it.

They had a fairly good show tonight: "The Imposter" with Ellen Drew and Jean Gabon. It was pretty good—have you seen it? That's the best show they have had this week.

It's another swell night. I wish I could spend one of these leisure days in Charlotte with you.

Yesterday was Independence Day, and instead of firing firecrackers we went out to the range today with Tommy Guns and Carbines—a safe 4th???

The war news is very heartening from all fronts. It may be a shorter time than we think before this war is ended and the Germans are "whooped." That will be a happy day, Cath, believe me.

They're playing an old hit parade program on the radio. They played "On Sunday, Monday or Always" – that is one of my all-time hits. Along with "Wait for Me, Mary"—that's tops.

How's everyone there—your mother and all? Tell them hello for me.

You know, Darling, it seems like years since I landed in North Africa. But it's really only about 8½ months of lost time—more like nine.

Darling, did you know that I love you very much? Buona Notta, Cath

All my love, Frank

*****

Saturday
July 15, 1944
2000 hours
Somewhere in Italy

My Darling Cath,

It's been rather a long stretch in which I haven't been able to write, but I will be settled in my new quarters again soon.

This country was rather a surprise to me. I had it pictured like Sicily with rocks a foot under the ground, but they have fertile fields, and as yet the kids have not learned to say, "Hey Joe, cigarette?"

How has my sweetheart been? OK, I hope? I've had enough of the sun. My face and hands are tan. If you remember last summer when I was at the beach, I acquired a very nice burn— but that I don't mind. I was fortunate when I got here—I had six letters from you. Boy, I was one happy guy! Darling, you're so darned sweet to me, and I love you so very much. Don't forget that, Cath.

I am getting a big head. I've been put in HG Company, and

the Major I was working for wanted me back to work for him. Well, I wanted to be with the Major, and I decided to see what I could do. So I went to the personnel office to see another Major who has charge of officers. I presented my problem. He flatly refused my transfer. He said that the company I am now in has priority on good men. Ain't that something? I did not know that they knew I existed. Darling, I was just kidding about the big head, but I just had to show you how Majors butt heads over Second Lieutenants. Well, enough of that.

I hope you have a good time at the beach, darling. I wish that it would be possible to spend a few days with you. That would be heaven with a fence around it.

I haven't seen many of the fellows lately. My work takes me away from the mainstream and the gang.

Darling, I guess sometimes you wonder if I forgot you because I can't write. Please don't think that because there isn't a day goes by that I don't think of you. I miss you so very much.

No, Cath, I haven't received the package yet, but sometimes it takes 3-4 months to reach here. It will put in its appearance one of these days. I hope the mail will be coming in better on your end, darling. Slow mail is a curse to mankind.

Cath, that cartoon is very much the way I look when I get mail all at once. Those cartoons were cute.

Darling, I would like some more pictures of you. I enjoy them very much. Yes, some in your bathing suit, also.

I must say good night, darling. I love you and miss you, Buona Notta

All of my love, Frank

*****

Tuesday night
July 18, 1944
2000 hours
Italy

Hello Darling,

Well, another week is rapidly slipping into oblivion. I'm hoping that there won't be many more before I am with you again. With all that lost time, I wonder how long it will take to make it up.

They're bouncing me around like a rubber ball. The last time I wrote, I was with HG Company. Now there is a change. I'm back with my old boss. I guess he pulled his rank. Anyway, I'm pleased to be at my old job. There have been some changes made, and it's not quite the same. "Improved" is the word for it. I'm just wondering if, by the next time I write, I'll be attached somewhere else. So it goes. After all, this is the Army. Enough of that.

How's my sweetheart tonight? OK, I hope. How's everyone there on the home front? I guess Dave is happy not having to report just yet. I did not know that he was inducted and in his training until I got your letter.

In a couple of days, I will be settled in my new quarters. There's nothing elaborate—just a floor with a ceiling over my head. It's funny what a fellow can adjust himself to. In the Army, one can expect most anything.

It has cooled off this evening, and I wish it would stay this way. We have to watch out for mosquitoes around this time of the evening. They're pretty bad, and this whole boot of Italy is subject to malaria. But as long as we take chloroquine there is little chance of getting it.

Ten months ago today was THE Saturday. The last Saturday we spent together—for the next day I left. Darling, it seems like ten years, not ten months. Cath, your letters have helped the time to pass fast. They've meant so very much to me, darling. You know, there's a guy around here that tells me he loves you. You know who he is? I believe him when he tells me that. I know he means it.

I haven't seen many of the gang lately. We aren't together like we were back on the island (Sicily).

Darling, I have to write to my brother. Buona Notta, I love you, Cath, and miss you so very much.

Love always, Frank

*****

Thursday night
July 20, 1944
2200 hours

My Darling Cath,

Well, I'm more or less settled in my new quarters. It's nothing like I had in Sicily, but it will do. I am used to anything by now.

This country is sure nice. Of course, any place in the States is better for my money. I have not seen much of my surrounding country yet but hope to get a little time to sightsee. The weather is certainly hot. We took a bath this evening—the first real one I have had in two weeks. It sure felt good. It's a luxury over here to get clean.

I guess you're making ready for your vacation around now. Gee, Darling, I would give a mint to be with you. It's almost a year since we met—one whole year. Does it seem that long? I'll be happy, Cath, when we can be together again. *I love you*—did you know?

I had Quinn move in with me today. He saw me start writing tonight and said, "There goes that Ward guy again—writing to his Cath." He's the card of A.B.T.C. (Airborne Training Center)

How's Dave making out? Have you heard any more of Forbes? You know, the Damn Yankee? Maybe I was lucky to get out of my old outfit when I did, or I would be going West.

Darling, I am an early riser tomorrow, so I've got to hit the hay. Good night, Cathy, I love you.

All my Love, Frank

*****

Monday night
July 26, 1944
2000 hours

Darling Cath,

I had a pleasant surprise today. I received two letters and a package from a sweet little girl in Charlotte. Darling, everything arrived in perfect condition. And it was grand. Items such as shaving lotion are very scarce, and the guy who gets a bottle at the P.X. is usually pestered. That pecan roll is delicious, Cath. Thanks for everything. You know you are spoiling me, but I like it.

This day has sped by exceedingly fast. I've been doing a lot of riding around. I guess that accounts for it.

The quarters I have are rather quiet. I don't see much of any of the boys anymore. I see some at the Red Cross sometimes. I do see Quinn and Russell quite often. That old gang of mine is getting scattered. Oh, well. "C'est la Guerre!" as the French would say.

Darling, I am glad the flowers arrived. Each time I send some—or rather order them—I wonder if the order will arrive. Best of all, Cath, I'm glad you like them. That's what matters to me: if my Cathy likes it OK. Just as long as it is me spoiling you, darling.

Darling, remember "Wait for Me, Mary"? They are playing it on the radio news. I like that tune especially well. I do not hear many new tunes.

It does not look like Germany will last much longer. Gee, I hope not. It will be a happy day when they throw in the towel.

Darling, I have to write to my folks. So I've got to sign off, Cath. I miss you very much, Cath. Buona Notta

Love always, Frank

*****

Friday night
July 28, 1944
2000 hours

Hello Darling,

Another week has nearly slipped by and another month is almost finished. This war can't last much longer, Cathy. Then I'll come marching home again. Happy Day!

Mail has been good lately. I hope, darling, that your mail is arriving better. I hit the jackpot yesterday—I received five letters from you and one from home.

I know what you mean, Cath, when you say "maybe tomorrow."

Speaking of jackpot—remember the time we went to the Morris Field Officers Club and tried to clean their slot machines out? We didn't succeed, but we had fun trying!

Darling, don't you listen to those old hens at the office. If all they have to do is spread idle gossip, it's a cinch they are not doing much to help the war cause. Anyway, it is not a French girl—it's an *Italian* girl—I am just kidding, Cath. It's really an American girl who lives in Charlotte. She's sure sweet, and I love her very much.

A nice ice-cold watermelon would sure go good right now. Yes, we get them now and again. Here they're just a little bigger than a cantaloupe but possess all the taste and other characteristics of a watermelon. Enough of that.

What I want to know is how my Cath is tonight? OK, I hope. I guess you are on your vacation right about now and by the time you get this, you will be back. I hope you had a good time. I'm sure sorry that I was not able to be with you.

Darling, there is one thing that is going to bust up the fighting fronts, and that is to hear that they're treating prisoners of war with lily white gloves and giving them dances. There is my Irish temper again, but Cath, it doesn't sound like a square deal to our boys. A good many of them shed good blood to take those prisoners.

I'm on the good side of the Mess Sergeant. I was just over there for a slight snack—a ham and pineapple sandwich. Nice guy to be on the good side of.

I've got to sign off, darling. I love you, Cath, remember my chin is up, darling.

Buona Notta

All of my love, Frank

*****

To Clinton from Frank:
July 20, 1944
2200 hours
Somewhere in Italy

Dear Clint,

This will be more or less a short letter. I'm writing to let you know every little thing is OK. I just finished a letter to the family telling about the trip to Rome. This is the sunny and beautiful Italy that you spoke of in one of your letters. It really is a nice country, but I'll still take the USA anytime. The roads are tree-lined just like some of our roads back home— nothing like our highway in width, but good surfaces.

I'm enclosing a money order for $100.00 bucks ... use it as you see fit.

My new quarters aren't anything to rave about. No electric lights—I'm writing by candlelight. I bathe in a creek, and it is refreshing—but boy, is it cold! And I have to walk about a mile for chow.

I received the package today. Many thanks, Clint. I'd like some writing paper and a few good books—maybe some best sellers. The candy was in good condition and was good.

How are the cars running—or are they? You should see some of the vehicular nightmares around here that they call cars. It would sure put a cramp in your side laughing.

Well, Clint, I hope everyone is well there at home. I trust that mom is going to have her eye taken care of soon. How is Dad? Fine, I hope.

Well, Clint, my candle is low, go I'd better sign off.

Your Brother, Frank

*****

Tuesday
July 25, 1944
9:30

Dear Mom,

I'm writing this as I'm waiting for our rations. We have to pick up our food ration every day, and there's usually a slight wait. I had a chance to visit Rome a while back. It's really quite some city. In fact, it reminds me a great deal of our own city. It is really a city for sightseeing—the wall of Rome, the Vatican, the ancient roads and old fortifications. The people are very much like our own—at least in outward appearances. The city has not suffered much from the war. It hardly seems like it was touched except in isolated areas. I hope I get a chance to go back for another visit real soon.

They have a Red Cross near us now. That's where I've been spending a great deal of my time. Most of the fellows I don't see anymore, as my work keeps me in a different part of Camp—but once in a while, we meet up at the Red Cross.

How is the home front? I trust everything is going well. Are you making arrangements to have your eyes taken care of yet? I am telling you I am going to harp on this until I hear that you are. How are Clint and his doc getting along? Is Dad still putting on weight? How is the rest of the clan?

I hear from Kop every now and then, but as for the rest of the gang, never a word.

The war news looks exceedingly good. With these internal revolts in Germany, it may not be as long as we feared it would be. But even then, it will be long.

I know, Mom, I have been a little slow in writing again, but moving can sure upset one's daily habits and routine.

The weather is hot and sultry. Sometimes it looks like rain, but even then, it seldom does. The last rain I was in, I got soaked to the skin. The evenings seem exceedingly long. It very seldom gets dark before 2100 hours, but that gives us light to read and write by. Otherwise, it would be candlelight.

Well, Mom, I guess that's the end for tonight. Love to all.

Your loving son, Frank

Thoughts for "July 1944, Italy"

Catherine was getting ready for her vacation to Myrtle Beach. We will never know if Catherine found it hard to vacation at the same beach where she and Frank had met eleven months earlier, while Frank was over in Italy, edging ever closer to the front lines. We don't know her feelings since we do not have her letters of July 1944, but I believe that her trip to the beach was a way to keep her mind and body busy so she would not miss her lieutenant so "darned" much. It had been nine months since Frank left on the 11:01.

On July 18, 1944, Frank writes that he has been away nine months since the last time he saw his Catherine on the train platform. He speaks of the day when he comes back on the train that stops in Charlotte. "Oh! What a happy-happy day!" He tells her to "have a good time," and, as always, he wishes he were there with her.

His eighteen-month tour is half over, but if Uncle Sam says to stay, Frank will remain. Catherine's letters give him the stamina to endure this war. He tells her that her words make his time go by fast. There is no doubt—she brought him home on a six-cent airmail stamp—*hundreds* of six-cent stamps!

And where was Frank while Catherine was on vacation? He was sightseeing in Rome only a matter of weeks after the Germans had made their exit. And Catherine was tanning on the white sands of Myrtle Beach, South Carolina.

Frank received a letter from Catherine in which she mentioned that some people at work were teasing her about the Italian and French girls who were trying to catch a Yank as a husband. She worried a little that he might like these Italian gals better than her and that he might not come home. His answer to her was, "No, she's not an Italian gal—she is a French gal!" Did he realize how he was playing with fire with his "just kidding" humor? We know for sure that Catherine was not able to take any teasing at all—and *especially* not from Frank. I'm glad I was not there when she read that part of his letter!

But after Frank's little joke, he consoled her and told her not to listen to those old hens since they were doing nothing for the war effort. And, of course, no "foreign gal" could take the place of his "little southern gal" in Charlotte in the good old US.

In a letter to his brother, Clinton, Frank writes a more realistic picture of his day-to-day life. Frank did not share certain details with his mom or with Catherine, such as the fact that he was bathing in a cold stream and walking a mile to "chow." But he knew he was lucky to be able to walk to chow when some of his fellow soldiers were trapped in foxholes, eating C-rations.

*****

In the last nine months of his deployment, Frank has had two major posts. When he first left the country in November 1943, he crossed over on a Kaiser Liberty ship. His unit was first stationed in North Africa—an assignment that lasted until the middle of February 1944. When they left that first post, they traveled the dusty, rocky roads of the North African Mediterranean coast in a convoy of open trucks. The journey must have been a long, exhausting trip over the rocky hills of Morocco, Algiers, and Tunisia on roads made for mountain goats. There were no five-star hotels for quarters along the way. No, they camped. The convoy's final destination? The city of Tunis was a significant port for all naval activity, which proved invaluable to the Allies.

From Tunis, Frank took a ship to Palermo in Sicily. He talked about how thankful he was to be out of the Dark Continent. During his time on the island of Sicily, his unit moved to three or four locations. In the first part of July, they boarded another ship and were sent somewhere in Italy.

The war was dragging on, but generally, the news was, as Frank says, "exceedingly good." On July 20, 1944, there was an attempt to kill the "Fuhrer" that plunged parts of Germany into civil disorder. In the unrest that followed, many entertained hopes that the war would soon be over. The Russian Front was going like gangbusters, and action on the Western Front in France was slowing down. If 1944 was going to be the year of victory, then this had better happen soon!

Frank wanted his piece of Hitler, and with the training he had received in the 17th, he knew he could achieve it. He wanted to make the Army his career. He jests in his letters about coming home as a first lieutenant or a captain. Yes, Frank liked the hierarchy of command, not to mention the order that the Army provided. But he kept wondering why he has not been in any action.

The 17th Airborne was a glider unit of motorless planes not used by paratroopers. These glider units were designed to be released by a mother airship to fly full combat-equipped troops and supplies behind enemy lines. They were instrumental in 30 missions in a variety of theaters: North Africa,

Sicily, Italy, France (on D-day), the China–Burma and India theaters, the Battle of the Bulge, and the crossing of the Rhine.

So far, the 17th Airborne had skirted around all of the action and big battles in the war. Frank and his unit often wondered what the Big Brass was saving the 17th Airborne for. It was a great source of disappointment for Frank and his men that they never had a chance to fly a mission in these gliders during one of these strategic engagements.

No. 1676 Twelve Men of the Airborne Troops Under the Wing of a Glider, Camp Mackall, N. C. *Signal Corps*

August 1944, Somewhere in Italy

The Eleventh Month of Deployment

Thursday night
August 8, 1944
Somewhere in Italy

My Darling Cathy,

Remember a year ago today, what fun we had? A sprained toe—a sunburned back—a captain and his camera—a nice strip of beach—a lovely girl named Cath—a boy named Frank (Jack)—a date in which I thought I was going to be stood up—a quiet moonlit ride—Dump and Dope—a second car with me in the driver's seat. The captain's rank—a barefoot boy – a soda pop in the town of Hamlet – the parting! But best of all, Darling, tomorrow is coming! Tomorrow will come and bring peace and time to do the things we want to do. It will also give us time to make up for the last time and forget the lost time. Darling, your love means so very much to me. I want you to know that. Cath, I will be back.

I am starting to get back in the groove. The Major finally discovered my hangouts.

They had a USO show here last night. It was pretty good. One of the best I have seen on this side of the pond. The show "Happy Land" with Don Ameche sure was good.

Hot in the day and cold at night. That is how our weather has been, and we still have to use our mosquito nets.

I see a little of Italy now and again. I have to go prancing over the countryside in pursuit of my work. This is a very pretty country, and it is a shame that it had to be torn by war. Darling, how do you like those "Yanks" storming through France?

Have you heard the song "Lili Marlen" (Marlay) yet? These Italians cannot understand why we sing a Tedeschi (German song). Darling, it sure has a haunting melody.

I received another Reader's Digest. Darling, I really enjoy that magazine, and there is already a waiting list for it.

You know, Darling, I think I have been forgotten. As the OD, I am about the only officer that hands out the orders for the day. I haven't had it but twice, and the rest of the fellows have had it four or five times. Oh well, when they do find out, I will be really hurting.

Honey, I guess that is all for tonight. Remember I love you, Cath.

Adios,
All my love,
Frank

*****

Sunday evening
August 13, 1944

My Darling Cath,

Sunday night and most of the gang is in town. But I do not mind an evening to be alone now and again. It gives me a chance to get things in order and take stock. How is my darling this evening? Did you go to church this morning? I was almost able to make it, but at the last minute, work put a stop to my plans. Next Sunday it will be a different story.

The news sure is scarce. Our lives have settled down to a dull routine which makes for much monotony. I went to town last night. They had a Red Cross dance for the lieutenants and the nurses. The music was fair, but to me, something was missing—and always is—at any of these dances. You know what I mean, darling? It's *you* I miss. I will never forget the dances at Scotty's. They were few, Darling. I had more fun that night than I have ever had at any of these dances over here. I remember that night very well.

Well, a year ago I was preparing to go on leave. I had just received a letter from a girl in Charlotte addressed to Jack Ward.

The evenings are growing shorter. It is only 2015, and the lights are already on.

Well, darling, I got out my winter clothes today. I guess in another month we will be going into them. That old patch (17th Airborne) sure looks good on it.

Cath, has your mail been any better lately? I hope it has, darling. Mine has. Good night, darling. There is a lieutenant somewhere in Italy that misses you very much. I love you, Cath.

All my love, Frank

*****

Thursday night
August 24, 1944

My Darling Cath,

It was a very funny day. It was one of those days when everything you want to do was wrong, regardless of how hard you tried to make it right. To top this off, it was exceedingly hot, and for the last little while, my work has been out in the open.

Darling, the mail has been good the last little while. I got two letters today. Both of them mailed from Myrtle Beach. Dear old Myrtle Beach. One of them contained four pictures of you. Cath, I like them so very much—especially the one of you on the beach and the one on the porch. Some of the fellows who saw them were very curious as to how I rate. My roommate said, "That girlfriend of yours is cute!" Also, he would like to meet you. I said, "Yes, but brother, you cannot move in."

Our section head gave a party for the officers in his department. It was quite a gala affair. There were 15 officers, about 10 nurses, and two or three Red Cross girls. About five of us got one lieutenant good and mad. When the dance started, we kept cutting in on him. When he'd cut back, someone else would cut in. He finally got disgusted with our tactics.

But darling, those parties lack a great deal as far as I am concerned. Because I'm always comparing those parties with the good times we used to have—and will have again. None of them can come close to the times we used to have.

Darling, we're going to get that extra pay that Congress passed for us. At least that's the current rumor. I won't know what to do with all of that money. None of us fellows around here spend what we get now. Guess most of us will send it home in the form of bonds or money orders.

I'm finishing the last of the ice tea we had for supper. It is nice to know the Mess Sergeant.

We have a pretty good bunch of fellows that live here in the warehouse. Every now and again we get together for a game of pinochle. That's what we were doing a while ago at our impromptu parties.

Cathy, I like that candy and would like some more of it. Thanks, darling.

A pup followed me into my quarters the other day, and he has been here ever since. We are thinking of adopting him for our warehouse mascot. We are stumped as to what to call him.

I sure hope those Yanks keep going through France the way they have been lately. Darling, I might be home before Christmas, but Cathy, don't count on it.

These quarters I have here in the warehouse are the best we have encountered since coming over.

Tomorrow is Friday and a big day on the calendar.

Goodnight, Darling. This lieutenant loves you very much,
    Buona Notta,
    All of my love, Frank
    PS: Thanks again for the pictures, love, Frank.

*****

Tuesday night
August 29, 1944
2245 hours

My Darling Cathy,

The mailman was good to me today. I received three let-ters—but what pleases me, next to the letter itself, is the short lapse of time it took to get here. It was mailed on the 22nd and arrived today. That is the quickest I have ever received any from the States. It sure makes my Cath seem closer. I hope when I come home that it will only take 7 days.

Work was unexpectedly slow. Quinn is working with me now. So I am learning his brand of wit, and he has promised to give me lessons in the art of gold bricking and work evasion. He is a past master of the arts in both. Only he claims it is a science of the mind. I guess he should know.

Darling, I remember that night at Scotty's well. I only wish that Smokey would have wanted to leave earlier. Then maybe we could have taken them home earlier. And I remember even better what happened after we had taken them home. I told you *I loved you.* I meant it, Cath, and I mean it *even more now!* Remember that, darling.

I went into town tonight; there was not too much doing. A couple of us joined forces and went to the R.C. Club and then to the show. It was Ray Malland's "Minister of Fear." It was rather mixed up, but not a bad picture. The grade of pictures is improving finally.

How is Dave doing in the Guard? OK? It is good train-ing. Especially these times; they always help out when one is inducted. You are two jumps ahead of the other fellow, which may eventually mean two or even three stripes ahead in the end.

How is my sweetheart tonight? OK, I hope.

Darling, my brother said that he was having prints made of those North Africa pictures, and would send you a set as soon as he got them. That was a week and a half ago. So you ought to have them by now.

Goodnight, darling. I've got to hit the hay. I love you.

Love always,

Frank

*****

To Catherine from Clinton:
August 6, 1944
Los Angeles, California

Dear Catherine,

Well here I am again—late as usual, but here I am. Received your letter and card some time ago, but am just getting around to answering. Of course, I have my alibis: my work at the office keeps me pretty close to the old grindstone, and then there is my beauty sleep to be considered, and I sure need that beauty sleep.

So you have been enjoying your vacation? I hope you had a good time and had a rest along with it. Lord knows a person needs a rest nowadays.

It is, as France would say, 1600 here on the broad Pacific slope. The scent of orange blossoms and jasmine are heavy on the onshore wind. Today has been a beautiful day. I gathered up my beach umbrella, thermos, and thoughts, and sallied forth to where the endless breakers pound out their age-old grudge against the white sands of the beach. I wondered what the kid brother was doing. And if he was thinking of the day that he could throw his big frame around the beach, and gulp down huge quantities of "pop and hot dogs." And I was even so bold as to wonder what you were doing—and there I had to stop because I couldn't picture you. But anyway, I hoped you were happy, and doing something you liked. The war seemed so far away today ... the kids romping around, their laughter sounding so un-war-like, and the smell of good things to eat. The jovial crowds, well-fed, happy-faced people, the air of plenty, and the quietness that pervades. But to fathom the ways of the like is far beyond my powers to comprehend. Anyway, it was a nice day, and I received a nice sunburn for my activities.

Now that it is night, the crowds have gone their respective ways, the beaches are deserted, and silence reigns. Silence except for the rolling waves coming in, and their song remains the same: Courage; it takes *courage* to have faith. So with that thought ringing in my brain (or what is left of it) I picked up my gear and sailed for home.

Now I am home, the applications of sunburn lotion have been made, the wise words of Walter Winchell have been digested, and the household has settled down to a long summer evening. Mom is furiously engaged in the construction of an afghan, Dad is mumbling over the intricacies of his nightly crossword puzzle, and the radio is tuned to some soft waltz music. I'm sort of glad to have you to write to tonight; it seems like it's a touch with something new, something more in touch with what used to be. Maybe it is a touch of the sun— or maybe it's the tall iced glass I have prepared for myself ...

After consulting the book of etiquette, latest edition, I learned that it is permissible to employ the use of a typewriter for personal correspondence. And because my new hobby requires the proficient use of this little mechanical devil, I am writing in this method. I hope you will bear with me and not judge too hastily my eccentricities. Unable to procure hardwoods to pursue my former hobby of woodworking, I have taken up journalism, a subject that I have always liked. So I have enrolled in a school for that purpose.

So, Catherine, it seems like I have run out of subject—so will end this letter here. Hoping that you can find time to write soon,

Adios amigo,
Clinton Ward

Thoughts for "August 1944, Somewhere in Italy"

On August 25, 1944, Paris was liberated from German control after four years of Nazi occupation. Thousands of American soldiers paraded with President de Gaulle down the Champs Élysées from the Arc de Triomphe. What a glorious sight for the Allies and for all who love freedom!

*****

The Yanks and the Allies in Paris after France was liberated by the Allies on August 25, 1944.

Catherine and Frank had met one year earlier, on the eighth of August 1943. Ten months into his deployment in the European theater, Catherine's letters kept coming, and the 17th Airborne was still being held in reserve.

Catherine had enjoyed her vacation and was back to her life of work, church, friends, and family. She had started a pen-pal relationship with Clinton Ward and mentioned that she is a little envious of his ability to write a letter. Not many people could write a letter like Clinton Ward. In the meantime, all Frank knew was that he wanted this "damnable war" to be over so that he could keep his date with Catherine at the Charlotte train station.

In the letters that they exchanged through the months, you hear Catherine and Frank ask each other, "Did you go to church today?" or, in Catherine's case, "I went to church three times this week—I was a good girl." They shared the same background of faith—something that was very important to both of them.

Frank had a strong faith in God. He did not follow the religions of man that believed in the "hell and brimstone" theory—but rather the religion of God. He was a Christian and believed in the teachings of Jesus. His God loved his children unconditionally. He respected people of different colors, religions, nationalities, backgrounds, financial status, and even different political views. He never passed judgment on another person, maintaining that that was a job for his God. On the other hand, he held himself to extremely high standards. Frank's words, thoughts, and deeds were all examples of God's love.

In one of the lighter notes of his letters, Frank mentions that he has made friends with a puppy that followed him back to the base one day—a base that is now an empty warehouse near Rome.

Frank mentions a German song he likes. Here are the words translated into English.

LILI MARLEEN

Outside the barracks, by the corner light
I'll always stand and wait for you at night
We will create a world for two
I'll wait for you the whole night through
For you, Lili Marleen
For you, Lili Marleen

Bugler, tonight, don't play the Call to Arms
I want another evening with her charms
Then we will say goodbye and part
I'll always keep you in my heart
With me, Lili Marleen
With me, Lili Marleen

Give me a rose to show how much you care
Tied to the stem, a lock of golden hair
Surely, tomorrow, you'll feel blue
But then will come a love that's new
For you, Lili Marleen
For you, Lili Marleen

When we are marching in the mud and cold
And when my pack seems more than I can hold
My love for you renews my might
I'm warm again; my pack is light
It's you, Lili Marleen
It's you, Lili Marleen

My love for you renews my might
I'm warm again; my pack is light
It's you, Lili Marleen
It's you, Lili Marleen

"Lili Marleen" was a universal song with a theme that reminded every soldier of the girl who was waiting back home. The Allies, Germans, and Russians were all enamored with this song. The lyrics were written by Hans Leip, a German soldier, and the music was sung by Lale Andersen, a young German in her thirties whose sweet voice echoed over the airways to all who were fighting in the European theater. The song was popular for many years during the war, and its melancholy words brought many a tear to a soldier's eye.

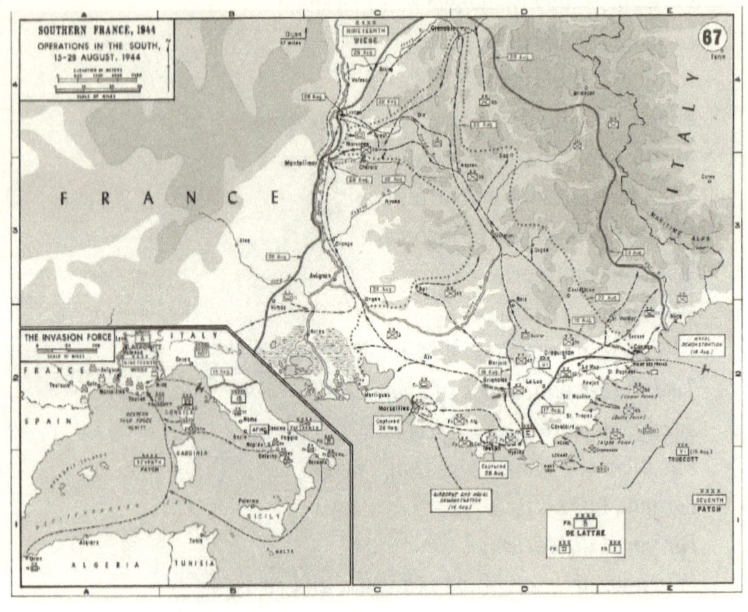

*****

It is fascinating to take a look back at what standard items cost in 1944. In the United States of America, the average cost of a new house was $3,450. For those families who could not afford a home, the average house rent was about fifty dollars per month. Average wages per year were $2,400. A loaf of bread was ten cents, a gallon of gas cost fifteen cents (when you could get it), and Old Spice Shaving Soap was a dollar.

WAR NEWS

The Democrats nominated Franklin Delano Roosevelt for a fourth term as President of the United States.

On August 15, 1944, the "other invasion" of France begun:

"Operation Dragoon." This thrust brings up the flank from the south, parachuting thousands of Allied Forces into southern France: the US 509th Parachute Infantry Regiment, the 517th Parachute Regimental Combat Team, and the British 2nd (Independent) Parachute Brigade. Added to these units are the 550th Glider Infantry Battalion and the 551st Parachute Infantry Battalion. This thrust, followed by an amphibious landing, has the Nazis running for high ground in the Vosges Mountains.

Operation Dragoon is not as famous as D-Day, but once again, the 17th Airborne was overlooked, and we assume that Frank and his unit were disappointed once again that they had not been involved in finishing this war. He was proud and happy that "... those Yanks are storming through France."

Italy, near Rome
July and August 1944

Lieutenant Ward with his men
and their adopted puppy

September 1944,
Italy and Southern France

The Twelfth Month of Deployment

During the first week of September 1944, Lieutenant Frank R. Ward had a few days left in sunny Italy before he and his unit were moved once more to Southern France. From this new position, they would reinforce those units that are pushing the Germans back to the Rhine River in the wake of the D-Day invasion of June 6, 1944.

*****

September 1, 1944
Italy

My Darling Cathy,

The mailman treated me good today. I got three letters—dated August 16-17-18. That's pretty good.

Thanks for the clipping, Cath; I always like to see what the US papers say about our hard work.

You know, Cathy, I also am rather envious of my brother's ability to write, but I'm more proud than envious. I've often been peeved at him that he didn't try to exert some of his talents. I remember he wrote me a letter at Christmastime while I was at Benning that I shan't forget. Growing up, he always referred to me as "the kid," but in this letter it was clear that he was trying hard to call me 'France' instead of "the kid."

From Benning on, he vowed not to call me the kid anymore. "A Lieutenant in the Army is not a kid," he said.

Darling, I bet your mother and everyone is happy to hear that your brother is coming home. But after two years and a third, he sure deserves all the time he can get—and more.

What's the new job you are after? And by this time, I guess I should ask instead—did you get the new job? If you got it, I hope you like it.

Yes, Cath, I've lived that day over and over many, many times—even cursing under my breath when the captain insisted on me driving home from the beach. It seems like a short time ago that all that took place. I hope that the time is even shorter until we'll be able to do those things again. It will be, Darling. It sure is a lovely evening here—a nice big moon and a cool breeze for a change. But please know, Cath—I love you. This war won't last forever, and this Lieutenant is coming home.

It was supposed to have been five years ago today that this war started. (Historical note to be filed.) I say there will not be another September 1.

Darling, I've got to turn in, so goodnight. Remember I love you.

Love always, Frank

*****

Sunday night
September 8, 1944

Hello Darling,

This weather is even more unpredictable than the legendary California weather. This morning I woke up to what I thought was a tremendous bombardment, but it turned out to be a hot thunder followed by a thunderstorm. For a while, I was undecided as to what sort of transportation to use. An amphibious jeep would have fit the role perfectly—but no such luck! So I was forced to use my water wings without board motors. Alright, alright—I ended up with a truck.

Darling, I received some more of the beach pictures today. The one in which you and your friend Charlotte stood by the 'no dogs allowed' sign, the picture of you along the fence—I like it very much. I took one of you there last year, remember?

I showed them to my roommate but told him that there were no dogs allowed, and told him that as far as I was concerned, that meant wolves, also. He said you were very cute and was coming back with me to see if the camera was lying or not. I assured him that the camera wasn't lying. He said, "Ward, you're a lucky guy." You're so darned sweet, Darling, and I love you very much.

You know, Quinn sure isn't afraid of work. He will sit and watch it all day! It's absolutely impossible to get mad at him. He's a good joker.

I went for some glider rides a few weeks back; it sure was fun. It was the first time I'd been up in a long time—got to earn my extra pay!

Thanks for pictures, honey. Goodnight, I love you.

All my love, Frank

*****

Saturday night
September 9, 1944

My Darling Cath,

How's my sweetheart tonight? Ok, I hope. Just a year ago tonight I had O.D. (Officer of the Day)—remember? You and Dump came down to Aberdeen. We had a nice steak at Scotty's and then a gay time dancing. "Sunday, Monday, or Always" was the song we danced to. Then Dump and Smokey took off for a little while. You know that story that you got out of me.

Anyway, in their absence, we had fun dancing. That evening Cath, remember what I told you? Darling, I mean it even more now. How's the home front, Cath? Did you get your new job? How are your mother and dad doing? You know, I think I'd be rather excited, too, if I had a brother I hadn't seen in two years. From experience, I'd say he's plenty excited himself.

Darling, the Russians are knocking on Hitler's door from the East. The British and Americans from the South and West. What he's waiting for? Maybe he still thinks he can get a negotiated peace. Well, negotiated or not, it's not far away.

Cath, have you received those North African pictures yet? I'm still working on mine. This is almost as bad as North Africa.

Well, tomorrow being Sunday, I think I shall go to town and really give it the once-over as to what makes it tick. Going to church tomorrow? I'll go with you.

Goodnight, sweets—this Lieutenant here loves you. Remember?

All my love, Frank

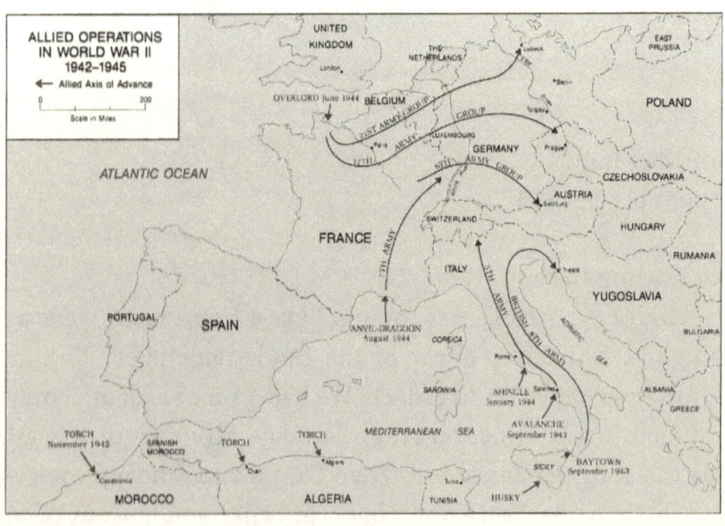

"Lafayette, I am here!"
September 1944, Somewhere in Southern France

On August 15, 1944, Operation Dragoon pushed the Germans further into the Vosges Mountains near the French border with Germany. Then, in September 1944, the US Navy transported the 17th Airborne to the South of France to help mop up after Operation Dragoon. The D-Day invasion of the Normandy Beaches on June 6, 1944, is so well known that this operation, the "other" invasion of France, is not as well remembered.

*****

Tuesday night
September 19, 1944

My Darling Cath,

Just a year ago tonight—one whole year has slipped by. One year that is forever gone. But Darling, this year has brought me lots of happiness and new experiences. By far, the most precious gift this year has brought me is your love. That means *everything* to me. The letters you have written, Cath—that's what keeps me going. When there isn't a letter for me, I pin my hopes on tomorrow. Darling, you have really spoiled me, but I like it. Everyone is envious of me because I get so much mail. I keep telling them that they just don't know anyone that can write.

I've been doing a bit of traveling. I've been to see a lot of the sights, and at present, I'm doing a little more traveling. "France, here I come!" or "Lafayette, I am here!" France is a new experience yet to be unfolded. What I was sent over here for, and what I've been waiting for almost a year for, is about to be realized.

Remember, Darling, our last Sunday together? It's one I won't soon forget. I told you I'd be back. Well, that I will, but if not as a Colonel, I will try and make it with at least a couple of bars. It's raining tonight—just as it was last year—sort of in remembrance of '43.

How is everything there, Darling? Did your brother arrive as expected? How's your work going? Going to church tomorrow? I'll go with you.

Good night, sweets—this Lieutenant here loves you ... Remember?

All my love, Frank

*****

Thursday night
September 21, 1944
Somewhere in France

My Darling Cath,

Tonight I'm somewhere in France, and I might say that it's really a nice country. The people and cities are by far more clean than any county to which I have been sent so far. But enough of that for the present.
They finally got around to issuing us our Wings. I'm sending them to you, as I want you to have them. I've sure waited a long time for them. Wear them for me, will you, Darling? I had these pictures made today in a town near here. For the pictures in general, these are a couple of good ones. I also took a roll of film in this town. I hope they're good.

I got one letter from you the day that I left my old station. It was dated August 3. Rather an old one, but it was never one bit less welcome. It was a sweet letter, Darling. Just like that Cath of mine. She's sweet, too. Darling, those days in August and September—I won't ever forget them. I'll be back, and we can have all that fun again.

Have you heard from my brother lately? I haven't heard for a couple of weeks. Well, it seems like it.

The rainy season has started to set in. It was really rough yesterday—wind and rain, and no raincoat. Boy, was I soaked!

I had chicken dinner with the Navy on Sunday, topped off with the best dish of ice cream this side of the Atlantic coast. Those Navy boys sure treated us swell while we were with them.

Also, here is some of the picturesque French Francs and some of our invasion "dough."

I'm with a couple of officers now that are really "très bon" (a very good vintage). One is a character from the Bronx; the other's a farmer from Kansas—but both are good eggs. I miss Quinn's wit. But this Bronx character is making up for it. He is Irish.

Darling, I'm going to get a chance to whoop those characters now. So Cath, if my letters are a little farther apart, remember I am using that time so I can get back to you sooner.

Those miniature pictures sure travel nice. I sure like them, Darling.

Well, Cath, tomorrow is another hard day. I love you, Darling,

Love always, Frank

*****

Friday night
September 22, 1944
Somewhere in Southern France

Sweets, I've had a long hard day, and I'm dog tired and ready for bed. This France is really a pretty country. I wish you could see it. I know you'd like it. The people are cleaner and better mannered than in Italy, and above all, they don't stand around waiting for someone to tell them what to do.

Darling, yesterday I sent you a small package with a set of my wings, a couple of photos, some invasion money, and a letter. I hope and pray, Cath, that this doesn't get lost in the mail. I hope you noticed my new address: A/B Infantry Battalion APO #512 c/o P.M: N.Y.C.—this is a surprise, yes.

Boy, it sure has turned cold these last few nights. The boys are digging for their red flannels and overcoats.

Darling, my eyes just refuse to obey me. So, I'd better sign off. Oh! One thing more—I love you and miss you.

All my love, Frank

*****

To Catherine from Clinton:
September 7, 1944
Los Angeles, California

Dear Catherine:

This morning I received a letter from France (Frank) and in it was a picture of you. It was a nice picture, and I am more convinced than ever at his choice of girlfriends. But the picture of you reminded me that I haven't heard from you for a long time, and that reminded me of an event that occurred about three weeks ago.

I had spent an evening writing letters—three of them: one to you, one to France, and one to a cousin in Utah. Two days ago my cousin in Utah wrote to me that the letter I had sent her was intended for France... I'm wondering if I have sent your letter to someone else? If so, I can plainly see why I haven't heard from you. But I was really sure that I had mailed it correctly. It was typewritten and described the beach where I had been that day, but if you didn't receive any letter from me, I am very sorry. It was unintentional, and just a sign that I am more stupid than usual.

You know, the way France writes about you and describes

you leads me to think that you are really a swell girl. France has always had a lot of girlfriends, but he's never said much in their favor. In fact, he's said he could take them or leave them. I told him that he had better use caution, then, as he would really 'get took' himself some day … and … well …

I did have a bunch of photos the kid brother wanted me to send to you, but they will have to wait till next time. I am writing this letter up at the office, and the pictures are at home, so next time I'll send them along to you.

It sure is hot here lately. The air currents moving in from Death Valley are just like gusts from a blow torch. How is the weather back in your town? Gee, everything here you touch, you stick to.

It is becoming more and more evident that the war in Europe will soon be finished and I've been wondering if France would be home soon after, but I don't believe he will. Anyway, the cessation of hostilities would help a lot.

Well, Catherine, I must get busy, so if you can forgive me for the blunder I made, somehow please write soon. Until then,

    Adios, Clinton

Thoughts for "September 1944, Italy and Southern France"

On September 1, 1944, the war passed the five-year mark. In August of 1939, Germany had invaded Poland in order to expand "their most perfect order." This provoked a declaration of war from France and England. The Third Reich declared war on the Soviet Union on June 22, 1941. The Soviet Union was shocked at this, as the Nazis were presumed to be their friends—or at least they had tolerated each other. The Russians then joined the Allies and fought with a vengeance against the Third Reich from 1941–1945—all the way to Berlin—and the rest is history.

The lieutenant from the Bronx whom Frank mentioned in his letter of September 21, 1944, was Frank Markey. Frank Markey and Frank Ward were "brothers in war," as I call them, and remained "brothers" for the rest of their lives.

The 17th Airborne Infantry was a special glider unit. It was highly trained at both flying in gliders and being Army infantry. In his letters of September 1944, Frank mentioned that he had trained in a glider four times in one week in September. This is his first mention of being in a glider, and he said that it was fun. The paratroopers named the gliders "the flying coffins," but Frank called it fun. He never spoke of the gliders again after his return to the US. As a matter of fact, there were many things he never spoke of again after returning home.

The 17th Airborne was assigned front-line duty in Southern France. Their first order of business was to help mop up after Operation Dragoon and then to continue to push the Nazis even further back into Germany. During the time he was en route from Italy to France on a US Naval ship, he wrote to tell Catherine how well the Navy boys had treated the 17th Airborne. He also lets her know that he is now going to accomplish the job that he has been training for, and he mentions that he would soon not be able to write as often as he had in the past. It was true he was moving closer to the front lines, where he would be met with foxholes and German artillery. You could hear the officer talking in these letters – there is no teasing, no playing, no joking, and no fear—just an Army lieutenant who wants to get this job done. The motto of the 17th Airborne was "Thunder from Heaven," and the storm was about to start for this unit of the US Army.

*****

Frank also writes that he is sending Catherine his glider Wings, and he asks her to wear them. For Frank, this was a

Airborne Glider Wings

little bit like asking her to wear his class ring or his jacket. He was proud of the wings he received and did not want anything to happen to them.

In one of Frank's letters, he mentioned "invasion money." This was a currency the servicemen received for pay when stationed in a foreign country that was under invasion. There were a few reasons why they were paid this way. One reason was that if they had been paid in hard currency, such as the dollar, it would have caused inflation in the local economies and would have facilitated the big risk of black market trading.

Invasion money

October 1944,
Somewhere in Southern France

The Thirteenth Month of Deployment

Frank was dodging "Jerry's shells" and is spending a lot of time in the foxholes of Southern France. He joined a group of distinguished American soldiers who fought in the foxholes of France in both world wars. The autumn days had turned into frigid cold nights, and most of the evenings were spent in a bedroll or a sleeping bag. Frank was one of the lucky ones: he had a sleeping bag. He told Catherine he was scared but mustn't show it because he is the unit's leader. The war was becoming extremely real for Frank.

*****

To Catherine from Frank
Postmarked October 5, 1944:
September 28, 1944

Darling Cath,

Tonight is going to be very cold. We've already put on everything available, including barracks bags—and we are still cold.

Darling, I managed to get another roll of film developed and here is part of the results. A couple of my buddies want to see the rest of them, and I'll mail those later. Some of them are pretty good, some so-so. I hope you like them.

I found out today that my mail is going somewhere else. I'm going to put a stop to that.

Darling, I have got a crazy crew and a good bunch of boys. One fellow was missed by a shell one day. He got out of his foxhole, looked towards Jerry, raised his arm and said, "Heil Hitler, you so-and-sos! You couldn't hit me if you wanted to!" Evidently, Jerry got mad because he started throwing things—and I don't mean pots and pans. I do not know all of the men, but will in time.

It's another beautiful night, big moon, bright sky. I wish we could spend it together. I wish we could take that ride through Brookgreen Gardens. Then from Myrtle Beach to Charlotte—that night was fun. That rainy Sunday and that 11:01 train. I wish it had been a later one ... oh well, Darling, it won't last much longer. Then Frank will be marching home again—Oh, happy day mañana!

How did your brother enjoy his stay? I know how he felt when it came time to leave. How are your mother and dad, Becky and David? Say hello to them for me.

Darling, some of the tales I'll have to tell when I get back will probably sound far-fetched, but boy, they will be good!

Goodnight, sweets, time to hit the road to dreamland. I love you, Cath.

All my love, Frank

*****

Monday night
October 2, 1944
2130 hours, Monday night

My Darling,

For a few days, I was becoming very adept in the art of dodging "Jerry shells." I got so that I could kiss the ground with the best of them and I intend to become a past master in the art. Though all that is necessary is to keep an ear peeled at all times. At a whistle, you kiss the ground. That's the main idea. But Cath, I'm still in one piece, and I have every intention of remaining in one piece. Darling, believe me, everyone says a prayer when those shells start to fly. I am not one to say I am not afraid—because I am. I'm *damn* scared, but my problem is not to show it. I've got an example to set. I've hit an outfit that's been called "Lucky." I hope that it remains that way. I met up with a couple of my old buddies in the outfit. It was sure good to see them. I will tell you all about my new outfit later.

You know, Darling, it's been over a year since I have even talked to you. Remember that day I called you? Then and now, I still have a lot of things I want to talk about. Cath, I don't think you ever did kick the so-and-so operator that interrupted our call and cut us short. That was funny.

It's raining tonight. I like to hear it rain because it reminds me of the last time we were together. Those minutes were all too short. We'll have to stop the clock when I get back, Cath.

Sweets, here are the rest of the pictures and very much to my surprise, I was able to pick up some more film here in France. I'm hoping to get some more.

Cath, I picked up a little something for you, and I hope you like it. I wished I knew what to get my Darling for Christmas— any suggestions? It seems funny to be talking about Christmas in October. I do wish I knew what to get for you, though. I guess these packages will take a while to travel.

Did you get the small package with the Wings in it? I hope it arrives soon. I'm sweating that one out.

Jerry threw a shell the other day. Now we don't have to dig out spuds—just go out and pick them up! Darn nice of him.

How is my sweetheart tonight? OK, I hope. Say hello to everyone for me.

The time has come to hit the hay. Cath, I love you and

miss you so very much. Goodnight, Darling.
Love always,
Frank

*****

Friday evening
October 6, 1944

Hello Darling,

Gee, this is a swell evening going to waste. I wished that you were here to help me enjoy it—although I dare say that the evening is just as fine there. The best part of this day has been mail call. I received two letters from you today, from early September. You know, Darling, one never really knows how much a letter means until he goes without one for a while. It's been almost three weeks since I received any mail. But those two letters from you today sure gave me a new lease on life.

I'm getting my chance at Jerry now and again. I'll give him 'hell' when I get a good chance.

It seems so strange to have my old platoon back again. I have to learn all over again those things I knew when I was at Mackall. I've been so used to looking after just me that the idea of looking after a platoon is strange. Oh well, it'll all come back. I have a darn good platoon sergeant to help me.

I have been driving quite a bit. It is fun. I have got to get more driving practice.

Cath, there is one tune that is still sweet music to my ears. We sang it coming in—"Wait for Me, Mary." Remember? I love you, Darling.
Love always,
Frank

*****

Monday night
October 23, 1944

My Darling Cath,

I am a tired and happy soldier today. The mail is coming in good now—the new and the old. It's wonderful, Cath, to get mail. And one doesn't appreciate it as much until he runs into a few weeks without.

The weather is holding good right now. It reminds me of California weather.

I'm becoming a bad boy. I haven't been to church in about a month. But I am going to try to go this Sunday. How's my sweetheart tonight? OK, I hope. Gee Darling, I wish I could see you tonight. It's such a swell evening. The moon is big and bright, and it is just like a summer night.

I got a letter from my brother today at this address—the first in a long time.

Darling, I was sweating out the arrival of that package—the one with the Wings. I was afraid that it might get lost. I'm glad you like them. I think they are pretty nifty myself.

Dancing in France has been forbidden until after the war is won. But that doesn't affect the GIs. They go on as before—only now they will get a little more drunk, a little more often. They do get a chance to dance it off.

This letter is being written in relays. I write a couple or three paragraphs and then things pop and then all is quiet. It is about time for the phone to ring because I am writing the fourth paragraph.

They have a Red Cross wort too far from here. As yet I haven't been able to do anything but glance into it. It's sure in a grand building.

This is one time I'd like to rob the icebox. We had fried chicken for supper, and they have got some left ... ah me, for a piece of chicken and a nice glass of sweet milk!

I'm going to another show tomorrow night—another

Durbin picture. They have a few more places that show English pictures. I hope I can get to see some.

No matter where you go, you can't get away from inspections. They have a big one slated for the near future.

The more I see "my boys," the more I'm convinced that I have got the best bunch in the outfit. That is not conceit—that's "esprit de corps."

Darling, I am almost asleep. I love you, Cath, with all of my heart. Goodnight, sweets.

All my love, Frank

*****

To Catherine from Clinton:
October 6, 1944
Los Angeles, California

Dear Catherine:

Received your letter today and after a hard day at the office, it was like sunshine after the rain.

I was beginning to wonder about France (Frank) as it was so long ago that I last heard from him. So was my mother. And like all other mothers, another day without a letter added another wrinkle to the brow. Mother wishes me to convey to you her thanks and appreciation for your kindness and thoughtfulness in informing us of what you know, and that goes for me, too. Thanks a lot.

So you put together a fruit cake! Gee, I bet he will go for that. Tomorrow is Saturday, and I'm going to go on the prowl once more to see what I can find for him. It is really a difficult task to get something for him—*especially* to get something that will be useful. When we send him packages, I have hit upon the idea of cleaning up an empty one-gallon can like a paint can, put in the articles to be sent, then soldering the can top back on. This makes it an air-tight and water-tight container.

So far, all I have got for him is a variety of candies and some lined leather gloves which he has often asked for. Like you, I am going to put off mailing the packages until the last possible day—in hopes a new APO number comes thru.

Say, I bet France is beautiful in the spring! At least that's what Charles Boyer says—and he is supposed to know.

I am holding down the fort tonight. Mother, Essie, and Addie have gone to the show to see "Gaslight." After four and one-half years of night shift, Dad now works days and is getting used to sleeping when white people do. So he is snoring away in his big chair. So it is pretty quiet at this time in the evening, 10:45. Except for outside in the palm tree, there is a mockingbird. He and his wife are having a song fest. They sure can sing, too. It is late fall, alright. We have to close the windows. Well, Catherine, seems like I run out of things to say pretty fast, too. I too must close here. So till next time—good luck, and thanks again.

As ever, Clinton

Thoughts for "October 1944, Somewhere in Southern France"

In October 1944, Frank was once again assigned to his old platoon of 30 to 40 men. This was also the first month when he saw real action. He was constantly saying that he had the greatest bunch of men in the Army. As a second lieutenant, he took his responsibility to model a commitment to hard work very seriously. He was proud to be a GI with the gold bars of a lieutenant—in other words, a "shavetail lieutenant."

He was finally getting a shot at "Jerry," and in return, Frank said, "Jerry is throwing everything but pots and pans." He continued, "If I get a real chance at Jerry, I will do some damage." He could not say what type of artillery or weapons either his men or the Germans were using because of the censor. However, historical accounts from the period tell us that the German pistols, machine guns, submachine guns, and anti-tank weapons were considerably more sophisticated than those of the Allies. In his letters, we hear Frank speak of his M1 rifle, Tommy guns, and the bazookas.

Frank's rifles and his handgun were surely next to his best friends in the Army. He had enormous respect for and knowledge of these firearms. He cleaned them, oiled them, took them apart, and put them together, over and over again. This cleaning and oiling was done with great respect and self-control, and for nearly three years while he was in the service, his guns never left his side. However, he never enjoyed or loved guns—they were just an essential part of staying alive in the war. He witnessed the harm these instruments of death could do, and after the war was over, these deadly weapons were never among his tools at home—they just weren't needed!

Catherine and Clinton had set up a "pen pal" relationship and began to exchange information regarding Frank's health and location, as well as overall information regarding the war.

War News, October 1944

- The Holocaust: Anne Frank and her sister Margot are deported from Auschwitz to the Bergen-Belsen concentration camp, where both girls later died of typhus in March 1945.

- Florence Foster Jenkins gives a recital at Carnegie Hall.

- **October 10**: The Holocaust/Porajmos: 800 Romani children are systematically murdered at the Auschwitz concentration camp.

- **October 21**: Aachen, the first German city to fall, is captured by American troops.

- In response to the Soviet Union who was coming on strong from the East, Hitler ordered the formation of a *Landsturm* (or a Nazi militia *Volkssturm*) to protect the homeland. The German Army has already been severely depleted in numbers and does not have enough men to counter the Russians coming from the East. As a result, the age of the civilians conscripted into this militia is between sixteen and sixty years old and consists of men who are either unhealthy, too old, or too young to fight in the regular German Army.

The two Franks

High on a pile of rubble...
the wins of war

The Jeep's name is "Leapin
Lena." Lt. Markey is in the
passenger seat.

A memorial to those who
did not come back in 1914

November 1944,
On the Front Lines

The Fourteenth Month of Deployment
Somewhere in Southern France

To Catherine from Frank:
Wednesday night
November 1, 1944

My Darling,

I hope to spend a peaceful, quiet evening listening to the radio and some good American swing. I heard your favorite this evening: "I walk alone." I agree, Cath, the words and music are very nice. I remember having heard it before, but I can't remember where.

It is cold this evening. The moon is up, now and then peeking through the cloud banks, showing scenic views of the valley. I've been wading in the snow. It is still the same old cold stuff it used to be, but now it is not only cold but also treacherous ...

We have electric lights of questionable quality. The volume of light will fluctuate 5-6 times every 10 minutes, but we manage to get along without candles. We also have in our room a stove that gives off a lot of smoke. We heat up our room, and then we open the window to let the smoke out. Hot, then cold—that's us ... but when it becomes too monotonous, we just hit the hay for a cozy sleep.

Cath, I would give anything I own if I could see you

tonight. I wish you knew how much I miss you, but I have to wait until this confounded war is over.

I'm tired tonight, darned tired. I didn't get to bed until 0200—that's rough. Then I got up at seven. Tonight I have a good chance to make it up since it is only 2000 hours right now.

Markey and Tare are still the cribbage players. We go at it whenever the situation presents itself or whenever we see one or the other. I still seem to be the "King of the Cribbage."

I did get a chance to visit Nice, France. Man, what a clip joint. Well, the whole city of Nice is nothing but a clip joint. Boy, the prices they charge down there are amazing. Maybe it is just as well I'm here. It is a lot cheaper and safer.

Darling, I am so tired, I think I'll hit the hay. I love you, Cath, from the bottom of my heart. Remember that, Cath.

All my love, Frank

*****

Saturday night
November 6, 1944

My Darling Cath,

Another couple of busy days have swiftly passed by. I wish this war would pass just as fast.

I was just about to say that today was a peaceful day—but then Jerry threw some heavy stuff over my way. It's sure an eerie sound to hear those shells whistle and fly over. But so long as you can hear them, you are reasonably safe. It's the one you never hear that has your name on it.

Darling, did you ever receive your mail at 0100 in the morning? That is what happened to me last night. Someone was coming our way from headquarters, so they delivered the mail to me.

My platoon medic is one character. I have him doing almost

anything and everything. He is also our cook. One thing in this war—I never thought that I would have pork chops or beef steaks on the front lines. Well, that's what we're getting along with. Fresh bread and butter—also fish, yes, indeed! This is a crazy war we are fighting.

I hope never to see this part of France again. Although I would like to see a bit of "Paree." Oh well, maybe I'll get a chance.

It has been surprisingly warm the last three days. In fact, I've even taken off my overcoat—but I can see that this won't last long.

I have not been able to get to church in a long time. It seems like I'm either up here, or I have some other work to do.

Incidentally, how is the war progressing? I haven't heard any news in quite a few days. I do know that the Philippine invasion was successful. How is the war over here coming?

Right now the bees are giving me more trouble than "Jerry." It is the first time they have ventured out since I've been here. I wish they would go back to the hive and hibernate. We still have fresh vegetables, but we have to dig for them. Jerry doesn't do it for us anymore. Fresh potatoes and fresh carrots. If anyone cooks them, they ought to be shot.

Darling, do you know that I miss you? I do, very much. Oh well, I will be coming in on one of those northbound trains someday soon.

Darling, I have a couple of guns to clean. I was out hunting today.

Goodnight, Darling. I love you very much.
Love always, Frank

*****

Saturday night
November 11, 1944

Hello Darling,

I'm numbered among the fortunate in this unit. I'm one of the few who has a sleeping bag. Believe me, one needs something like that up here.

The mail man came today. Boy, did he treat me swell—one package that my dad sent me, and about two dozen letters! Most of it was back mail, catching up for the latter part of September. Everything here is doing as well as can be expected. Cold weather is really setting in, although no one can complain about today. I was able to absorb some of the warm rays the sun so generously gives off.

Darling, I hope those pictures I sent you before don't give you a false impression of the way we are fighting this war. Actually, my pinks and greens are quite a distance from here now. Anyway, I was in a rest camp then. Boy, it was sure nice.

The people here continue to amaze us. They can be nice, or otherwise. Usually, they are nice. We bother them as little as possible—mostly because they do not want us to be here. But one thing that does make my blood boil is to see these young Frenchies around 21–24 walking around in civvies. I'm sure they can't all be 4-F.

Today was Armistice Day. I wish it were Armistice for this war. It would be a fitting conclusion to a bitter war.

Darling, that cartoon showing the censor cutting out the paper dolls is exactly how I feel sometimes. I showed it to my platoon. They sympathized with me, but they went right on writing letters. I have the writin'est bunch of fellows this side of the pond.

The clipping on the Airborne Infantry invasion was very interesting. I'm glad I wasn't on that glider. If there is another, maybe I will be in on it—*If* there is another.

I got hold of Bob Hope's movie, "I Never Left Home." It was pretty good. He's quite a character, and most of the boys enjoy his antics.

The Red Cross paid us a visit the other day with fresh doughnuts. They were pretty good, but we had to brew the coffee to go with them. The chow we get up here still amazes me. Tonight we are having fried chicken, mashed potatoes, corn and lima beans, fresh bread and butter, and coffee. Some menu! That is the way we have been eating. This is supposed to be the front lines, too.

The cribbage contest is still held whenever Lieutenant Markey and I can get together—which is next to impossible because one of us is usually away from the Command Post.

I guess David likes being in Fort Bragg. It's a short stretch of time, but when it gets into a year and then two, that's too long.

This country is beautiful to look at, but it is mean to climb and to fight over. Right now the leaves have put on their autumn colors, and the weather has turned its coldest. When the sun shines around here, everybody forgets Jerry and basks in the sunshine for a while.

Darling, this is about the first time in a few days that I have had a chance to write. Cath, when I can't write, just remember that I'm thinking of you and I love you so very much.

Well, after I censor the mail and write to my brother and do a few other odds and ends, maybe I'll be able to hit the hay. That is if I can get by the C.O. (Commanding Officer) without him seeing me.

There is one fellow in this platoon that is nothing but a character. He is a soldier of fortune and a wanderer. His life would make a good script for a movie. Well, enough about the members of my platoon.

How's my sweetheart tonight? I wish I could see you for just a while. I miss you, Darling, so much. Goodnight, Cath.

All my love, Frank

*****

"A Day on the Front Lines"

Monday night
November 12, 1944

My Darling Cath,

Along with darkness comes the cold. The later it gets, the colder. Right now I've crawled into my sleeping bag and am trying to get my feet warm. Every night after the evening meal, a few of my men and I sit around and just shoot the breeze. We then hold a postmortem over the day's events, and what news and rumors we've been able to pick up from passersby and our command post buddies. It's one of the moments of the day that I look forward to. It's one way I can find out about my men: their wishes, plans, and desires for the future. There is one man from San Francisco—we have started a feud, and it's a kick. Right now I hold the edge with a very unflattering remark about the people of San Francisco. But I do expect him to go me one better anytime. Up here, a lieutenant is just another man on the morning report. He sleeps with his men, he eats with his men, and in general is nothing but a GI with bars on. (It's still gold, but I'm hoping.)

Jerry got mean today and threw a few our way. No damage other than to the nerves—and believe me, it is one thing that can make a man wish he was down deep in mother earth. But when he quits, everyone makes some cracks, laughs off the whole thing, and continues with what he was doing. We may laugh and joke, but you can't forget what has just gone on before. Scared? Yes, each and every one of us is scared, but we manage to put up a front and go on to face our next task. So it goes. Some days no shells, other days, plenty—today, a few. Tomorrow? Who knows? Well, then comes the time of evening: the embers die down, everyone retires to their bedroll and crawls into deep warmth—so goes an evening here on the front. Well, Darling, enough about the war.

The mailman is treating me royally the last couple of days. I received your letter dated November 5th. That's pretty good. Also, I received one from my mother dated the 4th. That I consider very good.

I did not get to the dentist. It's something I keep putting off. I have still got to do it ... not a pleasant task. I think I'd rather hear shells whine than hear a dentist's drill. That gets me. I once had to leave a show because a dentist was using a drill. Funny? No!

How is my sweetheart tonight? Been working hard? Time is still flying by. I've already signed the pay voucher for this month. It seems like yesterday that I was signing October's voucher. Well, this is the fourteenth month I'm starting on, and it seems only like last month that I was checking into A/ OTC. (Airborne Officers Training Corp). Darling, I hope that I'll be able to see you soon. Did you know I love you, Cath? I do—very much.

Well, I hope the postman is treating my Cath as well as he's treated me. Yes, Darling, my mail is good.

How are Becky and David and all? Say hello to them for me. I'm glad the roses arrived, Darling. I wish I were where I could send them all the time. I like to send them, Darling, because I know that you enjoy them.

Cath, I've got to drop my brother a line yet, so I'd better sign off. Goodnight, sweetheart. I love you.

Love always, Frank

*****

Wednesday night
November 22, 1944
Southern France

My Darling Cath,
Down from "hell's acres"—it feels good to get back to

"semi-civilization." It also feels good to shave for the first time in two weeks. And best of all, I can go to sleep without keeping an ear open for guns. It is a strange life one leads up there: during the day you seek the shadows, at night you're afraid of a light.

Darling, I haven't been able to write any for the past week or so—maybe I'll be able to tell you why later on. But the mail-man has treated me good. I received a letter from you dated the 13th and a few from late September. Darling, that late mail makes the distance between us seem so short. I only wish it were shorter. I also received a package from my brother with a nice letter. Darling, I promise to try and restrain my sense of curiosity until the 25th of December.

I have a two-day pass coming up, but I can't say that I am exactly happy to get it. That doesn't sound right, does it? Well, I think I'll take it. Maybe I'll try to find something for my Cath.

Have you heard of pup tents? Well, that's my hotel for a while, and the ground is my mattress. That's where I'm writing this letter. Darling, if you can't read this letter, it's because I am lying down. It's cold here, and the warmest place is in bed. Oh, yes—I also have running water when it rains.

This month has sure gone by fast. It seems like it should be starting instead of ending.

The Army is sure planning a feed for the fellows over here—everything from turkey to nuts. What a feed!

I am one tired soldier tonight. We walked from sunrise to sunset—but not for exercise.

They still feed us good. We had nice thick steaks tonight with mashed potatoes and the rest of a good meal. Darling, that cherry pie sounds very good right now, but I will wait for it.

I still have mail to censor. That is a job that is becoming simple. I just spot the boys who violate censorship and check on them. I give a clean bill to the rest.

Darling, I love you very much, but I've got to go to sleep before I fall off. Goodnight, Darling.

All my love, Frank

*****

In the letter below, Frank speaks of his third Thanksgiving in the Army.

*****

Postmarked December 5, 1944:
Thursday afternoon
November 23, 1944

Darling Cath,

Happy Thanksgiving, Cath. Well, it is for us: turkey, cranberry sauce, ham, green peas, giblets, gravy, dressing, potatoes, and everything that goes with it except for the pie. Anyway, I'm waiting for a cherry pie! We have nothing to do this afternoon as the Captain has declared it "free time" – very generous of him. Some of the men have gone on pass, a few have hiked up into the hills, and a few of the men I and are holding down the fort. They have a radio going, and it is pouring out sweet swing. That's music to my ears and makes me want to walk home. They have played a couple of our favorites: "Constantly," "I walk alone," and "Sunday, Monday, or Always."

That pass I told you about? Well, it doesn't look like I am going to get it now. Oh well, so it goes.

Mail call was one package from home and two letters from my Cath. My mother sent me a feed fit for a king – everything from meat to nuts!

They had a show for us last night—one I hadn't seen—"You

Were Never Lovelier" with Fred Astaire and Rita Hayward. I really enjoyed it. It was the best show I have seen in over a month.

We are looking forward to a hot night. Everyone went out and gathered wood today, and I'll bet there are a lot of fires tonight.

Well, Darling, the afternoon is rapidly becoming dusk. The sun has sent up a beautiful sunset, glowing red. So according to an old and ancient prophecy, we'll have a good day tomorrow.

Cath, pardon the mixed stationery. I got it mixed on purpose—I ran out of the others.

Well, sweetheart, I have got to say goodnight. I love you, Cath, from the bottom of my heart.

Love always, Frank

PS: Darling, I wrote this and didn't get a chance to mail it—so here it is new from a week ago, love.

*****

Wednesday night
November 29, 1944

My Darling Cath,

I have been unable to write for a week, Cath, and if you promise not to worry about me, I will tell you why ... promise? About a week ago we were sitting around the fire having a bull session and playing cribbage, and well, I looked squarely into the fire when something exploded! Later we discovered it was a flashlight battery. Well, I got the full blast in the eyes. Well, when they got through bandaging me up, I probably looked like something out of a horror story. But everything is OK. My eyes are now normal, and I'm back to duty. I was wearing the bracelet you sent me last Christmas when it happened, and when I saw it a few days ago, I discovered it was black and pitted slightly. That happened in a split second when I put my hands up to my face—the bracelet caught the tail end of the blast. I considered myself very fortunate that nothing severe happened. I guess my "Guardian Angel" is watching out for me. Well, enough of that ...

News is so scarce around here that I hardly even know there is a war going on.

How is my sweetheart tonight? OK, I hope. It's a lovely night, Darling—clear sky and a bright moon—just like another night I remember. I wish you were able to see this part of France. It's really nice. They are playing your song right now. I sure like it—"I Walk Alone." Every time I hear it, I have to stop and listen to it. I think if I was in the middle of a firefight and I heard it, I'd still have to stop and listen to it. I miss you, Darling ... so very much.

Markey and I are still in the middle of our cribbage battle. I still hold the edge. He is a character from way back, but definitely a good egg. He has several good friends in Charlotte. He keeps kidding me about my wanting to get back to Charlotte, but I know he is just as anxious to get back as I am.

I'm sure embarrassed sometimes. I meet a lot of fellows that know me, but I just stand there trying to remember who they are. That is really embarrassing. Then about 2 minutes after they leave I remember who they are. I guess I'll have to take a memory course.

I hope you'll be able to read this, Cath. The pen is no good, and the table is wobbly.

Tomorrow is payday. There is going to be a hot time in the old town ... but not for me.

Darling, I love you ... remember that, Cath. I've got to get some shut-eye. Goodnight, sweets.

Love always, Frank

Lt. Wade and Lt. Wall
with Frank on leave in France

Frank in a rest camp

Snow in the south of France

Thoughts for "November 1944, On the Front Lines

In November 1944, President Franklin D. Roosevelt was elected for his fourth term.

The war was coming to a close, or at least that is what most of the pundits thought. However, for the men on the front lines, it was not closing fast enough. They called the front lines the "meat grinder." They were pushing back the Germans, one inch at a time. Frank refers to the Germans as "Jerry"—a popular slang name for Nazis. The Germans were armed with the new MK 44 (the first assault rifle 44), warmer uniforms, and waterproof boots—not to mention the German Panzers and Tiger tanks. Nevertheless, the US and its Allies were destined to outman this insidious foe with waves and waves of young, well-trained men—armed with fire in their bellies to defeat the Germans.

The pictures that we have of Frank during his time in southern France portray him as thin, even gaunt, and without a smile. In his letters, he often mentions that he has a lot of tales to tell, but the reality is that once the war was behind him, he chose never again to mention the foxholes or the front lines in Southern France. Even so, waking or sleeping, he was plagued with the whistles of "Jerry's shells" for many years after the war.

None of his family knew that he was even close to the front lines in Southern France—he managed to keep that secret very close to his vest. Did he choose not to tell his family all of his tall tales because it was just too much for us to grasp? Was he afraid we didn't even want to hear? I feel sure that he knew instinctively that the sights, smells, and sounds of war in his stories were just too graphic to share. Was this another of his heroic acts, protecting his friends and loved ones from the reality of the hellish experiences that he endured? Once again, his humble bravery speaks for itself: as he often said, he was a man on a mission, just doing what he had to do—alongside thousands of others of that "greatest generation."

Frank mentions that he sees many young Frenchmen, 21–24 years of age, walking around looking very healthy and dressed in civvies. He was just one of many who thought the French should be doing more to help the war effort and secure the liberation of France from Nazi occupation.

In a letter to Catherine, he mentions the time he spent in a rest camp, saying, "I hope those pictures I sent you before don't give you a false impression of the way we are fighting this war ... I was in a rest camp then. Boy, it sure was nice." The fighting was so intense that the US Army sent those who had been on the front lines the longest to a rest camp. The opportunity to spend 24 hours in one of these camps in France made Frank one of the lucky ones.

Frank suffered an injury to his eyes in a freak explosion of a flashlight battery, which had found its way into a campfire. As a result, his eyes were bandaged for about a week. Fortunately, he was able to report that his eyes were fine and that he sustained no scars from the battery shrapnel. He gives thanks for the "guardian angel" who was looking out for him that day. Indeed, his "guardian angel" did a very good job that day: it is remarkable that he never even wore glasses until he was in his fifties.

Again, he speaks of Frank Markey and what a good egg he was.

In November 1944, you could hear Frank growing weary of this conflict. On November 12, he tells the story of a day on the front lines, mentions that it is cold, and says how grateful he is to have a sleeping bag. Sleeping bags were not standard Army issue at that time. He is very careful not to worry Catherine, but if we read between the lines, we can tell that he is going through hell with his brothers in war.

Again, he talks about his men and how a second lieutenant is just another GI with gold bars. He sleeps with his men, eats with his men, and hits the ground with them when he hears the whistle of Jerry's shells. He speaks about how everyone was scared; however, after the shells had passed, his men just laughed it off and went on with their work. There was no denying that they were scared, but they managed to find a way to regain their focus and keep going. Once again, they had a job to do. Their only option—and their unshakeable resolve—was to get back to work and get it done.

As we read between the lines, it is easy to hear a weary second lieutenant who was down in the dumps. However, he could not tell Catherine he was tired because of her "chin up and work hard" theory. She just would not understand.

Unfortunately, many of Catherine's letters were casualties of war. In spite of the fact that she wrote and wrote, her letters from November 1944 were never recovered. We do know that it was her letters that gave him a reason to continue to live instead of just dying in the foxholes of France.

The pride that he feels for his men is palpable in all of his letters. At every turn, he speaks of his brothers in war as shining examples of the best and the brightest of their generation.

December 1944, Somewhere in Southern France

The Fifteenth Month of Deployment

In the early weeks of December 1944, Frank remained in the South of France. In the latter part of December, he and his unit were sent to England, where he felt right at home. He stayed in England from December 15–31, 1944, when the 17th Airborne was redeployed to Southern France.

He hated to move because it always delayed his mail. Besides, the front lines were not in England. He wanted to be out there, fighting the Germans, getting the job done!

*****

Friday night
December 1, 1944
Somewhere in Southern France

Dear Cath,
Well, there's another month overseas, and another month I won't have to worry about. Starting the 15th that makes 14 months that I have to my credit ... or three overseas stripes. I am back on duty, and my eyes are OK—for which I am thankful. Every time I go near a fire now, I always ask if there are any flashlight batteries in it.

What's my Cath been doing? I hope you haven't been working too hard. As for your Frank, he has been taking it easy for a few days. That pass is coming up again. I think I'll take it and get some rest—not that I need it, but it may come in handy.

Darling, there's sure not much news around here. Everything is quiet and almost peaceful. Yesterday was payday, and the boys took up a collection and bought our Sergeant a trumpet. Boy, he sure can swing with the blues. He used to play in one of the bands back in the good old USA.

Next month we'll get another boy an accordion, and then we'll have a company orchestra! Our company had a party the other night—man, what a blowout *that* was! The boys got a date, we had an orchestra, and the boys really had a good time.

How's everyone there on the home front? How's your mother, Becky, and the Kellys?

Our chow is still pretty good. We still get the luscious cuts of meat, etc. But I'd prefer to have C-rations in the States than to have steak in France. Oh well, I guess I can't be choosy about it.

My boys are rough. I've found out whom *not* to play football with. I played yesterday and got my lips bashed against my teeth. What a bunch of roughnecks!

Darling, it's getting late, and I've work to do tomorrow. Cath, I love you. That's the best news I know. Goodnight, sweets.

All of my love, Frank

*****

December 4, 1944
Somewhere in France

My Darling Cath,

It is getting cold enough to make me think that winter has descended on us. This morning the frost was thick enough to call snow. And I had to crack the ice to get water to wash and cook with. So it goes. Next thing I know, I'll be tramping in snow up to my hips. That's when I'll call the war off.

Darling, do not let this picture scare you. Just after it was taken, I became a normal looking human again. I shaved and washed. Boy, that was murder.

Lieutenant Markey got a plum pudding from home a while ago. Last night we ate it. Boy, was it good!

Every time I get near a fire now, I'm always suspicious of what may be in it. So far so good.

I manage to read part of a book now and again. "Shoe the Wild Mare" is pretty good. I also saw a good show last night, but it was old: "Here Comes Mr. Jordan." They're having another show tomorrow night: "Four Wives," which is also good.

Boy, when I get back to the States ... that, Darling, will be my happy day ... And they'll have to pull teeth to get me out again. Cath, I miss you so much—and Darling, I won't do like you said I did in your dream.

"I Walk Alone" continues to grow popular over here and then there's the ever-popular "White Christmas." They're playing both a lot. But the one I like is "Wait for Me, Mary." Remember?

Darling, everything we are doing is dull and routine, and boy, that gets monotonous. I'm hoping to get a pass.

Cath, this lieutenant loves you very much. I wish I could see you, Darling, and tell you how much ... But *c'est la guerre!*

Love always, Frank

Somewhere in England

Jolly old England, how nice it is! The chow is good but a little bland—the Brits always did eat a little boring. Frank now has wonderful quarters and even sofas, beds, and fireplaces—and people who really appreciate us Yanks. What a wonderful place to be for the duration—wouldn't it be nice?

*****

Saturday night
December 16, 1944
Somewhere in England

My Darling Cath,

You're nearly as surprised as I am. Thank God that we're now in a country where the people treat us royally. Well, this is one more country added to the list which I have visited—I'm sure getting around! By the time I get home, I will be referred to as a well-traveled man, but for all the traveling and all the things I have seen, I'd sooner never have left the States. Oh well ... *c'est la guerre*. (This is war.)

Well, Saturday night and I'm Officer of the Day. They're having a dance in the village near here. I have to make a check to make sure that our boys behave. I hope they do. I'd like to go to the dance, but I guess there are some officers who would enjoy it more than I would. They are up on the latest songs over here. They were playing "I Walk Alone" just as the Colonel took the radio to his quarters—worse luck.

The weather is cool, but strangely it doesn't seem as cold here as where we were. I've got a room with a couple of other officers. Quite nice ... a bath, closets, and—believe it or not—a real fireplace. What makes it complete is good food!

When we left our old territory, we were in one big fog as to where we were going. One of my boys asked, "Lieutenant, where are we going?" I said, "Can you keep a secret?" He brightened up and said, "Yes." "We're going where our advance party is." He was a little confused as to where it was and asked me, "Yes, but where is the advance party?" I then pulled it on him,

"Where we are going." I'm sorry, Darling. I know it is corny.

Darling, I've missed your letters so darn much. It seems like two months since I've received any mail now. It's hard to wait again for it to catch up with us. I'm becoming a regular bouncing ball. Here today, there tomorrow. I wish that tomorrow meant home. I miss you so much. I feel like catching the next plane west. I sure wish I could be there for Christmas. That would be the best Christmas present I could get. That would be wonderful, wouldn't it?

How's my Cathy today? OK, I hope. Not working too hard, are you? Darling, let me know when you get that package. I'd like to know how long it takes. I hope you like it, Cath. Say hello to everyone for me.

Well, a guard check and then maybe I'll have a chance to write home. Goodnight, Darling. I love you so much.

All my love, Frank

*****

December 23, 1944
Somewhere in England

My Darling Cath,

How is my Cath tonight? OK, I hope. As for me, I'm fine. I miss you so very much. Things in Europe do not look so good, but I think everything'll be OK.

There is so little to write about. No one has had any mail for a while and Darling, that doesn't do any of us any good. But I am sure that will be remedied soon. I saw a show last night: "Higher and Higher." It was pretty good and had some good tunes in it. We are going to have another show tonight. I hope it is one I have not seen.

I saw an old friend of mine, Captain Lyerly. He was sure glad to see me. It was like seeing someone from home. He is the one that took pictures of us at Myrtle Beach. And yes, he is the one that pulled rank on me and made me drive home that Sunday night. Boy, we had a good gabfest talking about old times. I think of those times so often. But more than that, I think of the day when I'll get off a train and meet a girl named Cath. That thought keeps me going.

Christmas Day is just two days away and gee, it isn't like any other Christmas I've known. Even at that, it has time to snow before Christmas.

How's everyone there, Darling? Say hello for me. Has Dave heard from the draft board?

The chow is still good, and that is one of the best features of being here in England. That, and sleeping in a warm room instead of in the icy cold.

The Red Cross still does a good job in England where there is plenty to do. It's funny to visit an English village and see how its people spend an evening. The men usually visit one of the pubs for their pint of bitters. The women have their gab-fests.

Well, Darling, I will write as soon as I can. Right now I've got work a foot deep. Cath, remember that I love you from the bottom of my heart. I only wish that I could hold you in my arms and tell you that. Goodnight, Darling.

All my love, Frank

*****

Monday evening
1944 (no date)
England

My Darling,

How's my sweetheart tonight? I miss you, Darling. The company just played a tune that always makes me think of you. It's really a beautiful tune. Our company is at a dance. I'm acting as a bouncer, checking refreshments, and trying to write to you. The former two are losing to the latter as I'm not one bit interested in this dance. They started off with "Sunday, Monday, or Always." That tune makes me only want to dance with one girl. Darling, I hope your package arrived safely. I wish I could have put myself in the package instead. I hope you like it, Darling.

Cath, forgive the paper as this is all I have here at present. Our mail hasn't caught up yet, but we're working on it.

How's work going, Cath? Not hard, I hope.

I saw Captain Lyerly again yesterday. Boy, he is a card. Still the same old guy.

We are having quite a few shows lately, and some good ones at that. Out of the six, I have seen only one of them before. That is something new. "Lassie Comes Home," "Higher and Higher," "Mask of Dimitrios," and "Music in Manhattan," etc.

Darling, I have got to sign off. I love you, Cath. That's the best news I know. Goodnight, sweetheart.

All my love, Frank

Somewhere in France

Frank's New Year's Day 1945 was spent traveling to Reims, France, in order to go into battle in Belgium. This is the first letter Frank wrote after being deployed back to the continent. It is also the last letter which was recovered from his time on active duty in Europe.

*****

Sunday night
December 31, 1944
Somewhere in France

Hello Darling,

Happy New Year, Cath. As you know, I'm spending this New Year's abroad. Although, Darling, I would sooner celebrate with you in the good old American style. I'm staying up an hour later instead of going to bed at 2000 hours; I am going to stay up to 2100 hours. There's no reason to stay up to see the New Year in as we have a blackout here. So we'll have to greet 1945 in the morning. Of course "spirits of fermenti" are lacking and we're more or less confined to apple cider. So the men who prefer a harder drink are just out of luck. I'll take cider. We are having turkey again today with the entire trimmings. Boy, I hope the fellows don't stuff themselves.

Darling, I hope you know why I have not been able to write. It's been just one of those things. I was thinking of you all of the time. Darling, the last letter I had from you was on December 6, 1944. Gee, Darling, I'm sure looking forward to that mail call. We've left some very luxurious surroundings: sofas, easy chairs, radios, fireplaces, officers clubs, theaters, etc. Oh well, "*C'est la Guerre*" (This is war!)

I have sitting in front of me right now two fresh eggs that I intend on having for my New Year's breakfast. Some of my boys gave them to me as a gift.

Darling, it would be wonderful to be with you tonight. I miss you, Cath.

Well, Markey just came in and challenged me to a game. He also told me to give you his regards.

Darling, I've got to sign off for now. Goodnight, sweetheart, I love you.

All my love, Frank

Thoughts for "December 1944, Somewhere in Southern France"

Frank used the phrase *"C'est la Guerre"* ("This is war") quite a lot in his final letters before he went into battle. Did he know that he was going to Belgium to fight in the Ardennes? I believe he did. In his letter of December 23, 1944, he told Catherine, "Things do not look so good in Europe right now. They will be better soon." Yes, he knew—and could not say a word. As he writes: "This is war." Even if he could tell, he would not reveal a word to Catherine, protecting her as long as he could.

Frank used to sign his letters with a lot of energy, saying, "This war won't last forever, and this Lieutenant is coming home." He sounded strong. He wanted to get his piece of the Führer, and he wanted to get the job done. In December 1944, he talked about being with her, if just for one evening. It was almost as if he were saying, "Isn't this war ever going to end? I need to feel human; I need to feel loved; I need to relax and have fun again; I need to say the things we have not had a chance to say. I need to see you now, Catherine, before I go fight this battle."

On December 31, 1944, the war was going badly for the Allies in Belgium. The weather was brutal that winter, and the fighting vicious. The American and Allied forces were going to neutralize the Bulge that the Germans had created. First, they would push the German forces back on the Western Front, then march straight on to the Rhine River, and then into Berlin. The 17th Airborne was instrumental in that conquest. I believe Frank knew of the battles that lay ahead of him.

At 23, Frank was weary and frightened, like thousands of other young men in the same situation. It was hard to be trucked or flown in and out of countries and then not receive his mail for weeks on end because the mail would take so long to catch up. In spite of the fact that Catherine had written a total of 24 letters that month, Frank received only two of them. This was indeed a "damnable war": no letters from Catherine and no letters from home. Frank just had to survive in the cold with his faith in God and in his men—his "brothers in war"—men whom he revered and trusted. At this most pivotal time in history and in this war, all the airborne troopers had to depend on was each other—and they did.

Frank really enjoyed his cribbage matches with Frank Markey. Their tournaments provided a great release and allowed them to escape the insanity of war for a few hours. They "kept each other's chins up," as Catherine would say. Frank Markey was one friend who was always "up" and always fun. His favorite saying was, "I wonder what the poor people are doing today?" We know that although he was not rich, Frank Markey never considered himself to be poor, either! I believe he had mastered the art of making every minute an important one and that he was thankful for the life and the time he had in the present moment.

Back in the US, the economy was growing. The war industry went a long way towards putting Americans back to work, making America a very wealthy country once more. Many vacation spots like Miami Beach were thriving because people were taking vacations again. Still, it had to be hard to think about vacations when hundreds of thousands of our finest young men were spending their "vacation" facing the Nazis or playing in the sand with Emperor Hirohito in the South Pacific. Everything was good for the American economy, but the US had to get rid of Hitler and Hirohito forever. It was a genuine oxymoron.

In Catherine's letters, she wrote about her Christmas social schedule and all of the things her church was doing for the Christmas holidays. Her Sunday school class was helping orphans in a girl's home. She was buying Christmas presents, wrapping them, sending cards, along with myriad other routine things she would write about. Those letters kept him going. But it is almost as if she had no clue about the danger he was in. Did she realize it but just refused to face it? Was she just unable to face the fact that her lieutenant was going into battle—the Battle of the Bulge? All she knew for certain was that he was in England. It sounded so safe. She was sure he would be just fine.

Dead Man's Ridge

January 1945

On January 1, 1945, General George Patton addressed his Third Army after delivering the orders of the day for the Battle of the Bulge:

> *I can find no fitter expression for my feelings than to apply to you the immortal words spoken by General Scott at Chapultepec when he said: "Brave rifles, veterans, you have been baptized in fire and blood and have come out steel."*

In the autumn of 1944, the Germans were retreating to the Rhine and their homeland. The Allies in Europe were secure in their victories in Italy, France, and Belgium, and they knew that the end of the war was in sight. Unfortunately, this may have influenced them to enter the next encounter with a somewhat false sense of confidence. At this strategic tipping point, while facing overwhelming forces, the Germans were desperate to defend their homeland and had no choice but to fight an organized retreat. History shows that the Ardennes had been the German military's chosen arena to stage an engagement in several previous wars, dating back to Karl der Grosse (Charlemagne) in the eighth century. This was precisely because they were familiar with the terrain and could predict the conditions and because they knew the conditions to be predictably favorable to whichever army was the *first* to take up a position there. Historically, the steep slopes with their thick forests had proven to be a fearsome battlefield where, time and again, the Germans had won major victories and their enemies had paid a tremendous price.

As such, the area was the best geographical point of defense for the German army at this turning point of the war. Add to this the fact that winter was setting in—something which gave them a significant advantage—because who wants to fight in winter?

Surely, the Allies' strategic planners were aware of these facts. However, it would appear that in their zeal to bring the war to a close as quickly as possible, Generals Eisenhower and Bradley chose to place their bets against these lessons of the past as they pursued their final push to Berlin. With this as their firm resolve, they gambled that Hitler would probably not attack the Western European line during the winter months. There were two main reasons. First, in addition to sustaining numerous losses on the Russian Eastern front, the Germans were suffering severe shortages of fuel and general provisions for war. Their priority would undoubtedly be to defend the Eastern front of their homeland. The second reason was that the Belgian winters were deathly cold. Even for the German soldiers who were well-equipped with heavy coats, fur-lined hats, and waterproof boots, it would prove to be a brutal fight. We have to wonder—did they know that this winter would be dramatically more brutal than normal?

Thus, the Allies were relatively confident that Hitler would leave the Western Front alone. Perhaps they forgot for a moment how extremely arrogant Hitler was. He regarded the American soldiers as crossbreeds and, therefore, lesser men than the soldiers of the Third Reich. Surely his pure-bred German soldiers would defeat this worthless half-breed Army with ease—even if some of his men were only sixteen years old.

Hitler planned the Ardennes offensive himself. In an effort to split the Allies, who were poised for a total triumph in the pines, he selected the thick Ardennes Forest as the stage for a strategic conflict in his desperate push back to the West. The numbers of men and armaments were staggering. He sent five Panzer divisions—roughly sixteen hundred tanks—to support fourteen German infantry divisions (approximately 250,000 men). Unfortunately, as Eisenhower and Bradley enacted their calculated risk for this engagement, there were a few factors that were not fully considered. Among others, they did not plan for a sufficient number of troops. Considering the extensive forces arrayed under Hitler's command, this one factor left our men even more vulnerable.

The Battle of the Bulge

The Battle of the Bulge began on December 16, 1944, with the American troops totaling 80,000. In the early stages, the Americans were forced to retreat a total of 50 miles, creating the "Bulge" in the Ardennes Forest.

With the Battle of the Bulge going his way in December 1944, Hitler was confident that the Allies would soon run in retreat all the way back to England. He would then use the American supplies that they left behind (American fuel, weapons, and provisions) to run his Panzers, arm his men, and secure the Allies' defeat.

By December 17–23, the 82nd Airborne Division, the 7th Armored Division, and the 101st Airborne Division had joined forces to stop the Germans at St. Vith, Belgium. Tired, sick, plagued with dysentery, and frozen to the bone with frostbite, these divisions were exhausted from weeks in foxholes and desperately in need of replacements. Frank's division, the 17th Airborne, had been held in reserve at Camp Chiseled in England for the last few weeks. Now, they would finally go into battle.

On January 1, 1945, the 17th Airborne troopers of the 193rd GIR (Gilder Infantry Regiment) were flown to Reims, France. A vital part of Patton's Third Army, they were fresh, not to mention extremely well-trained for this battle. They flew in on dramatic night flights in C-47 transport planes. Their ultimate destination: the front lines of the Battle of the Bulge. From Reims, this division was trucked across the Meuse River to a town called Neufchâteau in Belgium, where they set up their headquarters. Their objective? To repulse the German advance.

General George Patton ordered his Third Army to "take back the Bulge" by attacking from the south and thereby stopping the German assault. They were then to continue to push the Bulge back to the original line of demarcation and beyond, drive on to Berlin, and thus reclaim the contested territory behind German lines.

Two German-occupied villages that were vital to the recapture of Bastogne were Flamierge and Flamizoulle. The 17th Airborne's mission was to reclaim Bastogne by wrestling both Flamierge and Flamizoulle from German control. But it would be quite the fight: among other challenges, the weather systems were so unpredictable in the area that reconnaissance was close to impossible.

On Thursday, January 4, 1945, the 17th Airborne GIR started through the woods to take back these two villages. The Ardennes Mountains were beautiful, with thick pines that lined the hills and snow-laden roads, but the weather was gray and dark. The men were faced with knee-deep snow as they first headed for the town of Morhet. The combined perils of freezing wind, snow, and fog made the prospect of fighting in this icy nightmare nearly unthinkable—*but they had a job to do, and they persevered.*

The tranquil scenery was a stark contrast to the horrific scenes of war. As they penetrated deeper into the forest in their open transport trucks, the 17th's troopers were sickened by the eerie sight of dozens of lifeless soldiers, their frozen bodies scattered haphazardly along the roadside. They shuddered at the thought that they were there to replace those icy statues. They knew that even if they were fortunate enough to survive the upcoming battle, they would never forget those frozen forms in the snow. The chilling landscapes of war would be etched in these men's psyches forever.

The Bulge: January 4, 1945

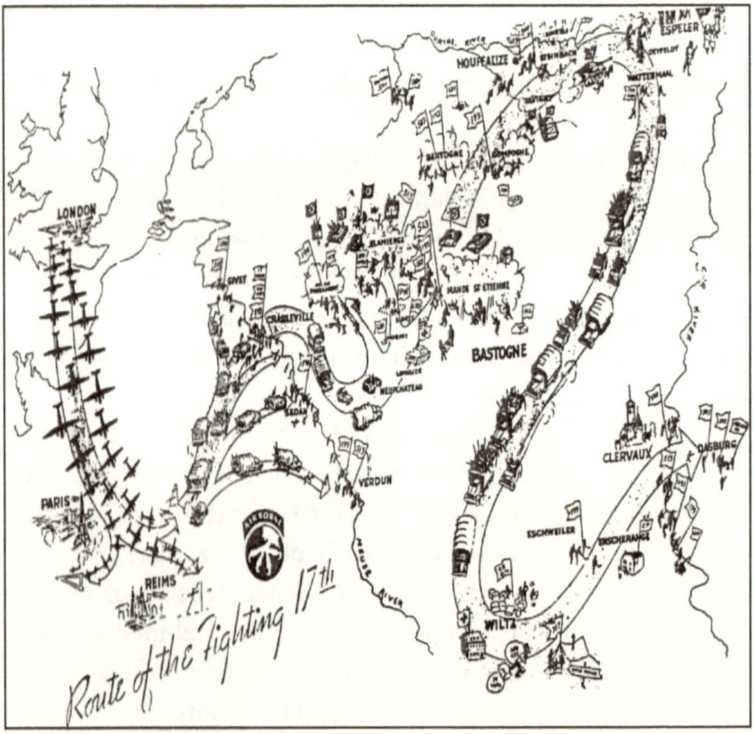

Above this road to Flamierge and Flamizoulle was a long, high ridge, soon to be known as "Dead Man's Ridge." High atop the ridge was a division of German tanks with a bird's eye view of these two towns that were so critical to the battle. Although the air troopers did not see the tanks hidden in the pines on the ridge, they knew they were there: beneath their feet, they could feel the rumble of the behemoth vehicles. Within moments, artillery shells began to pierce through the trees and explode in the snow, leaving great, deep holes mere inches from their feet.

Accompanying the German armored divisions were snipers that had been strategically and stealthily positioned in trees, haystacks, and random buildings—any place they could take good aim. *Highly refined marksmen, these "heckenschütze" rivaled our own snipers* and were trained to kill their enemy at great distances.

The US GIs proved to be clever in the art of camouflage, using sheets, curtains, and any white fabric they could find. The men in the armored divisions even covered their trucks and tanks in snow to hide the artillery. This is just one example of the Yankee GI's ingenuity in the face of the dramatic challenges they encountered on the battlefield.

The first task of these Airborne troopers—the job they had trained for—was to take the village of Flamierge. The village had been under German control for some time, and the Germans had no intention of giving it up. Dodging artillery shells and German patrols all the way, Frank's platoon finally reached the outskirts of Flamierge. At that moment, Frank thought back on the training he had received at Camp Mackall and all of the villages he had taken there. But none of their training exercises had prepared them for a moment like this— dodging shells all the way into the town. Frank thought about the two gold bars on his helmet. As Second Lieutenant, he was their leader and responsible for his men. They did their best to keep out of sight, seeking cover behind blown-out buildings—right under the noses of the Germans who were roaming the area.

It was nearly noon. The day was like nothing this unit had

ever seen before. The area was constantly being pummeled by the German Third Army Panzer Division with mortar, artillery, machine guns, and small arms fire. The hellish, incessant rumble of the German Panzers lumbering through the pines had to strike fear into the heart of even the bravest of soldiers. But the men of the 17th never wavered—and went on to accomplish unbelievable acts of courage.

As he reached the outskirts of Flamierge, Frank remembered the way he had been drilled about "quotas" during his training in OCS. *How can I reduce the lives of my brave men to such statistics?* he asked himself. Suddenly, that whole concept—so impersonal as a point of discussion in the classroom – now seemed utterly sacrilegious in the heat of battle. Caught up in the moment, Frank prayed, "God, please help me to keep my men alive." Nevertheless, over the next few hours, he saw most of his unit—his "brothers in war"—killed or wounded in this attack in the most horrific of ways. In much the same way as our lives flash before our eyes at the point of death, an uncanny clarity shaped his thoughts as he recalled all those times he had told Catherine that his men were the best and the brightest in the Army. His heart swelled with deep respect and gratitude for these men with whom he had slept, eaten, and fought side by side—for more than a year now. And today, he might die with them.

This was the day the "boy" in Frank died. He would never be the same.

The medics in these battles were heroes in their own right. They took endless chances, running in and out of buildings and into the streets—anywhere they needed to go to rescue the wounded. Add to this the fact that the extremely cold weather made it hard to tell if a man was dead or alive.

The Germans used everything they had, including the art of deception, to make the village streets appear to be empty— but our men knew it was not true. The wind blew, and ice collected on their helmets and guns as Frank's platoon fought for what used to be a side street in the village. They ran in and out of streets and buildings, claiming the area inch by inch, tree by tree—for the Allies and for humankind.

Then, the order came down for his unit to "fix bayonets." A chill ran up Frank's spine—and not from the icy cold. He hated the sound of that word: *bayonets*. He knew it meant hand-to-hand combat in the most gruesome of ways. It also meant the Germans were close—so they would have to tread softly. But at that moment, he could not think about the word, how it sounded, or what it signified to him—he and his men had an order to follow. So, they fixed the bayonets to their rifles and continued through the woods.

It was about 1400 when the snow stopped. The fog had finally cleared enough for the men to see the ridge above them. They still could not see the Panzers, for the tanks were hiding in the pines that lined the ridge. But they had heard the artillery and felt the rumble of the tanks from the moment they had reached the edge of town—so they knew they were there.

This was "Dead Man's Ridge." Again, the ground rumbled as Frank's platoon looked up at the ridge. They turned the corner of a blown-out shed. Shells were falling in torrents everywhere—bombarding the woods from which they had just emerged—and coming closer and closer to Frank's unit. The Germans must have caught sight of his men. When he spotted some blown-out walls across the road, he decided to lead the men in a dash behind these structures to remain out of sight of the roaming German patrols, the Panzers on the ridge, and the snipers just trying to take their shot.

As he rounded the bombed-out wall of a house, Frank suddenly saw him: a soldier who had been shot—and he was dead. Frank's first thought was, *Sniper!* He knew that these hidden expert marksmen were out there, just waiting to pick off his men.

Instantly, he raised his right arm to caution his men to stop; they stopped promptly at his command. They were well-trained to watch for his every command and were quick to obey. Then it happened—*In that very instant, Frank was shot by a sniper.*

Dazed, he grabbed his arm. Suddenly, everything became quiet and peaceful—almost like a dream ... How could this be? There, in the center of *hell*—how could there be such silence and peace? Conscious but still dazed, he battled the random, disjointed thoughts and sensations that left him bewildered, struggling to grasp the facts of the present situation. He knew he had been hit. He knew it was still day and that the temperatures were below zero. Beyond that, he was not sure what was happening. Dream-like thoughts mingled with the rational ones, threatening to undo his ability to take concrete action. Fortunately, his men were mobilized by the adrenaline of the moment and immediately mastered the situation. They killed the sniper, cleared a path, and rushed in to carry him away from the action to the shelter of a nearby open three-sided shed.

They sat him up in the cold and assured him they would call for a medic to find him there in the shed. Both Frank and his men still thought that it was only his right arm that had been hit and that his wound was only a relatively superficial shoulder wound.

Over the next few hours, he drifted in and out of consciousness, thinking of Catherine the whole time. He thought back on the fun they had had and the promise he had made to her, saying, "This lieutenant is coming home." He thought of her letters, always so cheerful and positive, and of the many times she had told him to keep his chin up. *I cannot die in this Belgian village,* he thought, as he focused on the future that he had planned in his heart. He was still aware of his surroundings but continued to drift in and out, losing track of how much time was passing. He *had* to stay awake! He had made a promise, and he *had* to stay alive. "Oh! Dear God, help me keep that promise to Catherine," he prayed. As he sat there, propped up in that three-sided shed, the minutes froze in time. But he clung to every one of them by whispering over and over, "This lieutenant is coming home."

Suddenly, something fractured the fragile peace that had blanketed him as he sat there in the abandoned shed—what was that sound? The unrelenting rumble of vehicles coming and going in this freezing winter purgatory—but from which side? The sound of the US jeep is completely different from the sound of German vehicles, so even in his half-stupor, he recognized that most of the ones that were passing his shed were German. He was careful to put his head down as they drove by, knowing that if he lay very still, they would think he was dead and continue on their way.

Frank knew that he would not last through the night unless help was to arrive, and it was getting darker and colder. He opened his eyes as if it could help him to distinguish sounds more accurately. After what seemed to be an interminably long stretch of time, he finally heard a different motor—was that an American or a German vehicle? *Wait! This time, it sounds and looks like an American jeep! They must have cleared out enough Germans to send in help for the wounded*, he thought. Yes—there it was—it was definitely the sound of a jeep—it was American! As the jeep approached, he tried to yell, "Hey, Captain!" but to his surprise, he couldn't speak—only a whisper emerged from his throat. Alarmed, bewildered, and discouraged, a feeling of desperation began to engulf him.

And then Frank moved.

The driver grabbed his gun ... *Was he American?* the captain wondered. Once again, Frank tried to yell, but all that came out was a muffled whisper—at least a bit louder this time. His life depended on it. "Captain, if you help me to the jeep, I think I can ride sitting up."

The captain looked at Frank in amazement and said, "Oh my God, Lieutenant, I thought you were dead." He helped Frank into the open jeep and made sure he was propped in an upright position.

A few moments later, the captain gave him some water. To his surprise, Frank could only spit it out. It dawned on him that Frank couldn't swallow. They didn't discover until sometime later that the sniper's bullet had actually penetrated his throat.

The amazing reality is that when Frank had raised his right arm to stop his men, the bullet had hit him off center, in effect saving his life. With just an arm movement to warn his men, he had not only saved them from an impending onslaught, but he had also saved his own life from a sniper's bullet. Not a bad day's work for this "ShaveTail Lieutenant."

Within a few hours, Frank was taken back to the battalion field hospital. Later on, the questions swirled—was it the cold weather that had kept Frank from bleeding out into his lungs? Or was it because he had sat in an upright position behind the shed that he had been kept alive? We may never know the natural circumstances of what it was that kept Frank alive that day. But we do know that he was in God's hands and that he would live to keep his promise to Catherine.

As for the rest of the 17th Infantry Airborne, they fought their way over "Dead Man's Ridge" and then went all the way to Germany. The ones who survived the Bulge (and other battles) took part in the occupation of formerly Nazi Germany after the war. The unit received two Medals of Honor and many other commendations for their bravery. But at what price? The 17th Airborne had lost a thousand men a day in the first three days of battle at Dead Man's Ridge. History records that the Battle of the Bulge was the deadliest battle of the war: among the 89,000 casualties, the Allies had sustained 19,000 dead. The Germans had lost 62,700 to 100,000 men in the Ardennes. The number of Allies killed did not surpass that of the Germans, but they were fueled by an absolute passion to win this war.

There were 610,000 Americans in this battle—all with fire in their bellies and determination in their soul. The Germans retreated, knowing these novice fighters were on their heels. They may have been replacements, but they knew they were fighting to stay alive. Our GIs stunned both the Germans and those who would live to record this day in history when they outfought the enemy and outsmarted them with their ordinary "Yankee know-how and common sense." These US servicemen paid for **OUR FREEDOM** with their lives, their wounded bodies, and their fractured souls and minds. Even so, after the fact, the majority of them would say, "We just did what we had to do."

Yes, Hitler found out what this half-breed Army could do when the chips were down and when life as they knew it was at stake. These men may not have had a pedigree, but the American GI proved his mettle by defeating the best Europe had to offer.

On January 4, 1945, the 17th Airborne 193rd Glider Infantry Regiment lost forty percent of its men on the first day of fighting. Most of Company B (Frank's Company) is listed as KIA: Killed in Action. Because of the number of men lost and wounded, the 193rd GIR was disbanded on March 1, 1945, and the remaining troopers were combined with the 194th GIR.

Yes, this war was over for Second Lieutenant Francis Royal Ward—or was it? This lieutenant was going home to his family, his beloved California, and to Catherine, the love of his life. He had kept his chin up, worked hard, and had been kept by the grace of God, which was with him always.

Thoughts for "Dead Man's Ridge"

JUNIOR 1944

There's a door that's idly swaying
In the breeze that's sadly playing,

Through the room that once was Junior's, long ago.
But the place seems quite forsaken,
For our junior boy has taken
Up a gun and sallied forth to meet the foe.
And has left us only sadness,
And an ache in hearts that once knew naught but joy.
Though his noisiness annoy us,
Yet the thought that buoys us,
Is that soon once more we'll see our soldier boy.

Sadly still the door is swaying
Mournfully the breeze is playing,
As though sighing for the boy who isn't there.
While our hearts are filled with sorrow
Yet we know some bright tomorrow,
He'll be coming home tomorrow and lift our load of care.
Oh! The days are long and dreary,
And our hearts are weary, weary,
Just thinking of the lad who's gone away.
How we hope he'll soon be homing
From far battlefields a-roaming
And bring his youth back home again to stay.

    – Frank R. Ward Senior 1945

Where is Frank?

January 1945
Los Angeles, California

For nearly six weeks, the Wards had not heard from their younger son. Unless someone has lived through it, they cannot imagine the anxiety and desperation the family faced—not knowing if their son was alive, wounded, or worse. Frank Senior (Papa Ward) wrote to his youngest son with a heavy heart but a light pen and a cheerful voice.

Frank was wounded on the day his dad wrote this letter.

*****

January 4, 1945
Los Angeles, California

Dear Frank:

It sure seems like nigh unto forty years since I heard from you and maybe you are thinking about the same thing. We are all through with the holiday season now and are settling down for another year of this thing called life. The holidays went by very quietly this year, although shopping was more or less of a nightmare. We went out to George's on the Sunday before New Year's, and on Monday we went to Ken's place. We had a surprise on Sunday, December 31st —Gail came to see us. He was on his way to San Diego from Albuquerque and had several hours to spare. Ernest also came during the week. Otherwise, everything was quiet. Clint and I enjoyed a few long weekends at home. We are hoping that a few of the packages caught up with you in time. We hear from Catherine occasionally, as she and Clint have been corresponding for some time.

Well, I am just on my noon hour, Frank, and it is just about shot, so I will sign off now and get this in the mail.

Good luck and best wishes from the folks at home,

Affectionately, Dad

Thoughts for "Where is Frank?"

Below are the first letters recovered from Catherine in eleven months. These letters were sent back to the US in 1945. It is especially poignant that this letter was also written on the day Frank was shot. On January 4, 1945, she was worried, frightened, and terrified beyond imagination, although she would always express a positive thought. She thinks he is in England and prays he is still there—but she can't understand why he hasn't written. She has not received a letter in her mailbox for weeks and admits that not hearing from Frank has ruined her Christmas. Frank's Christmas was not exactly a party. Why doesn't he write? Why? Why? Why? She sounds a little down-down-down.

*****

Thursday night
January 4, 1945
Charlotte, North Carolina

My Darling,

How are you this cold tonight? Gosh, it is cold here, down

to 14 degrees. Boy, did I hate to get out of bed and build a fire this morning. My dad spoiled me when he was home. He got up every day, made my breakfast, built a fire, and called me to get up. That was wonderful.

Darling, I took the terrible picture of you to the office and showed it to all the girls. They would say "Who is that ...? He is not as cute as Frank!" I told them you were camouflaged. I told them they liked you too much and I wanted them to think you were terrible looking—just kidding, Darling. I wish I could see you even if you did have a two weeks' beard. It breaks my heart to think of you being out in all the cold weather. I almost freeze to death when I walk to work in the mornings.

Frank, everybody down at the office is ahead of me in the mail situation. One girl got a letter December 22. I told her I was going to get one on December 25 or January 1—I didn't know which. I had a package on the way, and they don't have it. You should hear us—we are sometimes just like kids.

That girl in the office was worried about her husband, just like I was worried last week about you. Her husband is in the 82nd Airborne, and they are fighting in Bastogne, Belgium. She has not heard from him since December 11, 1944, but she will one of these days.

Darling, we got a letter from Bill today—the first we have had since before Christmas. He is fine. He was in on the Leyte Operation. That took place right after he was home. He went straight back to the Pacific. He sent me some Jap money. I am keeping a scrapbook for him.

Darling, tonight was my choir practice night. We have some pretty new anthems.

It is late, and I must get myself ready for bed. Remember, sweetheart, I love you. Wish I could see you tonight, good night, good luck,

All my love, Cathy

*****

Friday night
January 5, 1945

Darling Frank,

How is my sweetheart tonight? Your Cath is fine—just a shade tired. We have been working too hard. We had to take inventory of all our last year's claims ... That is a job!

Frank, one of the girls at the office got two letters today—December 26 and 27. I told them you were fighting. That little old "Eddie" started fooling around about who got mail ... or 'male.'

Say, how is that trumpet player doing? Tell him that I have a request: "Don't Fence Me In." That is a cute tune. Bing just finished singing it. I am going to send your boys a song sheet so they can play it. Another one is "I Am Going to See My Baby."

Frank, are you receiving your mail? I hope you are, even if mine is slow. I still haven't received the Christmas package. Have you received any of mine? I hope you received them on Christmas Day. I hope you like them.

I called Becky tonight, and little David answered the phone. He wouldn't let me talk to Becky. He is talking just like a little man. He said "Hello, Kay, what you doing? Why do you want to talk to my mother?" He is so cute.

Darling, do you know that I love you? Wish I could see you tonight.

Sweets, I still have a day's work before I can lie down to sleep. Goodnight and good luck.

All my love,
"Cathy"

*****

Saturday night
January 6, 1945

Hello Darling,

I had two surprises today. I received your letter of December 16, where you told me you were in England. I am so glad. Did you know that I was worried about you? In fact, it almost spoiled my Christmas because I couldn't hear from you. It had been a month since I had gotten any mail. Now I know why. You were moving. Darling, I am so thankful it was to England and not into Germany.

Frank, I also received the lovely bag today. It is just as cute as it can be. I like it lots. I needed a brown one. I can truthfully say it is different than any bag I have ever seen.

Thank you, Darling, you are so sweet.

Say—have you received any of my packages yet? I hope you have by now.

Yes, Frank, you will be referred to as a traveling man. You have really seen lots of different people and places, etc. What I wish is that you could travel towards Charlotte. That would be wonderful. I also wish you could be here for Christmas. Here's hoping next year you will be here for Christmas.

You are nearer to home in England. That is one good thing. I want you to watch those English gals—they really go for the "Yanks" I understand. You just tell them I said to leave you alone. I am jealous. They have some good dances for the boys in England, I understand. They also say the English girls can't dance.

Darling, I am so thankful that you have a nice place to stay. It made me sick to think about you sleeping on the ground in this cold weather.

Gosh, it is raining cats and dogs outside. I hope it stops before morning. I hate to go to church in the rain. I wish you could go with me. You did twice, didn't you, sweet? It seems so long ago.

Darling, thanks again for the beautiful Christmas present. You are sweet, and I love you. Good luck.

All my love always,
Cathy

*****

To Catherine from Clinton:
January 6, 1945
Los Angeles, California

Dear Catherine,

I received your letter today and your query re cigarettes. Yes, I received them, and I can assure you they were sure appreciated. Sure wish I could repay you in some manner. I'm working on it but in the meantime, thanks so much.

The last letter we have from France was four days ago. It was dated Southern France, December 2, 1944. Your letter from him dated Dec 6, 1944, is the latest. We sure had a very nice Christmas. Everything was super. How did you fare? You must have had a white Christmas by the cold weather reports. Did you? Gee, it's been so long since I've seen snow or experienced cold weather that every time I open the refrigerator, I don't have snowshoes and an overcoat.

Then came New Year's. I seemed to be engaged in a like manner as you were on New Year's Eve—I spent it writing letters in bed and dreaming of the Rose Parade by 11:00 pm. Then New Year's Day we all went up to a friend's place in Pasadena, where we had a swell dinner. Then a few of us went out to the archery range in the shadow of the Rose Bowl, where we shot a few rounds with a longbow. Did you ever shoot a bow? Lots of fun, and also lots of nasty bruises and cuts if you don't watch out. But it is a swell sport, and I sure go for it.

Well, Catherine, as we face this new year of 1945 it looks like we had all better adopt the outlook of 364 days of waiting and hoping. It looks like we tighten our belts and put the screws on our optimism and 'tho it's rather late in the New Year, I wish I to extend to you a wish of happiness—and some measurement of happiness that you didn't have last year.

Well, it seems like I'm running out of subject, so I will stop here.

Thanks again for your thoughtfulness for the cigarettes, and your nice card. Mother and Dad want me to thank you also for the card. (I live with my parents. I don't know whether you knew or not.)

Well, Catherine, you let me know when you hear from France and I will do the same.

Adios,

Clinton

*****

Letter from Catherine to Frank:
Thursday night
January 11, 1945

Hello Darling,

How is my Frank tonight? I hope that it is not as cold there as it is here. It was snowing here and 14 degrees! I had a letter from your brother—he received the cigarettes I sent him. He was glad to get them. He said they had a nice Christmas. He went to Pasadena on New Year's Day. He had a swell dinner and shot bows. Darling, are you still in England? I sure wish I could get a letter. I got one last Saturday—it was written December 16. I want another one now. I hope you are on your way home. That is a good thought. I only wish it were true.

Darling, Charlotte was over tonight. I showed her my Christmas present. She had a fit over my bag. She thought it was the prettiest bag she had ever seen.

Have you received your package? How about your mail? I hope it is coming through better than mine. Goodnight, Darling. I love you with all my heart. Good luck,

All my love,

"Cathy"

*****

Monday night
January 17, 1945

Hello Darling,

How is your mail? Are you receiving any? I hope so,
Darling. If not, it is not my fault—I do write them. I sure wish I
could hear from you. It will be one month tomorrow since my
last letter was written. But Darling, I know it is not your fault.

I know you are in there, fighting. I was just reading in the
paper tonight where they flew in the Airborne from hundreds
of miles to save the day in Belgium. These Airborne guys—you
can't beat them. I have been telling the people at the office
that the Airborne is going to win this war. I pick up the paper
every day to see if there is anything about the Airborne.

Sweet, I didn't write to you last night. There wasn't much
news except I love you. I will just have to tell you that twice
tonight. Yesterday was a terrible day—it rained all day. I went
down to the club for a little while. I wish you could have gone
with me. I am listening to the Lux Radio. It is a German story
but a very good one. It is a story of a German who wanted to
be an American.

Frank, David still has not gone to the Army but expects to
go in February. I hope he doesn't have to go.

Darling, the war news sounds good tonight.

Frank, it is late—I must roll my hair, etc. and write my
brother a note. Remember wherever you go, sweetheart, I love
you. Good night and good luck,

All my love,
Cathy

*****

To Catherine from Clinton:
January 15, 1945

Dear Catherine:

Received a letter from you today—sort of a welcome treat after a day at the office. Judging from your office address I can say, "I bet you know the trials and tribulations of an under-staffed office."

Note with interest your declaration of receipt of a letter from France on the December 16. Mother received a short typed written letter from him dated 'England.' A Master Sergeant friend of mine told me that men were transferred to England for just three reasons: reforming or regrouping, rest, or clearance to the United States. I have received no letter from him since Dec 2, 1944.

Gee, your brother is sure going to town—right where it hurts the Japs most.

One of my secretaries at the office is the mother of 4 sons—3 in the service. Has a son presumably now on Luzon (the largest island of the Philippines).

I can't tell you how much I appreciated your kindness for the present of those Camels. Gee, I feel like a millionaire or something. We even have ads in the Sunday classified section that read, "Will trade two packs of Camels or whatever you can offer." No fooling—they even list cigarettes as assets now. So you can imagine how I felt—the possessor of *a whole carton!* Until my slow brain gets to going and I can think of a more suitable reply—again—thanks so much.

Gosh, what does 14 degrees feel like? It was 78 here today. The coldest I get now is when I open the refrigerator door.

Well, Catherine, that's about all the dope from this drip. So until the next time, good luck and as ever,

Adios,

Clinton

*****

To Frank from Catherine:
Saturday night
January 17, 1945

Hello Darling,
  This has been a busy day for me—How about my Frank?
Gosh, Darling, the war news sounds bad on the Western Front.
It worries me to death. I know it will be OK, but it is going to
be so awful.
  Frank, I went to the movies today. Becky and I went to the
2:30 show. We waited until four to see "Thirty Seconds Over
Tokyo." It was wonderful. If you get a chance to see it, don't
miss it. It has a wonderful love story. You know me.
  Frank, I received a letter from your brother today. He is
fine. We can't figure out the reason for your being transferred
to England. We are hoping it is for the best. He sure did enjoy
his cigarettes. I will have to send him some more when I can
get them. He said the weather is wonderful in California—it
was 78 degrees the day he wrote to me. It has been so cold
here.
  Darling, guess what was first on the hit parade today?
"Don't Fence Me In." It is a cute song.
  Frank, it is late, and I must get up early in the morning—I
am going to church. Goodnight, Darling, and good luck,
  All my love,
  Cathy

The Telegram

January 25, 1945

On the morning of January 25, 1945, it was so cold that Catherine did not want to get out of bed. However, she forced herself, started the fire, and dressed for work. It was not as cold as it had been—brrr!—but cold, nonetheless. She ate a quick breakfast of toast with a little homemade strawberry jam and orange juice and then hurried to the corner to catch the bus. It was an "OK" day—so-so as days go. All of the trees were so naked now, and the winds so bitter. She longed for the light spring breezes to replace the cold, northerly winds that froze her to the bone—breezes that would bring the heavenly fragrances of crepe myrtle, jasmine, and magnolia. Catherine had never been a winter type of gal. Thank goodness, it wasn't raining that Thursday and it had not frozen the night before. She hated to be out in the rain and ice—well, she just hated being out in the cold at all.

She was still working on the year-end bookkeeping and inventory at her office at Associated Transport in downtown Charlotte. *It will be so nice when February comes,* she thought. *Oh! And by February, I know I will have heard from Frank,* she said to herself while she waited at the bus stop.

It had been weeks since she heard from him. *Maybe he is on his way home,* she consoled herself. She stepped onto the bus and was glad to come in from the cold air. It was warm inside; she hoped that Frank was warm today. *Well, at least he is in England, where it is just foggy,* she thought. *But the front lines are not in England?* It was a confusing thought—one she did not want to entertain too carefully for fear of where it might lead. *Oh, please let him still be in England*, she prayed—and shivered.

She knew Frank was in England, but she also knew the Airborne was in Belgium. When she thought of Frank being in Belgium, her stomach did flip-flops almost to the point of nausea. *I know he is in England*, she kept telling herself. The paper said the fighting was atrocious. The Nazis were throwing all they had into a last push in the Ardennes Mountains, but the battle was looking better on this twenty-fifth day of January. *Nevertheless, where is he? Why doesn't he write?* She was scared, and her 'chin-up' resolve was not working anymore. *What is going on in Belgium? If he could write, he would*, she told herself. With that thought, her eyes burned with tears—tears that ripped at her heart and rolled down her face. It was getting harder and harder to shake those confusing thoughts, and she started shaking with shivers again. The fear and pain of not knowing was the worst. How was she going to work or even *live* if she didn't hear from Frank? *No! No! He will be alright—he is too good for anything to happen to him.* She told herself that over and over until she had to believe it.

The bus had almost arrived at her workplace. She had to shake off this overwhelming anxiety. *He is in England!* she told herself one more time.

At work, Catherine's morning was just like any other. It was Thursday—Friday was almost here! *Goody*, she thought, and she wasn't too busy—not like Mondays. She balanced her books and joked with her friends in the office. Catherine had a talent for not letting her emotions show. She was always up and happy when she was at work with her sidekicks: Charlotte, Ruby, Ann, and Margit. The girls all kept a running tally of the mail they received from their boyfriends and husbands overseas. Her friend Ann had received a letter from her boyfriend in England the day before. But during the last few weeks, Catherine had been losing in the "letter lottery." She hoped beyond hope that she would receive a letter today.

She had just finished all of her morning tasks when it was time for lunch. *Oh, good! she thought, It's lunchtime. I could use a break.* She chatted with her friends as they took a brisk walk to Woolworth's for a sandwich (Catherine's favorite was bacon and tomato) and a "Coke-Cola" at the lunch counter. She left half of her sandwich—she didn't have much appetite these days—but finished her Coke. Catherine loved her Cokes.

She got back to the office at 1:00 p.m. and started her usual afternoon work. She joked with the girls and told them she knew there would be a letter for her today when she got home. Suddenly, the phone rang on her desk. Busy working at the filing cabinet, she ran to grab the phone. "See, what did I tell you? I bet that is my mama calling me right now with a letter from Frank," she said, smiling as she spoke. She picked up the receiver and was surprised to hear that it was Becky's voice on the other end. *Oh good, she thought, I got a letter from Frank!*

"Hey, Cat," Becky said. Catherine could tell by the sound of her voice there was something wrong.

"Hey, Beck, what's wrong?" The two sisters could read each other immediately. "Where are you?"

"Cat, I am at Mama's. You have a telegram here with two stars on it."

"What?" Catherine sputtered, bewildered, a slight crack in her voice. "What?" she asked again, hoping that she had mistaken Becky's words.

"Cat, it is a telegram."

Catherine instantly knew it was about Frank. She caught her breath and slipped into her chair. Catherine's head started to swirl, remembering the instructions that Frank had given to Clinton in case something happened to him. Clinton was to telegram her at once.

"Becky, read it to me. What does it say? Open it, please!" she cried almost hysterically.

Becky read: "Regret to inform, France seriously wounded,

Belgium January fourth; no details; letter follows this—Clinton Ward."

Catherine fell back in her chair and slipped straight to the floor, fainting dead away. Her co-workers immediately guessed what was going on and called for medical help from the company's health office. Then they went back to check on her and sat her up carefully.

When the nurse arrived, she waved the smelling salts under Catherine's nose. Her head jerked back in reaction to the smell of the salts. She came to and just sat there, in a blurred haze of confusion, rubbing away the irritation caused by the salts.

What had just happened? *He was in England! How did he get to Belgium? she wondered. I knew the Airborne was in Belgium, but not Frank, not my lieutenant.* She sat up and looked around at the sea of faces crowded around her. Slowly the news penetrated her thoughts and sketched out her new reality: **Frank was seriously wounded.** *What a nightmare! I must be asleep,* she pleaded with herself—*this can't be real.* Slowly, the tears of unbearable pain smarted in her eyes until she almost could not breathe. *How do I know he is going to be alright? How do I know?* As the reality set in, her cries of anguish kept coming out in unrelenting waves of pain. Never until this moment did Catherine know she could feel so devastated, so broken—and now all she wanted to do was curl up in a ball and cry.

In the days that followed—days so full of uncertainty, verging on despair—she worked hard to keep her chin up. She wrote to him every night. This could not be happening to her lieutenant! She went to church; she prayed and prayed for him. She did everything there was to do. One of the first to practice the power of positive thinking, she never let a bad thought get to her—never. *How could God let this happen to me?* she kept asking herself. *He's too good to be shot, and he is supposed to come home. He promised to come back to me on that train—the same train that he left on at 11:01 on September 19, 1943—in the rain. And we have all that time to make for ...*

But for now, she was still slumped in a heap at work, surrounded by friends who were doing all they could to comfort her. Dazed and confused, in one part of her mind, she kept thinking, *This cannot be happening. This is a mistake ...* But in another part of her mind, she knew, *No, it can't be a mistake!* The reality was that he was wounded in Belgium. That was the reason she had not heard from him and that she had heard from Clinton instead. Then she thought about the date—January 4, 1945—the day he was shot. *He was shot over twenty-one days ago,* she muttered over and over—*He was not able to write.*

Finally, the tears slowed enough for Catherine to catch her breath. Deep gulps of air escaped her, sounding as though they were coming from her broken heart. Suddenly, she realized that a nurse was holding her and her girlfriends were stroking her hands. Slowly, she settled down enough to breathe more normally and regain her focus. They helped her up into a chair, and after about twenty minutes, when her head had stopped whirling, her friends Ann and Marge took her home. Catherine called her sister Becky to let her know.

As she walked up the stairs of the porch at her parents' home, she thought of the day that Frank left for Fort Meade on Sunday, September 19, 1943. That was the weekend he had asked her to wait for him. How that moment and that simple request had changed everything for her. She had never been serious about any one man before her lieutenant. She had played the field, dated, and kissed the boys goodnight at the door. She had danced with many soldiers, and written to many of them, and had had nothing but fun—but now? That girl— that flirty little tease with the happy, carefree façade and the sweet Southern accent—well, *that* girl didn't exist anymore. At this point in time, she was a mature woman, in love with a wounded warrior. She was waiting to know if he would live or die—and if he would be scarred or disabled from fighting in this war. But one thing was sure: his fate was inseparable from her own because, at this point, his fate was to be hers—forever.

Catherine had great friends at work and at church. And, of course, she had her sister Becky and family. Over the next few days, they did not let her stay alone for many nights.

And Catherine continued to write to Frank every night—even though she did not have an address for him. She wrote and wrote and wrote.

*****

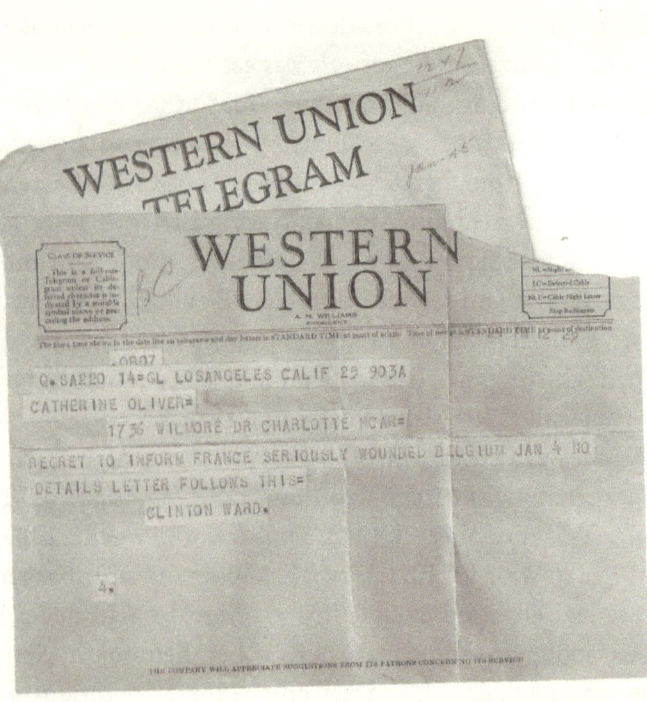

To Catherine from Clinton:
January 25, 1945
Los Angeles, California
1:00 PM

Dear Catherine:
I am very sorry that I had to send you that telegram, but

I was following France's instructions. You see, just after he landed in Africa, he sent me a letter explaining what I was to do—in case he was killed or injured or among the missing. The first thing he requested was that I notify you immediately ... the telegram which we received this morning at just 8 am read exactly: "Regret to inform you that your son, 2nd Lieutenant Francis R. Ward, was seriously injured in action in Belgium January 4, 1945, address and details will be sent direct from the hospital." Dad and I were at work and Mom answered the door. She saw the two purple stars and believed that the stars indicated death—well, she had a few tough moments. Dad and I came home from the office, and I immediately wired you. I sincerely hope that you'll forgive my rather abrupt manner ... but it seemed that I could just hear the kid telling me to do so.

Two facts in the gram give us hope ... The words "address" and "details to follow," and the fact that the injury took place way back on the 4th. We naturally are all rather upset; however, we are constantly watching for the mailman.

Received your last letter this morn also. As always, I am glad to hear from you.

I will keep you posted on all events as soon as we find out ourselves. So let's hope and pray that all will be OK.

Adios, Clint

*****

To Frank from Catherine:
Friday night
January 26, 1945

My Darling Frank,

I wonder how my Frank is tonight. I received the message yesterday from your brother about you being wounded. Darling, I only hope it is not serious. Becky called me and told me I had a telegram with two stars on it. I fainted at work. I had to go home. But Darling, I am trying to be a brave soldier like you would want me to be.

Everyone at the office has been wonderful to me. Ann came over to see me last night and stayed with me until eleven o'clock. Ruby and Margit come over tonight. Ann made me go out for dinner and a picture with her. We saw "The Very Thought of You." It was wonderful. I thought about my Frank all through the picture. They won't let me stay by myself.

I have too much time to think. I am out at Ann's house now. She made me come home with her. She is so sweet. I want you to meet her.

But Darling, I want you to know, where I go or what I do, my thoughts are with you. I love you so much. I only wish I could be there to help nurse my Darling. I hope those nurses will do a good job. Not as good as I would do, but they will have to do.

Frank, here is hoping you are not hurt too bad. I can't wait to hear from you. Your brother said he would write just as soon as he heard. He was so nice to wire me. I sure do appreciate it. I am going to write to him tomorrow; I can't tonight. Frank, I hope you can read this. I am trying to write on my knees in bed. I love you. Keep your chin up.

All my love, Cath

Thoughts for "The Telegram"

Frank received only three letters at the end of December 1944, before he went on attack: two from Catherine and one from his family. Catherine's letters from January 1944 through December 1944 were never recovered.

Catherine did not have his address after he was wounded, but she still wrote almost every night. He wasn't there to talk to, so she wrote. In a way, writing to Frank was similar to writing in a diary or journaling. This was the way she could let go of her feelings: the things that worried her and the things that made her feel good or made her feel angry, sad, or happy. Her letters were almost ordinary or monotonous at times, but he loved them because in them, she wrote of everyday life, and it helped him to feel connected to the woman he loved and all the things of home. Yes, Catherine's letters may have been ordinary, but there was nothing ordinary about their love.

February 1945,
The Recovery in England

The Seventeenth Month of Deployment

It was dusk in the bitter ice-cold of Belgium before a medic noticed Frank and took him to the battalion field hospital. From there, he received emergency care and pain medication: morphine and sulfa. At the field hospital, they discovered that Frank had been shot through the throat, not through the shoulder, as was first thought. Soon afterward, he was transported to the airfield and then flown to the Army hospital in England on a C-47 air ambulance. The C-47 was notorious for being cold in the winter and hot in the summer. Nevertheless, it was the backbone of all medical air transport in WWII. The flight was long, rough, and cold, but the medical flight crew and nurses worked tirelessly to keep the wounded soldiers alive and as comfortable as possible. The weather systems were particularly bad that day, and Frank was just a lucky man that the air train was flying at all. Otherwise, if they had not been flying, he might have died right there on the airfield.

It is estimated that Frank arrived at the hospital in England on Saturday, January 6, 1945. Considering his injuries, it was questionable whether he would make it at all. Nevertheless, he was young—23 years of age—in the best physical shape of his life, and one of America's best.

Frank had a "sucking wound" in his shoulder where the bullet had exited his body. A "sucking wound" refers to a chest wound. His lung immediately became infected, and his fever went sky high. Since his lung had been hit, he was in a lot of pain, and the high fevers caused periods of delirium. (In many cases, delirium is God's gift to the seriously ill.) The fever went on for days, and the pain was at least a nine on a scale of ten. Fortunately, they were able to control the pain with morphine. He lost 25 pounds, and his right arm was almost useless for a long time, but Frank was one of the lucky ones to receive a new miracle drug called penicillin. In a letter to Clinton, he says, "I am really a very fortunate fellow."

During his time in England, his wound had to be dressed and cleaned at least twice daily and medications applied. He received morphine as needed for the pain. There were days when he did not even wake up. The doctors probably did not know whether or not Frank would get home to Catherine and his family at all. Maybe that is why the telegram came three weeks to the day after he was shot.

Maybe Catherine was right; he was too good to die in this war.

Waiting

The Wards finally found out why Frank had not written. The War Department notified them by telegram that he had been seriously wounded in the Battle of the Bulge on January 4, 1945. When Mama Ward answered the door and saw the stars on the envelope, she completely fell apart. Even though the servicemen who delivered the telegram told her that Frank had not been killed in action, but rather he was wounded, she went into hysterics. She was still reeling and in shock when Papa Ward and Clinton arrived home.

When we think about the way we communicate these days, it is hard to fathom the agony the servicemen's families experienced in 1945. It was almost five weeks before they heard the whereabouts of their son who had been severely wounded in the Battle of the Bulge. Then, it was another three weeks before they finally heard from the War Department that he was progressing normally in an Army hospital in England and they received Frank's new address. Although Catherine did not have his address, she continued to write to her lieutenant and sent all her letters to the address she had for him in Europe.

*****

To Frank from Catherine:
Friday night
February 2, 1945

Hello Darling,

How is the wounded Lieutenant tonight? I sincerely hope you are much-much better.

Darling, I just got home from Becky's. She came over after me and wanted me to make her some candy. I can make good candy if I have time. So I went over and made it, and it turned out pretty good.

Frank, I got the pictures today. The ones I made for you. They are good—in fact, the best I have sent. I think I will send them as soon as I get an address. I have a sack of letters with no address. You will get a lot of mail at one time. You will have time to read in the hospital.

Darling, I got a nice letter from your brother today. He has been swell to me since you got wounded. He tried, as soon as they got the message, to let me know that you were wounded. He has written me several letters. That has helped me a lot. I wrote your mother a long letter last Saturday. She said she enjoyed hearing from me. Your brother said your ex-boss, Mr. Bernstein, had a fit when he heard you had been wounded.

Guess what your brother made me? A pair of candlesticks

out of some of his hardwood. I can't wait to get them! I know they are beautiful. I am going to send him a couple of the pictures I took Sunday. They are the best I have ever made. I want him to see just what his brother's girl looks like.

Frank, I have a lot of little old things I want to send you when I get your address. I wish they would just send you home. I think they should. I am going to talk to the "big boys" and see what I can do about it.

Darling, it is that time again. I love you, did you know that? Keep your chin up. Mine is up. Here is hoping you are on your way home.

Love always, Cathy

*****

Thursday night
February 8, 1945

My Darling,

How is my soldier tonight? I only wish I knew. I bet you don't know where I have been tonight. I have been talking to Lieutenant Wace, a recruiter. Don't get excited—I am not going to join. I wish I could work in some of those hospitals to help with the wounded boys. It breaks my heart to think what they have to go through.

The only thing is, if I would enlist, I couldn't get out when you get home. That would not be good; that ain't my plans. I want to be free when you come home. I don't want the Army telling me what to do. It is enough ... them telling you.

I will say it again; I would like to help because they really need nurse's aides badly. I think I will work on in Memorial Hospital in Charlotte. That is important, too.

Darling, I got a letter from you today—written the night before you went into Belgium. I think it was December 31, 1944—is that right? Anyway, my mother called me at work.

I have been waiting so anxiously to hear how badly you are hurt. I just knew this was the letter I had been waiting on. I got home and found it was written December 31st. I was terribly disappointed that the letter did not inform me of your progress, but maybe I will get that letter tomorrow.

Darling, I only hope you are getting your mail, even if I can't get mine. It is more important that you get yours. I got a letter from your brother today. He has really been swell. I don't know what I would have done without him. Anyway, he had contacted the Red Cross. They told him that your mail will go straight through without a delay. So here is hoping. I mailed 14 letters today. I numbered them so you can tell which one comes first. I have been saving them until I got your address.

Darling, did you know that I love you more and more each day? I can just see you lying up in bed with some of those cute nurses waiting on "My Frank." Gosh, it makes me so jealous. I hope this letter will speed you back to health again.

I love you, Cathy

Thoughts for "February 1945, The Recovery in England"

When Catherine received the news of Frank being wounded, her life was immediately turned upside down. She did not know if her lieutenant was coming home the same way he left for war, if he was disfigured, or if he was going to come home at all. All that Catherine and the Wards knew was that he was recovering and that an address and further information would follow.

In the letters of February 2–8, 1945, Catherine still speaks of being a nurse. Along with being anxious about Frank's condition, she sincerely wants to help him recover. She is still in touch with Lieutenant Wace, a recruiter who would love to sign her up for the Army Nurse Corps. This was a program that was developed in response to the severe shortage of medical help for the wounded towards the end of WWII. At one point, the War Department was seriously tinkering with the idea of drafting RNs, LVNs, and even nurse's aides into the Corps—but that never came to be.

Looking back, it is clear: Catherine should have been in some type of health care. This was the path not taken—a possible path that would have completed Catherine in so many positive ways and brought a new balance to her life. She loved to help people.

It was a common practice of the War Department to delay notifying the family about a wounded serviceman's condition until he was relatively stable. They didn't want the families to believe their servicemen were alive and recovering, only to get a four-star telegram in the next few weeks. This explains why it took three weeks after Frank was wounded for the telegram to arrive. It had taken three weeks of intense medical care before the doctors knew whether he would live or die.

*****

Below is a letter that Frank wrote when he was still in England, recovering from his wounds.

To Catherine from Frank:
Sunday night
February 3, 1945
England

My Darling Cath,

I hope you know, Darling, why there has been so long a silence from this end. I trust my brother didn't let us down. Anyway, my story is the same as many. Sniper! Yes, Cath, it was my misfortune to stop a bullet addressed to yours truly. I assure you it was delivered with dead intent. But they should have used something bigger if they wanted to put me out of the way. It was funny—after I was hit, nothing seemed to matter, everything was very peaceful right in the middle of hell. It put my arm out of whack, as you can see by my scribbling. Cath, I'm getting along swell, but I miss you so very much. I went to a Communion service today. There isn't much for me to do except to sit around and rest. I lost about 25 pounds, and they're trying to make me gain it back. I've received my Purple Heart, a very pretty medal. Oh, yes—and I've a few stars on my ribbon. I guess I've lost my film and camera, to say nothing of those snapshots you sent me. I still have the miniature portraits you sent me for Easter. They fit very well into my shirt pocket, and I value them very highly. They mean very, very much to me, Darling. I received a letter from you just before we went into the attack. I should say many letters, the latest of which was postmarked December 20th. That was the first mail we had had in about a month. Darling, I hope you can read this. Happy Birthday, Darling—I wish I were there to celebrate with you, but Darling, they tell me there is still a war on. Our day will come—you just wait and see. Unfortunately, I can't write much. But Darling, I will write as often as possible. Goodnight, Cath ... I love you very much.

Love always, Frank

Address: Dept. of Patients, #4152 plant #4152 APO #63 c/o P.M.N.Y.C.

The following is a letter which Frank wrote to Clinton and the whole Ward family. They were thrilled to receive it, even though his handwriting was extremely shaky. This is the last of Frank's letters that were recovered from WWII.

*****

To Clinton from Frank:
February 12, 1945

Dear Clint,

Here I am again. I'm progressing to the doc's satisfaction. So I guess I will live. I told you we'd frame that letter. Were you notified by the War Department about my being wounded? If so, I sure hope that you notified Cath. It's been a long time since she's heard from me. I wrote a few days ago. As you can see, I still haven't got control of my arm and hand. The doc says it will be quite a while before it'll be normal. I am really a very fortunate fellow when you consider that I was shot through the throat and it exited at the shoulder. It developed what is known as a "King Wound," or a penetrated lung. That has practically healed. You can use your own discretion as to what to tell mom. Most of all, impress on the whole family that I am doing OK because I am.

I saw a very good musical show last night: "Rhapsody in Blue," George Gershwin's life, but it was the music that was so darned good. That seems to be about all there is to do. I'm becoming very efficient with my left hand. I shave with it and my table manners, though a little rough, are 100% improved as compared with the first time I tried to use it.

How's everyone there? Boy, I sure wish that my mail would catch up to me. I like to know what the news is. How's the Chrysler running nowadays? OK, I hope. How much gas do you get nowadays? How are the Crocketts? I hope you can read this, but I doubt it.

That's all for this time, Clint. Love to all.

You Brother, Frank

*****

To Catherine from Clinton:
February 19, 1945
Los Angeles, California

Dear Catherine,

This is a hastily written note and in pencil also, but I have no time or inclination at the moment to adhere to formalities, and I feel sure that you will forgive me when you read further.

We received a communique from the Adjutant General this morning. Mother just called me here at the office. It reads, quote: "We are happy to inform you that your Lieutenant Frank R. Ward is showing normal improvement as of this date. His wound consists of a penetrating chest wound" unquote and the address as follows: Lt Francis R. Ward # 01313830, 4152 US Army Hospital Plant APO 63 Post Master, New York City, New York. And a serious wound. I cannot tell you the relief all felt this morning, and I'm sure that everything is on the upturn.

I didn't want to telegram you as those stars give a person a bad jolt. So I am sending this note by airmail. So chin up, and I'll write later.

Bye for now,

Adios as ever, Clinton

*****

To Frank from Catherine:

Monday night

February 26, 1945

My Birthday

My Darling,

I have had the best birthday ever. Today at lunchtime my mother gave a surprise birthday dinner and invited the girls from the office. We had a cake with candles, etc. In the midst of the meal, the postman came and brought me that long-awaited letter from my Darling. I was so happy! You should have seen me! I couldn't get it open quick enough!

Yes sweets, I understand why you haven't written. Your

Sunday Night
Feb 1, 1945
England

My Darling Cath,

I hope you know darling why there's been so long a silence from this end. I trust my Brother did let us down. — Anyway my [illegible] the same anyway. Sniper! You catch [illegible] my misfortune to stop a bullet, addressed to yours truly. I assure you it was delivered with dead intent. But they should have used something bigger if they wanted to put me out of the war — It was funny, after I was hit nothing seemed to matter, everything was very peaceful — right in the midst of hell — [illegible] wheel as you can see by my scribbling. — Cath I'm getting along swell but I [illegible] you very much — I [illegible] communion service today — there isn't much for me to do except sit around and rest. [illegible] hand and about a [illegible] [illegible] it back. — I've received my purple heart. — Very pretty medal. — oh yes and I've a few stars on my ribbon. — I guess I've lost my film and camera to say nothing of those snap shots you sent me. I've still the miniature portraits you sent me for Easter — they fit very well into my shirt pocket. — and I value them very highly. They mean very very much to me darling. — I received a letter from you just before we went into the attack. I should say many letters, the latest of which was

The portrait of Catherine that Frank carried with him in WWII and the Battle of the Bulge

brother wired me just as soon they got their wire from the War Department. I can't tell you how I felt when my sister called me and told me I had a two-star telegram. I knew it was you before she read it. That was a terrible day for me—and for your family. But we have kept our chins up and prayed for the best. Darling, you told me all of the time that you were going to be OK. You have got to get better! I know you will. Your brother has written many times when he found out any good news. I did the same. Frank, I don't know what I would have done without him.

I sure would like to see your Purple Heart. I know that goes to your mother. I have never seen one.

You said you had a few stars from where you have been. Have you been in more than one battle? Why didn't you tell me? I knew you were in Southern France but did not know that you were fighting. Tell me more.

Darling, I am sorry you lost your camera and pictures. But I am so happy you weren't hurt any worse than you were. We have a lot to thank God for.

So happy to hear you got some mail before going into combat. By the way, have you received your Christmas packages yet?

Frank, you have no idea what your letter meant to me today since today was my birthday. It is the nicest present I got. Yes, Darling, I know even though you couldn't be here, your thoughts were with me. That's what counts anyway. Don't hurt your arm trying to write—just write when you feel like it. I will understand. I wrote to you all of the time. I didn't get it back, so you have a lot of mail somewhere—Lord knows where!

Honey, the girls at the office gave me a dinner party tonight and took me to the show. We saw "Tonight and Every Night." It wasn't so good, but the food was delicious. They were pinch-hitting for you. I hope next year we can celebrate together. Oh! Frank, I got so many pretty gifts!

Well, Frank, it is late—I do mean late. I had to write your brother let him know that I heard from you. I love you with all my heart. Wishing you a speedy recovery, good night –

All my love, Cathy

The US and the Allies were heading toward the Rhine and Germany. They had been bombing Berlin. Belgium was completely cleared of all Nazi Germans, and the United States, the United Kingdom, and Russia were meeting in the Yalta Conference in Crimea to discuss post-war Europe. Most of the neutral countries were now declaring war on Germany and Japan, now that the Axis powers were definitely losing the war. It sounded like some of these countries were waiting for the chips to fall before they committed to joining the fight. Or perhaps they were just waiting for the Allies to do all of the fighting and dirty work before they spoke out against the tyrants of Nazi Germany and Japan. Finally, these malicious enemies were almost gone forever.

Frank was still recovering in England from his wound at the hands of a German sniper. To me, it seems terribly personal when a person is shot by a sniper. Surely, there was more than flesh and blood that needed to heal after being shot in that way.

In 1945, the wounded servicemen were getting the best treatments available. While in the Army hospital in England, Frank did receive penicillin, the new "miracle drug." This drug was extremely new during WWII and was used in England for the wounded Allies. His lung infection was slowly healing, but for some time, he continued to have problems while writing, eating, and shaving.

There were five reasons that Frank's life was saved.

First, when he was shot, his right arm was over his head, warning his men of a sniper. This movement turned his body off-center, causing the sniper's aim to miss the target, which was the center of the throat.

Second, the weather was freezing cold, which allowed him to avoid bleeding out and dying right there in that Belgian village.

Third, his men propped him up in an upright position on the side of an old shed while he waited for help. If he had been lying down, he would have bled into his lungs.

Fourth, the penicillin he received at the Army hospitals stopped the lung infection that otherwise would have killed him.

Fifth, he was absolutely determined to keep the promise he had made to Catherine when he said, "This Lieutenant is coming home."

While in the hospital in England, Frank received the Purple Heart Medal and two stars for the battles in which he had fought. He was also promoted in rank to First Lieutenant. His medals were sent home to his mother, which Catherine said she understood!

When Frank moved to Sicily from North Africa, he sent his footlocker back to Los Angeles. In that footlocker were the letters from Catherine from August 1943 to January 1944. When he was wounded, all of his personal belongings were lost, including his camera, letters, and the pictures he had taken. Those pictures that were found were sent to Clinton and Catherine. All of Catherine's letters and his family's letters from January 1944 to December 1944 were lost. It was war, and Frank had traveled from North Africa to Sicily, Italy, Southern France, England, France again, and then to Belgium. His belongings could have been lost anywhere. As he recovered in the hospital in England, he wrote two letters: one to Catherine and one to this brother Clinton. These are the last of his letters that I have from the war.

From December 1944 to March of 1945, Catherine wrote to

Frank almost every night. He had received only a couple of letters before he went on attack in Belgium. What seemed to be
hundreds of letters were sent to every address in Europe and
finally made it back to the Baxter Army Hospital in Spokane,
Washington. Frank received them in late March 1945.

359

Home Again!

Back in the United States
March 1945

Papa Ward answers Frank's letter of February 12, 1945, when he was recovering in the Army Hospital in England. In his letter, you can hear the joy, relief, and pure thankfulness that his youngest son is recovering as expected.

To Frank Junior from Frank Senior:
March 6, 1945
Los Angeles, California

Dear Frank,

You have no idea how happy it made us all feel to receive your letter. And to know that you are continuing to progress so nicely. It would perhaps be a superfluous remark to tell you to take good care of yourself. We are praying for your speedy recovery.

We got a letter yesterday from Alma K. He is still over in the Pacific. He says he surely enjoys getting letters from you. Mother and I have been sending him some little gifts occasionally, and he is very appreciative. We also heard yesterday from Juanita and from Catherine. We are all well here and are looking forward to Spring, which seems to be just around the corner. We are hoping that your mail will be catching up with you right soon. There should be quite a stack of letters on the way.

Well, things are running along about as usual here at home.

But we very seldom have any visitors aside from George and Virginia. Of course, the two little old ladies who live across the street, Mrs. Holmes and Mrs. Avery, come quite often. They have been very nice to Mother and are so solicitous about you. One would almost think they were your two favorite aunts. Mother and I have been going to the Presbyterian Church at the corner, and she sees one or two shows a week. The past week she has attended a broadcast, and she went to Earl Carrol's. (*Earl Carrol's was a glamorous theater supper club, famous and fashionable at the time.*) So you can see she does get around some.

Well, Frank, that will be all for now.

Love from all, and good wishes galore.

Affectionately, Dad

*****

To Frank from Catherine:
Sunday night
March 4, 1945

My Darling Frank,

Yes, just two months ago today that old sniper got my Frank. How are you feeling tonight? Are those nurses good to you? I will say it again; I wish I could be there to nurse you. How is that arm doing?

Darling, I didn't go to church today. My mother is still sick. I wouldn't let her do anything. I cooked dinner and cleaned up the house. I had a good dinner, even if I did make it. Becky and David ate with us. David said I hope in a few more weeks Frank will be eating with us. I told him, I surely hope you will also. Wouldn't that be wonderful? That sounds like a dream.

Darling, I got letters from my brother yesterday. He is fine. They were written February 22–24, and that was good delivery from the Pacific. He has been in plenty of action. He sent me some money for my birthday.

Say—a fortune teller told me yesterday that you were coming home in May. I don't believe in fortune tellers, but that sounds good to me. I hope it is true, don't you?

Darling, I love you with all my heart and wish you the best of luck. Keep your chin up. I will be pulling for you. Good night.

All of my love, Cathy

*****

Tuesday evening
March 6, 1945

Hi Sweetheart,

How are you feeling tonight, and how is that arm? I hope it is much better. I know it is, because you can't keep a good man down. Darling, I didn't work at the hospital tonight. Becky, Nancy, and I went to the movies and saw "Here Come the Waves." Well, it was not such a good picture, but Bing Crosby can sing for me anytime. He sang "Let's Take the Long Way Home." But I would rather that Lieutenant Frank Ward sing "Let's Take the Long Way Home." Would you mind? I remember you sang "Wait for Me, Mary" to me one night, coming home from the beach. Those were the good old days, weren't they, Darling?

Becky is learning how to drive. We had their car tonight. Much against David's wishes, but we got home safe. She does fine, I think. But he doesn't think so. She drove uptown in all the traffic and parked. She backed out of the parking space just as pretty as you please.

Guess what, Darling? David got his orders today. He leaves for the Army March 21, 1945. Becky sure hates to see him go. He sure hates to leave her and little David. I hope and pray he won't have to go overseas. That may sound selfish. I guess it is selfish. Darling, he is no better than you and thousands of others. He has been looking for these orders for almost a year now. He had his exam last May. Becky doesn't know what to do yet. I wish she would come home, but there is not enough room for all of her furniture.

Darling, are you receiving any mail? I hope and pray you are. It is about time you are getting some. It has been a long time without mail. If they do not do better, I will have to come and deliver it in person. I think it would make it in better time.

Well, sweetheart, it is that time again. I have to do so many things before I lay down to sleep. Good night, dream boy, and good luck. Remember I love you dearly, and you are my dream boy, mind?

All my love, "Cathy"

Telegram for Miss Catherine Oliver
Wednesday, March 21, 1945

Catherine had just arrived home from work and was going to help her mother with supper. The baked chicken was in the oven, and the green beans with potatoes were cooking on the stove with fatback. That was the only way to cook green beans in the Oliver home. There was cornbread almost ready in the oven. Catherine made the sweet tea and set the table; supper was ready.

"Betty Jean, come on and eat—it's suppertime, y'hear now?" Mama Oliver called in a stern but sweet voice.

"But, Mama, I need to finish this homework before I eat," Betty Jean replied in a whiney voice.

"You can finish after supper, child. We are not cooking again tonight," raising her soft sweet voice again. "Now come on!" Betty Jean had always been a little on the spoiled side since she was the baby. But she did finally come into the dining room to eat—with a pout.

"Oh boy, Mama, this looks good!" Catherine said. Dora May was a true Southern cook. Usually, there were just the three women for dinner: Mama Oliver, Catherine, and Betty Jean. Papa worked in Tennessee most of the time and only came home for a weekend once a month or so. He had worked out of town since the crash of 1929, but at least this year, he was blessed to be able to work in his own trade as a plumber.

Mama Oliver was nearly disabled, and even though Catherine worked full-time, she was a huge help to her mother with all of the daily chores. From the time she was a child, Catherine had always taken care of her family. Her mother was her mainstay, and she would do anything her mother needed.

Ever since Frank had been wounded on January 4, 1945, he hadn't been able to write. She needed his letters just as much as he needed hers, and her heart felt empty without them. The love they had shared for the last nineteen months had unfolded and deepened "via airmail"—and now the mail had stopped. In the absence of his letters, Catherine was battling a deep heartache. She understood why he couldn't write (or at least she tried to understand), but it didn't make it any easier. The only thing she could do to keep her chin up was to keep writing a steady stream of letters to Frank.

*****

Yes, these letters were the lifeblood of their relationship. During these months after his war injury, Catherine kept writing to keep their hopes alive. Writing letters was the only way she knew to fight back. She did not know where, when, or *if* he was coming home. She knew *nothing!* What if the Army sent him back to active duty, like Clinton had mentioned? *Well, I can't worry about that now,* she would say to herself, *and that just won't happen*, sticking to her old "chin up" resolve. She knew that worry would get her nowhere.

Oh, she knew he was alright—at least she thought so. At one point, she even wrote Frank a letter while he was at the hospital in England, asking him why he didn't ask a nurse to help him write a letter to her. (As luck would have it, he never did receive that letter.) In reality, the nurses were probably way too busy to write letters for the wounded servicemen.

There were thousands of other girlfriends and wives with men in the service overseas just like Catherine—all of them waiting for their men to come home. The waiting had been so hard for Catherine; she had never been a patient person. And now that he was "almost home," she found herself wondering what it would be like when they actually saw each other again. Would he still be the same person who had left on that 11:01 train? How many times has she thought back on that late night in the rain! She hadn't been ready to tell him that she loved him that night—their relationship was still so young—but in recent months, she has come to regret it. Nevertheless, she has told him thousands of times in her letters. It seems that Catherine has matured in the last nineteen months, and even if she did hesitate that night so long ago in Charlotte, she now knows that she is ready to let go of her independence and embrace this as the love of her life.

They were just about to finish supper when the doorbell rang. "I'll get it, Mama," Betty Jean called out.

Catherine smiled to herself as she started to clear the table, thinking back on the time when Frank had chased Betty Jean down the block to help with the dishes on his last visit. "He fits so well into the family," Mama always said. "He is a sweet soul who makes you feel good just to be around him."

Betty Jean opened the door. The young man handed her a telegram, saying, "Telegram for Miss Catherine Oliver." Instantly fear gripped Betty in the pit of her stomach. She couldn't help but recall the last time "Cat" had received a telegram, and how she had fallen apart at the news that Frank was wounded. She held her breath as she searched the envelope. Then came a sigh of relief; there were no stars.

Only then did she call out, "Cat, you have a telegram!"

Catherine also searched the envelope when she arrived at the door—no stars. Still, she shuddered as a huge wave of relief swept over her.

"Are you Miss Catherine Oliver?" the young boy asked.

"Why, yes, I am," she said.

"Miss Oliver, would you please sign here?"

She felt slightly faint, and her hand shook as she took the pen. She mumbled a word of thanks to the messenger, turned, and tore open the telegram as she walked back to the dining room. It read: "Darling: just arrived Baxter General Hospital Spokane Washington; will write and call soon; Love, Frank."

"Mama, Mama! Come quickly! Frank is home! He is in Spokane, Washington, at the Army Baxter Hospital!"

Dora May came as fast as her little round body would take her. She had not seen her daughter that happy for months. "Praise the Lord!" Mama said in a soft voice. "Thank you, Jesus, for this blessed day!" Mama Oliver prayed again. She was so relieved to know that Frank was finally home. Of all of the boys that Catherine had dated, Frank was her favorite. Catherine hugged her Mama, and together they cried with joy.

Catherine was almost beside herself with joy and relief. Caught between shallow sobs and chuckles of delight, a confusing jumble of thoughts and questions tumbled out as she took in the news. "But Mama, why would Frank be in Washington State? Do you think it's because that is where his family is from—the West Coast? Isn't that wonderful? He said he is going to call. Oh, I hope he calls soon. It will be so great to hear his voice again with that accent of his," she laughed through her tears.

Suddenly the phone rang, and Catherine nearly jumped out of her skin. It was Becky. Still overwhelmed with the news, Catherine blurted out her good news and told Becky that

Frank was going to call. Sharing in her excitement, Becky told her she would be over after a little while.

She could hardly believe it! Frank was home in the good old US! For the first time in months, Catherine's heart was singing. And the best thing was that she was going to see him soon. She just knew it. It had been eighteen long months since he had been sent off to war and nearly three months since that sniper had shot him. *If he is here in the US and is healthy enough to travel, he will be OK,* she thought. *Now, we will be able to finish what we started.*

She just knew that if she stayed positive, kept her chin up, and worked hard, everything would be OK, and Frank would come home. Not to mention millions of prayers and thousands of tears. But now the waiting is almost over. Now there were only tears of joy.

What a blessed day this was! Frank was finally home.

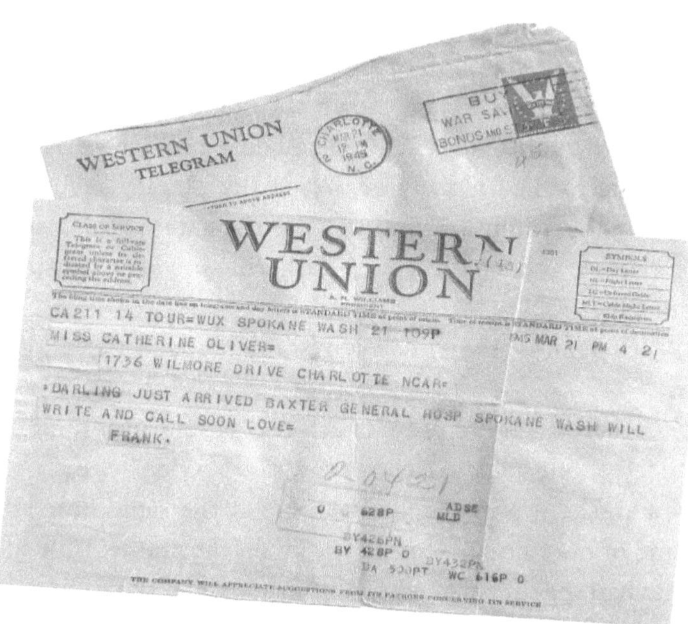

The Western Union to Catherine from Frank: March 21, 1945

March 24, 1945

It was hard waiting for his call. Every time the phone rang, Catherine jumped and ran to the dining room, where the phone sat on a telephone table with an attached seat. It had only been two days since the telegram, with no further word from Frank; however, it seemed like two years.

This Saturday night, Catherine would not go to the movies with her friends or to supper with her sister. She asked her sister Becky over to eat with her and Mama, while she waited for Frank's call. It was about 6:30 p.m., and the women were clearing the supper dishes away when Becky said, "Well, it looks like the dishes are all done except for that last pan—let's just leave it to soak." Little David, who was three years old now, was in the living room, playing with his toy train under Mama Oliver's watchful eye.

Catherine was wiping down the counters in the kitchen when the phone rang. Before she could run into the dining room, Becky had already answered the phone. "Hello?" she said sweetly, smiling at Catherine as she entered the room.

"Hey, Frank, how are you? Catherine has been waiting for your call."

"It's Frank," she whispered as she handed the phone to Cat.

Catherine took a deep breath and settled into the seat at the telephone table. "Hello?" she said anxiously. Before she knew it, she was crying and smiling at the same time at the sound of his voice. It was really him on the phone! How many times had she dreamed of this moment, when she could finally hear his voice? "I almost can't believe that I am talking to you. How are you doing? Welcome home! I love you, Frank—

so much. ... How are those old nurses treating you at the hospital?" It was as if she couldn't say things fast enough—as if she could keep him on the phone with her forever if she just kept talking and asking him questions. Finally, she stopped long enough to take a breath. "I wish you were closer to me," she said softly.

"I love you too, Cath. How are you, darling? I cannot wait to see you." She could hear his smile over the phone. "I have missed you so very much."

There it was—his Yankee accent. He sounded so good to her!

"Well, I am just fine—now that I am talking to you! I have missed you so much. How *are* you?" she asked again.

"I'm doing well," he said. "I wanted to give you the dates of my leave, and I had to wait for Uncle Sam to approve those dates. It looks like I can get a thirty-day leave or more, starting in April. Could you meet me in Los Angeles? I would like you to meet my parents, and I would like them to meet you so they can fall in love with you, too. There is plenty of room at my parents' house. Can you take the time off work?"

"Why aren't you able to come to Charlotte?" she said, a little confused.

"Well, darling, if I go to Charlotte, it would take me twice as long as it would to get to Los Angeles, and we will have more time together in Los Angeles. Cath, I need to see my family. And I am excited for all of them to meet you. So, will you meet me there?"

"Alright, that will be OK. Yes, I will meet you in Los Angeles. I can't wait to see my Frank again. What are the dates of your leave? Are you sure it's OK with your family?" Catherine asked. "This is all like a dream," she said, getting more and more excited. "Oh! Frank, I just can't wait! I just can't wait! When is your leave?"

"I think it will begin on the 1st or 2nd of April, and my folks can't wait to meet you. You can probably make train arrangements for the trip on or about April sixth. I should be in Los Angeles by then. I will let you know if there are any changes. Uncle Sam can take his own sweet time, you know ..."

"How is your shoulder?" she asked. "And how is the nerve damage in your hand? I have so many things I want to talk to you about. Where do I write you? And should I write your mother?" she blurted, trying to make sense of her jumbled thoughts. "I know I will love Los Angeles and California," she added hastily with all of the excitement of a child at Christmas.

"I am OK, darling—but my wound has a way to go before I am a hundred percent. Of course you can write my mother. She would love to hear from you. Now, do you have a pen? I will give you my address: Lieutenant Frank R Ward #1313830, T-18 Ward, Baxter General Hospital, Spokane, Washington.

"Darling, I have some good news! I have received a promotion. I am now a first lieutenant. I know that it is not a colonel or a major, but it is a promotion in pay, also." Frank told her proudly.

"Oh, that's wonderful! You know that I'm so very proud of you. And it doesn't matter about the promotion so much, as long as you are going to be OK. Are those nurses treating you well? Do I need to come up to Spokane and take care of you myself?" she offered with a teasing smile in her voice.

"No, Cath, I am just fine, and I am receiving great care. Don't you worry about me," he replied.

"Oh, Frank! I just can't wait to see you. It's like a dream! It's not Charlotte, but Los Angeles is wonderful, and you are home!"

Thoughts for "Home Again!"

In March 1945, the war news was good. The Allies in the Pacific were bombing the large cities of Japan, including Tokyo, while the Americans and the Allies in Europe had begun to cross the Rhine into Germany. Patton's troops had captured the German town of Mainz, and the Germans were under attack from enemy forces on two sides of their country. Much to Patton's dismay, the Allies slowed down the advance into Germany, which allowed the Red Army to take Berlin. Speaking from a position of strength, General Eisenhower broadcast a demand for the Germans to surrender.

Oh yes, the war news was excellent, but the best news to Catherine was that her lieutenant was home. On the other side of the country, perhaps, but he was home in the United States of America.

The Wards had also just received the best news of their lives: Frank, their second son, was alive and safe in the US, and they would see him soon. It had been a long three years for the Ward family. They had paid their dues in this war. Now it was nearly over, and Frank Jr. was home, in the United States of America.

Catherine was beside herself with happiness. Frank began to work on his plans for Catherine to meet his family, and for his family to meet his Catherine. Nevertheless, it was not easy to make these arrangements—mainly because of the Army. First, he would have to wait for the Army's official approval of his leave, and then wait for his release from the hospital. He would have to arrange for the ongoing care of his arm and manage Catherine's schedule and the trains. Wow! It seemed to Frank that it was easier to run a platoon of men up a hill in a battle!

Oh yes, Frank was home. But now what? Were the Wards going to have a Catherine in their family after all? Frank's mother had posed the question to him in one of her letters when he was still in North Africa. Would Catherine charm these Westerners with all of her Southern ways?

If there was any doubt that Catherine would go to California to see Frank, that question was answered in a heartbeat with the telephone call on the twenty-fourth of March.

It took her a millisecond to answer Frank—and it was "Yes!"

What about Frank? He had made plans for an extended leave—did they include plans such as shopping for a ring? Or would he take it one step at a time? No one really knew. The only thing that was important to him right now was to see his Catherine.

Frank was unable to write letters because of nerve damage when he was shot. His right hand was almost useless and remained that way for a long time to come. But the lung infection that had almost killed him was almost totally healed. And apart from a large gaping scar on this right shoulder, the shoulder wound had almost healed as well.

HEADLINES FOR MARCH 24, 1945:

- The Allies storm across the lower Rhine.

- The last big battle is underway in Europe.

- Thousands of planes strike the Allies' biggest blow on Germany.

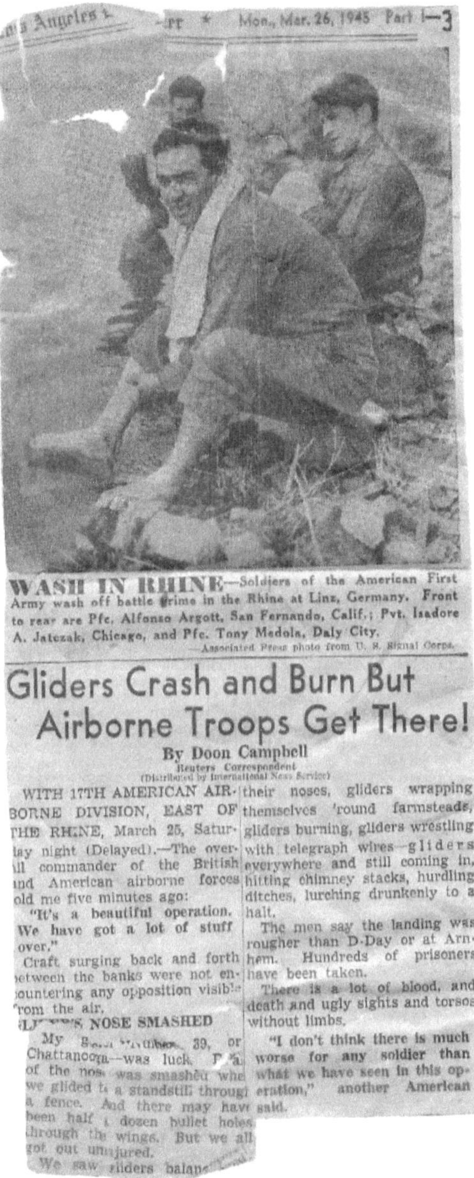

The USA Glider Army Infantry Air trooper
Cross over the Rhine and into Germany.
March 26, 1945

California, Here She Comes!

April 1945

Frank had just finished his dinner at the hospital in Spokane. Eager to talk to Cath, he was heading to his room to gather a few coins to use the pay phone in the community room on the third floor. On the one hand, he couldn't wait to talk to his sweetheart, but on the other hand, he was struggling with some mixed feelings. His leave had not yet come through, and he would have to tell her about the change of plans. Even though their relationship was still young, he knew this would upset her—and he hated the thought of delivering this disappointing news.

The orders for his six-week leave were still in limbo. Apparently, they had been trapped in the halls of red tape, mired in the department of "hurry up and wait." And once they came through, Catherine would have to change her train reservations to another week.

It was hard to secure a long-distance phone line during wartime, but that day, the call went right through. He gave the operator the number, and then, before he could even gather his thoughts, he heard Catherine's voice at the other end.

"Hello?"

"Hello, Cath, darling," Frank said.

"Frank, darling—are you OK? Is everything alright?" Catherine answered, surprised to hear his voice on the other end of the line. In 1945, long-distance phone calls were usually reserved for emergencies or some kind of bad news.

"Oh, I am fine, darling, but the Army is not. I haven't

received my orders yet. I didn't want you to arrive in Los Angeles before I did, so I had to call. It looks like I won't be able to leave for another two weeks. You will probably have to reschedule your train reservations for some time after the thirteenth of April."

"Gosh, Frank! I am so disappointed! I could almost cry. Well, I think I *am* going to cry. I want to see you so badly. What is wrong with that old Washington, D.C.? They shouldn't treat their wounded soldiers like that. I am so mad!" She sounded off like a spoiled little girl.

"I know, darling; I feel the same way. I want to see you as much or more, believe me. I am very sorry for the reason for this call, but I still love talking to you and listening to your voice. I wish I could hear your voice in person. You are so important to me, sweets. I miss you so much," Frank said with an apologetic tone.

"It seems like it has been a year since you called me in March. I just don't know if I can wait." She fell silent for a brief moment. "Alright, I will change my reservations, and then I'll write as soon as I know what they are," she said with a pout.

Just then, the operator came on and asked for five more quarters, and Frank put the money in the slot.

"It will just be a few more hours we have to make up for, darling. Remember how much I love you," he said, doing his best to calm her down.

"I know," Catherine told him, "I will be OK if you are OK. We've waited this long; I guess we can wait just a bit longer. I love you and just can't wait to see you! I'll let you know when I've had a chance to change my reservations for those days."

They were just starting their lives together, and already Frank was learning the knack of charming her and calming her down. And it worked—even in these early weeks of their relationship!

The letter below is one that Catherine wrote that evening

after the phone call had ended. Her "Ha! Ha!" humor was a thinly veiled but brave attempt to cover up her deep, deep disappointment in the face of this change of plans. Catherine never did like surprises—especially bad ones. It was just like her to flare up when disappointed, but fortunately, her quick temper was also quick to burn out.

*****

Monday night
April 2, 1945

My Darling Frank,

It was nice talking to you tonight. It really was a surprise because I thought you were already on your way to California. Why don't they get on the ball and get those orders to you? I am going to write to Washington myself if they don't get on the ball right soon. Ha! Ha!

Darling, I can't wait until Friday-week, and then—just think—it will only be a few days until I will see you! It has been so long. Yes, I know I will like California. Frank, if you are there, that is all that matters to me. I guess you know that.

I am anxious to meet your family. They have been swell to me, Frank. You don't know what it has meant to me to come home to no mail from Frank. No mail from Frank for weeks— then a letter would come from Clinton, telling me about your latest letter to your family. And when you were shot, he was wonderful to me.

Becky said to tell you it was nice talking to you again. She likes to hear you talk. I love to hear you talk too, but I want to *see* you.

Yes, Frank, it seems like months since you called me the first time from Washington. We will have 30 days and maybe more in California. Isn't that wonderful? It seems like a dream. Everybody at the office envies me. Yes, I remember those three hours that I waited—and I got so mad! Then I said, oh well, that will not do any good. I know you couldn't help it.

I was making myself a dress tonight when you called; the dress is turning out right cute.

The other day I was writing a letter to you when little David asked me, "Kay, are you writing to my daddy? If you are, tell him to come home. I really miss him." He is so cute, and talking so good.

Did you have a nice Easter? Oh! How I wish I could have been with you. It won't be many Sundays until I can go to church with you in California. Frank, I am over at Becky's. She has a three room apartment with David's mother—a real cute place.

Becky and I went out to the hospital tonight to see a couple of our friends who were sick. We have done our good deed for the day. I wish I could have gone to Baxter Hospital. I bet you can't guess why?

Well, Darling, I am writing with Becky's pen. She is going to write to David. I love you, Frank—did you know that? Good night,

All of my love, "Cathy"

*****

To Frank from Catherine:
Monday night
April 9, 1945

Hello Darling,

This time next week I hope to be in California with you. Oh goodie!

Frank, I had a sweet letter from your mother yesterday. She said that she was glad I was going to pay them a visit— that made me feel good. Darling, I can't wait to meet your family. They were all so nice to me when you were shot.

Gosh, today has been a hard day for me. Mondays are always hard for me, but today was worse than usual because I was off for three days. But my shoulder is better. The doctor said it was just a cold in it, but I haven't had a cold.

Darling, do you know that it has been almost a month since you landed? It seems like a year since you called me the first time after you got home. I can't wait for Friday to get here. That is a long trip, but it will be twice as long for me, knowing that you are to meet me when I get off the train. That sounds like a dream, doesn't it? But this time it is true.

Yesterday I had a letter from my brother. He said to tell you he was glad you are home and he hopes that you won't have to go back. He also said congratulations on your promotion. You deserve it, and he hopes to meet you someday soon.

Darling, one of my girlfriends just called and told me that her husband has been liberated by the Russians. Isn't that wonderful? He has been a prisoner for two years! I am so glad he is coming home. He is really a swell person. He will be home by Sunday!

Frank, I mailed you something today. Now, I will do you like you did me, and not tell you what it is. Goodie! Goodie!

Darling, I want to write your mother a note. I am going to a shower for Annie tonight. I love you,

All my love, "Cathy"

The Golden State Limited

It was Tuesday, April 17, 1945. Catherine sat on the edge of her bed, looking at the things she still had to pack for her trip to Los Angeles. As she tried to picture what the weather would be like in California, she took a sundress from the bed and hung it back in her closet. *Hmmm, should I take something that's a little warmer?* she wondered. *After all, it isn't summer yet.*

She finished her packing and looked at her ticket. It was for 9:00 a.m. the next day. *It is actually going to happen,* she thought. *By Saturday, I will see Frank.* She wondered about the future and what would become of their love. She didn't want to expect too much at this point in time; he was just recovering from a horrific wound. She wouldn't let herself think about a ring ... But given all that they had shared and the love they had pledged to one another, what else could there be in their future? All this thinking was making her crazy. *I am going to see my lieutenant—that is the most important thing.*

The next morning when Becky took her to the train station, Catherine was as excited as a child on her birthday. How could she sit on that train for three days? She would just have to find a way. First, she was to take the Southerner to New Orleans and then to El Paso, and from there, she would take the Golden State Limited to Los Angeles, California.

This trip was a new experience for this Southern gal. She had seen quite a bit of the South and had always enjoyed the train, but she had never journeyed so far west. Once she left the lush green countryside of her treasured North Carolina, she was both stunned and captivated by the endless stretches of desert landscape that followed—it felt so stark and barren in comparison with the rolling hills of home. Suddenly, the larger reality of the changes that awaited her was staring her in the face—and her heart ached for all that she might be leaving behind.

The last night on the train, Catherine had only had a little sleep, there in her coach seat. She awoke before dawn when the train was about three hours away from Los Angeles. She wished that she could get a bit more sleep, but she knew it would be impossible. Her head was spinning, filled with thoughts, questions, and a great longing for the reunion that was now only a short time away. She tried to quiet her restless mind by gazing out the window into the dim pre-dawn light, but the landscape was hardly comforting: still desert, as far as the eyes could see. Sparse, barren desert. Weary from days of travel and racing thoughts and already feeling a bit disoriented in this foreign land, she closed her eyes and strained to picture the faces of all the loved ones she had left behind in Charlotte, aching a little for the familiar things of home.

Just then, the train gave a jolt, her eyes popped open, and she was jerked back into the present moment. To her amazement, everything around her had changed! The sun had begun to peek above the horizon, transforming the black-and-white landscape into a blaze of color! She watched, breathless, as the lifeless expanse that had surrounded her just a few minutes before now came alive with brilliant hues. Was this real? The desert floor and hills were suddenly painted in wonderful shades of pink and orange that broke into bright yellow—everywhere! What a sight to behold!

Catherine was used to riding on trains, but that day, she was as nervous as a bed bug when she thought about seeing her lieutenant again—and meeting his family! Of all the family members, she felt that she knew Clinton the best. They had kept up quite a correspondence during Frank's deployment overseas, and he had been so good at writing to her when Frank was shot. Just the thought of him being shot was still a bit surreal to her. How many times had she muttered under her breath, "It makes me mad to think of that old sniper shooting my Frank!"

She ducked into the restroom to freshen up for the big moment. After she had washed her face, brushed her teeth, fixed her hair, and applied a little lipstick, she pinched her cheeks with a little lipstick on her finger and dabbed a little White Shoulders perfume behind her ears. *There is no reason to be so nervous,* she thought. Then she chuckled to herself, knowing that it was a happy, nervous excitement for the future. "Is there going to be a future?" she wondered out loud to herself. Oh! She hoped so. They had never actually spoken of a lifetime ... but was it understood? He had asked her to wait for him, and she had. She hadn't thought about their future then, but now, it was the only thing that was important.

The sun was much higher in the sky by then, and she could tell that they were nearing the city. Cute little neighborhoods and the occasional industrial building had replaced the colorful expanse of desert that had so delighted her an hour before. She changed into one of her favorite dresses—a little, dusty aqua number with a matching jacket. The skirt opened into a soft flare at the bottom, hemmed at the knee. A simple string of cultured pearls at her neck was a nice complement to her white gloves and the off-white headband hat, which showed off her thick, dark, shoulder-length hair. Her brown shoes were a perfect match to the lightweight wool coat she carried, and she had made sure to bring along the brown purse that Frank had bought for her in France last Christmas. The whole ensemble flattered her trim figure and accentuated her best features, and the aqua dress brought out a green glimmer in her eyes. She was truly the picture of loveliness and excitement.

Suddenly, Catherine was overwhelmed with an anxious thought. She had worked with many of the servicemen who had returned with horrible injuries during her time as a volunteer nurse's aide at the Red Cross, and she had listened patiently as they told their gut-wrenching stories. For so many of these young men, life would never be the same. Some had deep scars from shrapnel in their face and bodies, and some had been badly burned. Some had lost eyes or lost limbs, and some had lost their hearing. The ride was getting a bit bumpy then, tossing her from side to side as the train passed over one track merger after another, coming closer to the city. She caught herself wondering if Frank would have scars like those she had seen in the hospital. But she quickly pushed that thought right out of her mind. After all, that just could not happen to her Frank. In the midst of all these anxious thoughts, it never once occurred to her that there might be even deeper scars—ones that no one could see with their eyes—scars deep in a soldier's heart and soul. Not once did she think of that.

It was almost time to pull into the station. Her stomach flipped with excitement again. She knew that she should have a bite of breakfast before they arrived. She did manage to force down a piece of toast and sip some orange juice in the dining car, but she was really too nervous to eat. She strained her eyes to see the platform where Frank would be waiting. *Will he be the same? Is he physically OK?* Once again, she tried to quiet her mind, focusing on what she knew to be true: she loved him, and that was all that mattered.

Even though the train was already slowing its pace, she could see that it would be a few minutes more before she would be able to catch a glimpse of the platform. She took a deep breath, closed her eyes, and laid back in her seat as she said a little prayer of thanks. Just then, the porter's call jarred her out of her reverie as he shouted, "Next stop, Los Angeles! Los Angeles, up ahead! End of the line! Next stop, Los Angeles!" When she opened her eyes, she was amazed to see dozens of train tracks parallel with those of the Golden State Limited, all converging into the massive station ahead. She had never seen so many tracks lead into one station! Suddenly, she heard the hiss of the brakes, and the air outside her window filled with rising steam, blocking her view. She struggled to peer through the steam as it slowly dissipated—then there it was! The platform! But was he there? She still couldn't see. *Oh! Where is he?* she thought.

Then the train lurched and started to move again—backward this time. *What is this?* she wondered. *Are we pulling out of Los Angeles before I can even get off the train?* Slowly, it pulled away from one platform and up to another, stopping again with a soft jolt. *How many platforms does this old station have?* she thought, slightly exasperated at the delay. Once again, she peered through the window, scanning the crowded platform.

One last jolt, then more steam ... *Oh, where is he?* she thought somewhat frantically.

Finally, the steam cleared, and there he was! She pushed her way to the door and through the open car. There he was, waving to her with his left hand. "Frank!" she called. He stood there, beaming and looking as handsome as ever. A huge wave of relief swept over her as she tumbled out of the train, elated to see her lieutenant.

They fell into each other's arms, and he held her as if he would never let go. "I told you this Lieutenant was coming home," he said softly as he smiled and kissed her. This was the embrace they had both been looking forward to for nineteen long months. An embrace neither of them would ever forget.

"Oh, Frank! I can't believe it's really you! Please tell me this is not a dream! You look so good! Oh, I love you, Frank! I have waited so long to tell you that!" This was the first time she could say those three little words to him in person. She had told him hundreds of times in her letters, but so many of those letters had been lost in Europe in the wake of the Battle of the Bulge.

They stood there for a long time and looked at each other. Oblivious to the fact that the platform around them had cleared of all the other travelers and their families, they just stood there, first looking at each other, then holding each other, drinking in the moment they had waited for for so long. The love they had shared in their letters—so tangible and warm—was still there after all those months of separation. In their hearts, they knew that if it had already lasted through the battles of the war, it was destined to last a lifetime.

One more time, he let her go, just long enough to take a good look at her beaming, tear-stained face. "Darling, you are beautiful," he whispered.

"And you are just as I remembered you, darling," she said, wrapping her arms around his neck. "Just like when he said so-long on the 11:01 train in Charlotte, the Frank I love."

Suddenly, she stopped herself. "I'm not hurting your shoulder, am I?"

He smiled at her with a reassuring smile, saying, "You could never hurt me, darling."

Now, it was Catherine's turn to let go and stand back for a good look at her lieutenant standing before her. There he stood, her dashingly handsome young man, all dressed up in his "Pinks"—his dress uniform. This was their dream come true: Frank meeting her at the train station to finish what they had started. The only difference was that this station was in Los Angeles and not in Charlotte, as they had both envisioned a thousand times since that rainy night when he pulled away on the 11:01. But it didn't matter. They both knew this was a day they would always cherish. This was the day they had written about, fantasized about, and longed for—for nineteen endless months. This is why he had come home: to meet her at the train station. The fact that the train station was all the way across the country from the spot where they had said their so-long really didn't matter. All that mattered now was that they were together.

Eager to get on their way, Frank grabbed her suitcases and loaded them into the car. It was a fifteen-to-twenty-minute drive from downtown Union Station to the Wards' home on West 53rd Street on the West Side, but Frank and Catherine were happy for the short drive. It would give them a few minutes to be alone before having to share their time with the rest of the family. Full of the excitement of finally being together, they chattered happily as the miles flew by. She couldn't help but notice that his injury was affecting his driving, but he seemed to drive well with his left arm while shifting with his right. She relaxed into her seat and just stared across at him as he drove, still pinching herself at the thought that their day had finally come. He loved to drive, and he loved her. It was the first of many, many rides they would take together. As she watched the downtown office buildings give way to charming little neighborhoods, as she and Frank drove into their future.

There is nothing like spring in Los Angeles, California, but this was Catherine's first glimpse of its wonders: temperatures in the 70s with clear blue skies, and everywhere she looked, palm trees were swaying in the light breeze that swept in from the ocean. It was truly the City of Angels.

Frank could hardly wait for his family to meet his Cath. They drove straight to the Wards, and Frank introduced his Southern gal. "Mom," he said, "this is Catherine." From the moment Mama Ward laid eyes on Catherine, she was amazed at Catherine's loveliness and her poise. Mama Ward gave her a warm hug, showed her to her room upstairs, and helped her get settled for the time she would be staying. Mama Ward was glad to finally meet the gal that had swept her son off of his feet, but she couldn't help but wonder in the back of her mind if this lovely Southern gal would be here forever.

Within her first few minutes in the Ward home, Catherine also met Frank's father; his brother, Clinton; and his two aunts, Addie and Essie. From the very beginning, the family was duly impressed with Catherine. She was quite charming and pleasant, and her sweet Southern accent kept them smiling in spite of themselves.

As much as Catherine and Frank were glad to all be together as a family, at this moment, they were eager just to have some time to be alone.

Thoughts for "California, Here She Comes!"

Six days before Catherine and Frank were reunited, the United States had lost its beloved president, Frank Delano Roosevelt. He had served for twelve years over three terms in office. Both Catherine and Frank felt a deep sense of loss as they mourned the only president that they had ever known to care for the average man. He had brought the country through the Depression and a tough World War. In spite of tremendous personal and physical challenges, he stood tall as the only president who completely understood how to work around the world of politics as he navigated through daunting economic times in the midst of global conflict. Both felt as if they had known him personally, and to lose him so unexpectedly almost felt like losing a father in the White House. For years, President Roosevelt had spoken to his countrymen through his radio-broadcast fireside chats as a loving father would speak to his children. He had explained the pros and cons of the challenges they faced together, and no matter how dark and oppressive the circumstances that beleaguered the nation as a whole, he always served as a beacon of hope. They were saddened at the thought that he had not lived to see the Allies win their hard-fought victory. These were the Allies that he had worked so hard to coalesce and to support through thick and thin, personally sharing in every phase of their struggle to neutralize the oppressive forces that so threatened the world as they knew it.

Yes, the country mourned their beloved president. It is true that our country would not be the same today if it were not for FDR. Indeed, perhaps America as we know it might not have even survived at all.

Frank and Catherine
in the Wards backyard,
April 1945

Our Day Will Come

May 1945

Frank's "little southern gal" did charm the Wards. They loved her sweet Southern accent, her naïve ways, and her sweet smile. Besides being extremely pretty, she was gracious and a perfect lady at all times. Catherine was not a princess; she helped around the house, did the dishes, and even fixed a few meals for the family, like her "Southern fried chicken" dinner with all of the trimmings. Both Catherine and her dinners were a big hit.

Catherine had her own room upstairs in the back part of the house. It was a nice room, beautifully decorated with embroidered linens lovingly made over the years by Mama Ward. Catherine was comfortable in her room, but the most important thing was that she could now be close to Frank.

For the first time in months, Frank and Catherine began to get to know each other in person again. It was heaven, just being together. There were long rides to the Hollywood Hills and Frank's beloved Pacific Ocean. It seems that Clinton had been saving all of his gas coupons for when Frank got home. They laughed, went out for suppers, and took in a few shows. They sang songs and danced to "Wait for Me, Mary." And when they had some quiet time alone, they just sat and looked at each other for hours. For two straight weeks, there was never a moment when they were apart except at night when they each went to their own rooms. And on Sunday mornings, they walked to the Presbyterian Church, where they gave heartfelt thanks for Frank's safe return and for the chance to finally be together again.

May 8 was Victory Day in Europe. After Frank had served eighteen months in this war of horrors, it was so fitting that he and Catherine were able to spend this day together—the day that victory was declared. Catherine felt that she had taken every step with him, and with every day of his deployment, Frank had missed having her with him. On this special day of victory, they celebrated with Frank's family and some of his friends. After holding each other's hearts for so many dark and anxious months, America was finally once again a land of joy! It was like nothing they had ever felt before!

This conflict made the US the first superpower of our time and would not have been possible without the dedicated efforts of every GI, sailor, Marine, and Army doctor and nurse. They all worked together to bring about the victory we were able to celebrate on VE Day 1945.

They are all heroes in time, and although many are now gone, they are never to be forgotten.

Five days after Catherine arrived in California on the "Golden State Limited," Frank asked her to marry him. He had decided many months before that he never wanted to be away from his best friend ever again. And of course, she said "YES!" because she also knew that she did not want to be away from Frank. His future with the Army was unclear; however, their future together was certain. They started to plan their wedding right away and decided to have it in Los Angeles—not Charlotte.

The Wards were shocked by this rush for the wedding. After all, they had had precious little time with their son who had just come home a war hero. For over three years, they had lost sleep with worry for Frank. They had prayed, cried, and written hundreds of letters to keep his spirits up while he was away. And now they had to give him away to this Southern gal? It's true that they were already very fond of Catherine, and they certainly enjoyed her sweet Southern ways—but marriage? **WOW!** They hardly knew her! Marriage was for life. And how well did Frank really know her? They had only spent time together for a few short weeks in North Carolina before his deployment. *Why don't they wait?* they wondered. However, in spite of their questions and concerns, they were very careful to keep their feelings to themselves.

The Wards finally concluded that Frank and Catherine had actually been courting for the full eighteen months of their separation—through their letters. And they knew that those letters were the driving force that had brought him home again. Nothing could be better ... Their son was home, and they knew how blessed he was to be in one piece and doing so well, considering the wounds he had endured.

But the most compelling reason to support their decision was that they were obviously so much in love. Anyone could tell that just by looking at them.

So, like all good in-laws should do, they helped with the wedding plans and even gave them some financial help along the way.

The announcement from Catherine's parents read:

Mr. and Mrs. Edward James Oliver
wish to announce the marriage of their Daughter
Mary Catherine Oliver
to
First Lieutenant Francis Royal Ward
on
May 22, 1945
Forest Lawn, Glendale, California
at the Wee Kirk of the Heather

****

Catherine and Frank were married on May 22, 1945, at the "Wee Kirk of the Heather," a beautiful little chapel at Forest Lawn Memorial Park in Glendale, California. Frank was 24, and Catherine was 26. Frank's brother, Clinton, was his best man, and Catherine's maid of honor was Selma, the wife of one of Frank's good friends. The wedding was small and included only a few close friends of the Wards as well as all of the aunts, uncles, and cousins who were not overseas in the Armed Services.

This wedding was not just a ceremony of marriage. It was a celebration of a miracle and of God's grace, which had brought him home to Catherine. Only five months earlier, Frank had sat propped up against a shed in Belgium after being shot through the throat. There he had sat in a state of shock and gripped by fear as he spent hours slipping in and out of consciousness. As he waited at that shed, hoping that the medics would arrive in time to save his life, he kept his thoughts focused on Catherine and how he would marry her when he got home to California. The very thought of her had kept him alive long enough to get the medical attention he needed. Indeed, this was a day to treasure for the rest of their lives.

As Frank began the long, slow process of physical recovery from his wounds and the dark realities of war, new glimmers of hope emerged with every passing day. And here they were, a few short weeks later, celebrating their wedding day in Los Angeles, California. Their dreams of being together again were finally coming true. How many times had he encouraged her to hang on, reassuring her with the words, "Our day will come!"—and now it had. They were grateful for so many things on their wedding day, but perhaps they were most grateful to God for Frank's recovery.

Of course, Catherine was sad that her own family could not be there on her special day. However, she was overjoyed to be marrying her Lieutenant after his eighteen months overseas. In the years that followed, Catherine often said that her mother would not have let her go if she had known that she was going to get married during her "visit" to California. Nevertheless, Catherine was 26, and there was not much that would have kept her from rushing out west to finally be reunited with her lieutenant. Indeed, the Olivers were deeply disappointed to miss their first daughter's wedding, but they loved Frank, and they could not have been happier to have him as their new son-in-law.

Even a bride-to-be in 1945 had to have coupons to buy a wedding dress; the war effort made it hard to purchase garments of any type. During the 1940s, clothes were purchased with practical considerations in mind, as most people expected to wear them for several years. To spend precious coupons on a wedding dress would have been a frivolous and extravagant expense during wartime. Most of the servicemen's brides wore somber suits, but it did not make them any less happy or in love. So, Catherine wore a stunning, aqua, light wool gabardine suit whose stylish lines flattered her shapely figure. A brown pillbox hat lay on her thick brunette hair. A lovely pair of brown heels and a huge white orchid brought the ensemble together in the most fetching way. But the loveliest thing that she wore that day was her radiant smile. And Frank was movie-star handsome in his dress uniform "Pinks."

Their wedding reception and dinner were held at one of the Wards' favorite restaurants. After the reception, they left for their short honeymoon at Hotel Laguna at the Laguna Niguel, where they could look out at the beautiful green-blue-gray Pacific. They cherished every minute as they drove down the Pacific Coast Highway, enjoying the coastal landscape.

Clinton was able to reserve a comfortable room for the newlyweds—a quaint honeymoon suite with an unbelievable view. During the day, they enjoyed walking among the little shops along Highway 101, occasionally stopping for a bite to eat in one of the local places. They found a nightclub with a band and again danced their nights away to big band sounds and their favorite music.

Catherine quickly discovered that these Pacific beaches were nothing like the beaches she was used to on the Atlantic coast—especially Myrtle Beach. The weather was always overcast in the mornings, and she was curious and amused to discover that the locals even had a name for this morning weather: "May Grey." She was a little disappointed that it made it hard for her to "toned up," but once the clouds had cleared away, the days were beautiful, warm, and sunny—perfect Southern California weather! One thing is sure—we know that Frank did *not* drag Catherine into the surf this time—not at *this* beach!

Yes, this honeymoon was their chance to finally have all of the fun they had dreamed about for the last eighteen months. Here was their chance to make up for all of that lost time— starting with their very first date, when Frank arrived three hours late!

They did not know what the Army had in store for Frank in the next few months. After all, he was still in the service and at the beck and call of Uncle Sam. But nothing could dampen their happiness. They knew beyond a shadow of a doubt that they would be OK now—just because they were together, and that is all they wanted. Their future was bright and happy.

Thoughts for "Our Day Will Come"

May 8 was Victory Day In Europe—the happiest day in Europe in almost six years. Frank and Catherine celebrated with the rest of the free world. It was certain that this insidious enemy— this motivator of hate—had been stopped. This mastermind of inconceivable atrocities against mankind finally died as he had lived—a coward. Hitler and his wife, Eva Braun, committed suicide, never to see the daylight of the world again. The world danced and gave thanks to God, whichever God they chose to worship. *The war in Europe was over!*

It was another four months before the stubborn Empire of Japan finally surrendered on August 15, 1945.

The Wishing Chair
Mr. and Mrs. Francis Royal Ward
May 22, 1945

Epilogue,
May 1945–October 2001

Frank and Catherine: Happily Ever After!

Los Angeles was a dream come true. But dreams aren't reality, and the real world is always waiting when you wake up. For the moment, it was just enough for Frank and Catherine to cling to the memory of their wedding and to continue to spin new dreams of the life they wanted to build together. At least they had the assurance that from now on, they would be together forever. Yes, *that* dream had come true.

Frank returned to Spokane at the end of his leave in California. However, this time, he had the pleasure of his wife's company. He decided to drive his own car back to Washington so that they would have transportation during their time there. Housing was in short supply all over the country, so the new couple chose to rent a room for their stay.

They rented a room with kitchen privileges in Spokane, Washington, from a lovely and helpful landlady, Mrs. Kowalski. It didn't matter where they lived. They were in newlywed bliss.

It was cool and rainy in Spokane, and Catherine wasn't sure this weather agreed with her. This "little southern gal" wasn't quite used to a cool summer and felt she might be coming down with something. In addition to having to grapple with these new weather conditions, she had been sick every morning. As soon as she ate breakfast, it would come back up again. She thought she might have the flu—but why was it lasting so long?

When Catherine confided in her landlady about how sick she was in the mornings, Mrs. Kowalski stunned her with the words, "My dear Catherine, I do believe you are going to have a baby!"

"Oh, no!" Catherine shrieked. "I can't be, Mrs. Kowalski! I just got married! I haven't even seen my parents yet. I haven't even been home! How am I going to go home expecting a baby?"

Catherine was very naïve when it came to the facts of life. Was it possible she was already pregnant and expecting a baby? In the 1920s, '30s, and '40s, pregnancy was something of a forbidden subject in many homes and families—mostly for reasons of piety and propriety. Most of the young women learned about the facts of life from their husbands when they became pregnant! Catherine was mortified even to think that she might be pregnant. *This baby will ruin me if he comes early,* she thought. *How did this happen so soon?*

"Now, honey, it will be OK," Mrs. Kowalski reassured her. "This baby will be the best thing that has ever happened to you! You'll see! I know it is a little soon, but you have a wonderful lieutenant for a husband, Cathy! This will *complete* you ... you'll see! Now, let me fix you something to eat."

What am I going to do with a baby, Catherine wondered. *People back home are going to think I <u>had</u> to get married!* She was crying hard now, with big tears rolling down her cheeks. "Mrs. Kowalski, I am so frightened. My Frank is wonderful, but I am so far away from home—what am I going to do?" Catherine hiccupped.

"You will be a wonderful mother, and you will love this little baby. I just know it. You are a sweet young lady, and I'll help if you let me."

"Why, thank you, Mrs. Kowalski. You are so kind."

Mrs. Kowalski was a lifesaver for Catherine. She helped Catherine through her first weeks of pregnancy as if Mrs. Kowalski was Catherine's own mother—maybe even better! And long after the couple moved away from Spokane,

Catherine wrote to Mrs. Kowalski often—up until her passing, years later.

A few weeks later, Catherine went to the Army doctor to confirm her suspicions. Sure enough—she was pregnant! The due date was to be sometime in late February 1946. They lived in Mrs. Kowalski's rented room in Spokane from June until October 1945. But when Catherine became homesick on top of being pregnant, it all became a bit too much for her. All she wanted to do was to go home.

In October 1945, Frank's future in the Army was still unclear, so he arranged for an extended leave to take Catherine home to Charlotte, where his baby would be born a few months later. Catherine's family welcomed her home with open arms and was thrilled and surprised about the baby who was on the way. Somehow in the 1940s no one spoke of being pregnant.

While Frank was in Charlotte, he received notice that he would receive an honorable discharge from the Army in November 1945. He remained in Charlotte with Catherine until the first part of January, where they were able to celebrate Christmas and New Year's together for the first time. At least they were finally able to get a running start on making up all that time that they had lost while he was away!

Frank knew his future was in Los Angeles. He needed a good job with promotions and housing for his new wife and baby son, James Francis. California was home, and there was no doubt—he was a real Westerner. He knew there were job opportunities waiting for him in Southern California, and he was eager to return home and land a good job. It was hard on both Frank and Catherine to be apart during this time; however, Catherine was not able to travel in her current state of "mommyhood." Even if she had found a way to travel, she would have been miserable beyond belief.

In 1946, women did not travel in the late stages of pregnancy. Besides, the Olivers were delighted to have Catherine at home with a new baby coming. It almost made up for not being at her wedding in California—almost.

*****

This is a letter Catherine wrote to Frank on February 19, 1946, two days before their baby was born:

*****

Tuesday night
February 19, 1946

My Darling Frank,

How is my sweetheart tonight? Your fat wife is feeling pretty good. Darling, I am not much fatter than I was when you were here. I only weigh 146. I weighed 145 when you were here. I gained 2 pounds, and then I lost one. But the doctor says that is OK. If I am not so fat, I won't have a big baby. It will be easier on me.

I didn't get any mail today. You said you didn't write Saturday, so I guess that is the reason. Today was a terrible day; a letter would have helped. It rained all day—and I mean *it rained!* I have never seen it rain so hard. Therefore your wife had to stay in all day.

Tomorrow is my brother's last day at home. I hope if they send him to the West Coast they will send him someplace near L.A., so he can come over to see us often.

Darling, I laughed so hard it hurt. Bill told me that one of his old friends was bragging about how much his family has. So Bill just up and told him that his sister lives in Beverly Hills. And that it's nothing for us to go out and talk to Bing Crosby or Clark Gable. He is so crazy. I told him you had seen old Clark, but I have never seen him. I sure would like to.

But most of all, I would like to see Frank Ward. To me, he is better looking than any of those old movie stars. I have that man.

Darling, I have been cleaning out my chest of drawers

today, to make a place for Junior's clothes. I also pressed all of my bed jackets and gowns, etc. I am getting ready to go one of these days. Monday is Ruby's birthday, and Tuesday is mine. She wants me to have "James Francis" on her birthday, but I told her I was going to hold out for my birthday on February 26. Gosh, Darling, your wife is getting old. I will be 27! Oh, that sounds awful. But that doesn't matter, as long as you love me.

My mother is going to buy a bed for Junior and Eddie when I leave—one like little David's. That's the kind that I want. You can raise the springs up and down so you won't have to stoop so low while the baby is little. Do you know what I am talking about?

Well, sweetheart, there is no more news from this end; just remember that your wife loves you, and wishes she could see you tonight.

Good night and sweet dreams,
All of my love, Your Cath

*****

Mary Catherine (or "Baby Kay") was born on February 21, 1946. In spite of the fact that I was supposed to be "James Francis," Mother was surprised at how much she loved her baby girl, and I was soon forgiven for my gender. Below is a letter which Mother wrote to Dad just after I was born. In this letter, she mentions Eddie, Becky and David's new baby boy, born in September 1945.

*****

Sunday night
February 24, 1946

My Darling Frank,
Yes, your mommie is doing fine. How is my daddy? Gosh, I

400

sure wish I could see him tonight. Darling, this is the first time I have felt like writing. In fact, it is the first time they would even raise me up. They did not raise me very far.

Darling, I came to the hospital about the same time that Becky came over, but Darling, I was in the labor room for 14 hours. See, Darling, if you had been here, you would have had 14 hours to walk the floor downstairs. I had a terrible time, sweetheart. I was too small to have the baby normally. I didn't dilate enough. They finally had to take her with forceps. Gosh, Darling, I have never been in so much pain. But she is worth it all.

Darling, she is the prettiest little thing. Eddie was cute, but our little girl is pretty. She looks just like her Daddy. Her little face is shaped like yours, and she has my nose and mouth. My dad picked her out of all of the babies in the nursery. She is so sweet. When they bring her in to nurse, she will nurse for a few minutes, and she cuddles up to her mother and goes to sleep. Darling, I could eat her up. I can't wait to get to where I can hold her. Frank, you will love her to death. The nurse told me she was the prettiest in the nursery. They have her on the front row. You know they always put the prettiest babies on the front row. She is darling.

Sweetheart, I have a nice private room at the front of the hospital. It is pink with little white curtains at the window.

Yes, my darling Daddy, I received the beautiful red roses. They are still pretty. I cried when I got them. I love you, Frank. All my nurses want to know how I rate those beautiful roses. I told her my sweetheart loves me.

I received your letter of Feb. 12 today. You can tell Dan just wait and see our "Little Rebel." Now she is a "Rebel" too. She is darling, sweetheart, and I know that you can't wait to see her. I bet your mother is just about as bad.

Frank, I will pay the hospital bill and Dr. Matthews what I can. I don't think he will fuss. Don't worry, Darling—you send what you can, but keep enough for your sweet self. I love you.

I wish you didn't have to work so hard.

What are we going to call her—"Kay" or "Cathy"—since you call me "Cath"?

The doctor said I am doing fine, but I have a lot of stitches. I am going to be OK.

Darling, you wouldn't know me—I have lost so much weight Ha-ha! How about you? I am about Becky's size now. You know how good she looks.

Frank, you have the sweetest mother. She sent me a beautiful birthday card with $5.00 in it for me to buy something for my birthday.

It is hard to write lying down, but I wanted to write to my Darling. Let him know how much I love him. Let him know that I am doing OK.

Sweetheart, I will kiss our little daughter for you when they bring her in. She is so sweet I wouldn't take a million dollars for her. Everybody has been so nice to me. Millie just had a fit over the baby. Ruby said to tell you she is so glad it was a girl. Darling, I am tired. I love you and I will write again soon.

All my love, "Cath"

*****

It seems that Mother had some health problems after I was born and was not released by her doctor for a while. It was some type of back problem that kept her down. In 1946, the recovery time for a pregnancy was different than in today's world. Bed rest was the panacea, although she was anxiously waiting to join her new husband in California and start their new life—or was she?

If the truth were known, Mother had ambivalent feelings about living in Los Angeles. The South was everything she knew. Besides, she loved showing off her new daughter, "Kay," (who did not ruin her reputation)—and I looked just like my daddy, Frank. To leave all of Catherine's friends and family would take a lot of courage, love, and faith in God.

She was torn between her Southern family and her new husband in Los Angeles, whom she loved deeply. But she made her choice, and it was her lieutenant. Now was the time for her to step up and be the woman she promised to be when she married her lieutenant. Mother and I stayed in Charlotte until late May 1946. It was almost three months before Dad met his baby daughter, "Kay" (me).

They decided to call me "Kay" so there would not be any confusion—it was sort of a nickname.

Mother and I flew into Los Angeles, and from there, we started our new life together as a family in Southern California. Dad soon became my hero; what a change from a hero on the battlefield to being the hero of a little girl who insisted on going everywhere he went.

Mother did become homesick, but her wish concerning her brother Bill's post came true because he was stationed at Long Beach Naval Station, close to Los Angeles. Uncle Bill (I called him Uncle Bull) would visit our new family often on weekends. The brother-and-sister pair also drove every year across the country to visit family and friends in Charlotte for six weeks at a time. It was always hard for Mother to leave her Charlotte family at the end of these visits, but she had made a new life in California with her lieutenant. And of course, she still lived by her philosophy to "work hard and keep your chin up." All in all, it took a long time for Mother to adjust to her new hometown. Dad tried to help, but she often resisted.

In May 1946, a new house was a luxury. There were not many to rent in the Los Angeles area, and those which were for rent were outrageously priced. All of the servicemen were coming home, and there was little housing available. So, Mom and Dad moved into Dad's parents' home. Mother was very happy and elated to present the newest addition to the Ward family, and the Wards were over the moon with joy to meet their new granddaughter "Kay." I was the first grandchild, and

I looked just like Frank!

Was this house going to be big enough for these two women? Well, that might have to be another book.

During the year of 1946, Dad looked into many types of careers before taking a job with the Bernstein Brothers Original Fabrics Company. He worked in Los Angeles and was happy in his position while Mother was home with me. But after a few months, Mother decided to go back to work as well, leaving me with Mama Ward.

In 1944, FDR signed the GI Bill, which was designed to make certain practical provisions and ensure the welfare of all returning servicemen. One initiative in this bill involved the building of new houses during the late forties and early fifties. These homes, called "track homes," were built with the GI in mind.

Our first home was in Whittier, California—and for my parents, it was a dream home. I was five when we moved there, and I remember how beautiful the house seemed to me at the time. Mother worked hard to make sure that all the drapes, furniture, and accessories were tastefully coordinated. The kitchen had lovely ivy wallpaper with delicately ivy-patterned dish towels and dishes to match. Throughout the house, the windows featured tie-back sheers with lots of ruffles, and there were custom-made drapes in the living room.

Our home was surrounded by an orchard of orange trees, and there was fresh orange juice every morning. Just outside the windows, we could see our lovely orange trees with white blooms that smelled glorious. Dad planted pansies in rows and sweet peas that grew on a trellis the full height of the garage wall in the backyard. The smell was heavenly—especially when the scents of sweet peas and orange blossoms mingled together in the spring. It wasn't quite the crepe myrtles and magnolias of Charlotte that Mother was used to, but she was happy. And as a little girl, I remember it being wonderful. I often took huge bouquets of sweet peas to my teacher when

I was in the first grade. She always loved getting the flowers, and it made me feel special to be able to do this for her. I'll always be thankful to dad for these great memories.

Mother blessed the Wards again with another granddaughter on July 12, 1952. The new house was built just in time for the new arrival. Terry had red hair, adorable dimples, and Dad's blue eyes. She was the apple of her daddy's eye, and the Wards were in love all over again. Dad never did get his "James Francis."

Frank Royal Ward Junior

A hero is no braver than an ordinary man, but a
hero is braver five minutes longer.
– Emerson

Dad was honorably discharged from the Army in November of 1945. Along with the discharge came a total change in his life's plans. He had intended to make the Army his life's work. He had done well in the Army and often wrote, "Being an officer is not for the lazy." Dad liked the order of the Army, the discipline with the hierarchy of rank, and his experience was impressive. However, he was a wounded warrior, and in the years following WWII, the Army had a surplus of wounded warriors.

Dad did not go to Germany. He didn't get the chance to face down Hitler the way he wanted to. But there is no question that he did his share for the war effort.

His wounds from the Battle of the Bulge would affect him for years to come. The lung infection that set in after being shot left him prone to additional infections and pneumonia for the rest of this life. He lost sixty percent of his hearing in his right ear, with a constant ringing for the rest of his life. He never fully recovered from the nerve damage in his right arm; he just learned to manage it. But the real damage was to his soul.

The Army was able to treat the physical wounds that Dad sustained in the wake of his injuries. However, the loathsome sights, sounds, and smells of the war continued to haunt his soul. When he could not forget them or block them out, he did his best to ignore them. Still, they would not go away. For years, he lived with post-traumatic stress disorder (PTSD), or "battle fatigue," as it was called in the 1940s and '50s. This affected all of us in the family immensely. Some nights were filled with nightmares and night sweats. He spent many sleepless nights sitting up in the living room, reading for hours on end, trying to take his mind off the memories that overwhelmed him. And sometimes he just sat there in a stupor, watching a blank TV screen.

Dad was not alone in this. The flashbacks and nightmares throw many veterans into a downward spiral of depression and even psychotic breaks with reality. Some found that long periods of bed rest helped them to regain their bearings. A number of them sought treatment in mental hospitals to restore their ability to function in normal daily life. Others needed a more aggressive approach. One of the best cures they had in those days was electric shock treatments. The electric shock jumbled their memories and lessened the relentless effects of the trauma they had experienced. A lobotomy was used in the most extreme cases—a practice that continued until the early 1950s. However, even with the best treatment available at the time, many found it impossible to live a normal life after returning from war. Many turned to alcohol or drugs in order to cope, and addictions among our brave warriors were rampant. Unable to escape the recurring images of the carnage they had witnessed on the battlefield, some even committed suicide—just to make it stop. And, as always, so many were plagued by the question: *WHY did I make it home?*

In the 1940s and 50s, there was a stigma attached to mental health issues, and no one talked about it at the weekly bridge games or in any type of everyday circle. It was considered a weakness. In those years, the effects of such trauma were referred to as "a soldier's heart," "shell shock," and "battle fatigue."

General Patton brought the term "battle fatigue" to the front pages after an incident in a hospital in Sicily. Patton was reprimanded for slapping a young GI who was suffering from shell shock, and Patton was subsequently instructed to apologize to the soldier's whole Plattoom. We now know that whereas PTSD most noticeably occurs during the weeks and months immediately following the trauma, it may take years for it to fully surface in the soldier's life. It often leads to additional disabling conditions such as depression, anxiety, night frights, and other psychological disorders. Regardless of when these conditions first appear, the disorders usually take years to overcome.

It took the mental health experts years to realize that this trauma was not a mental illness like schizophrenia or bipolar disorder. It was not until after the Gulf War in the 1980s that PTSD was recognized as a psychological condition brought on by trauma and, as such, was defined as a mental disorder, not a mental illness.

Dad's struggle went on for years—well into the late 1960s. One great blessing was that Dad had always been a man of God, and his faith was instrumental in his recovery. He was a quiet man who kept his problems to himself. When people looked at Dad or talked to him, they never knew that he was suffering. Even those of us who knew him best, never knew how much he suffered. However, the truth is that Dad fought depression, anxiety, panic attacks, and night frights for the rest of his life.

No, the war did not end for Dad on January 4, 1945. WWII

stole the innocence of that happy-go-lucky young man and turned him into a depressed and wounded warrior who no longer knew how to identify his mission in life ...

Perhaps the hardest part for Dad was that Mom was unable to understand his struggles. During their long separation and courtship, both had bravely soldiered on with a resolve to "work hard and keep their chins up." When this did not work as an antidote for Dad's post-traumatic stress disorder, Mom suffered her own set of wounds and took it very personally. There is no doubt that she tried to comprehend what he was going through. They had been through so much together, even when they were apart. *Why isn't he happy?* she kept asking herself. *Why can't I fix this?*

Mom would have nothing to do with any counseling or therapy. In her mind, she was not the one who was broken. It would be a long time before Dad's problems lessened, and they never completely went away. The one constant was their love for each other. Through it all, she stayed with Dad and loved him the only way she knew how.

I remember that Mom always pleaded with him to talk to her. But because Dad always did his best to protect her at all costs, he was especially vigilant about shielding her from the effects of his depression and anxiety. Convinced that she would never understand, he lived by a steely resolve not to expose her to the fallout from the realities he had experienced in battle. He felt sure that she would say, "Why don't you just forget it, Frank? The war is over but it was not over, it was still living in Frank's psyche. It is true that she never did understand that there are some things a person cannot escape just by pushing them way down. This approach was very unhealthy, both for Mother and for those around her—but it was the only way she knew how to cope with the adversities that she found too overwhelming to manage. She also did not understand that all things were not about her.

In today's world, the Army regards post-traumatic stress

disorder as a treatable condition. However, in the years following WWII, thousands of servicemen had no choice but to suffer in silence. I know that Dad was happy that, in the closing decades of the twentieth century, our servicemen were finally able to get the help they needed.

In spite of his inner turmoil, Dad was still able to provide for his family. In 1952, he was hired by a large textile company, Crompton-Richmond. Both Mom and Dad were delighted that he had been given this opportunity to have a promotion within the industry that he loved. From the beginning, Dad did well and was soon given a territory of his own in San Francisco and Northern California. There, he flourished selling his corduroy, velvet, and velveteen to retail stores and clothing manufacturers. There is no doubt that this success helped him to cope with the debilitating effects of his PTSD. It wasn't long before Dad and Mom were able to buy a home by the bay in beautiful San Mateo, California.

The years of 1954–55 were extremely hard for Dad. He managed to go to work every day and to keep his life and family going, but in reality, he was haunted deeply by the horrors of war.. At one point, he began to have panic attacks, and his anxiety eventually resulted in some physical ailments. When he tried to get help, the doctor assured him that there was nothing wrong and he was fine. This only compounded the problem and drove him into a deeper depression. One night in 1955, the angst and pain became so acute that he told Mom to take the girls and go back to Charlotte.

Mom was terrified! She could not see his wound—this wound that she could never have imagined. It was as if an invisible dark cloud hung over him, trapping him in a dark sadness. She realized that after all was said and done, the war truly **had** broken her Frank—and she did not know how to fix it! He was her protector ... she wasn't his! She felt so alone. Of course, she had some friends but no family—and in so many ways, she depended on Dad. She couldn't even drive to the beauty shop on her own.

I remember having hot dogs and beans for dinner that night. The supper dishes were still on the table. It was a beautiful spring evening, filled with the filtered day light that I so loved as a child, and my daddy was watching TV. I looked at my mother and said, "Mommy, you are different now. Why are you so different now?" I had seen the bottle of bourbon on the counter before and noticed that she talked funny when she drank from that bottle. Suddenly, I was filled with an odd feeling that was so frightening, "You talk funny, Mommy," I said, almost shyly.

I was too young to understand it fully but I know now.

I knew that things were sad for my mother because she was crying. In spite of the fact that she thought her life was coming apart, she would not understand that it was the war that tortured her Frank. Her "chin up and work hard" approach to life was no longer enough to appease her personal demons, to lessen her pain and confusion or to control the situations that faced her. She was finding it increasingly difficult to hold it all together and to keep things in their personal lives stable. She felt lost and helpless and missed her family in Charlotte desperately. Just to make the situation bearable she started to drink to and lose herself in her numbness

Now that I am an adult and able to look back, I feel such sympathy for the state she was in at that point. No matter what she tried, she felt as if she were losing her lieutenant. She only had her eight-year-old little daughter and a bottle of bourbon for companions. Quite a fall from grace for the teetotaling Sunday school teacher from North Carolina.

I was really scared. All I could do was stare at her, wondering why her face was distorted and her normally confident eyes were searching for answers and brimming with pain. She started to cry again and said, "Kay, you are the only one I can talk to. I am so far away from my family, and ..." She stopped and swallowed hard, wondering if she could speak the words that raced through her troubled mind. "You are such a big girl now ... It's your Daddy," she blurted out, almost unintelligibly. "I am afraid he is going to kill himself. He wants me to go back to Charlotte and take you and Terry with me." She looked down at the counter as if she could hide her tears from me and bury them there in her apron. But it was too late. Her words terrified me for years after that conversation. A long moment passed. She took a deep breath and looked up again. Her eyes were red and swollen, and I could still see her shaking, but there was more composure there than I had seen a moment before. A stray thought darted through my confusion: "There is no one else for me to talk to about your daddy," she said in something of a rambling tone. "I am so afraid he is going to kill himself."

"But why, Mommy—why?" I asked, innocently

"He's just not himself these days. I am afraid that he is going to have a nervous breakdown." She looked away again, afraid to give words to everything she was thinking. Suddenly, her voice got very quiet. "I'm really afraid he's going to kill himself."

I had never seen Mom like this. Suddenly, I wondered if it was my fault. Struck at the thought, I finally stammered, "But why, Mommy? Did I do something wrong? Was I bad? What did I do?" To my surprise, that just made her cry harder.

I was a big girl, alright—about eight or nine. But what was I to do with that kind of information?

We didn't leave for Charlotte. We were able to find an understanding doctor in San Mateo who helped Dad come back from the brink. We also had Ann, a good friend from Charlotte who lived in Menlo Park. She was married to a doctor, which gave her special insight into Dad's condition, and she had a very calming effect on our whole situation. Her husband gave Mom other names of people who could help Dad. Ann also took Mom to some classes at the Catholic church, where she gained some new ideas about how to be a good wife. The classes seemed to help for a while, and Ann had a very reassuring effect on Mom.

Mom started selling Avon, which added an important new purpose to her life. more than her job as a mother and housewife. It was through her new friends at Avon that she met Bonnie, who invited Mom and Dad to try the Baptist church in San Mateo. In the months that followed, they threw their hearts and souls into that church, and the fellowship and teaching they found there helped a great deal with Dad's healing. They sang in the choir, helped in the kitchen during special events, and taught in Sunday school. Once again, their faith had seen them through another storm.

Nevertheless, the conversation with my mother that day was devastating to a little girl of eight who totally adored her father. I had long since shed the night fears which so often plague small children, but all of those fears returned to pester me in new ways. As I struggled with chronic bouts of nausea and insomnia, I started looking for the monsters in my closet, and I was terrified of being in the dark. Sometimes when my dad was asleep in the den watching TV, I would sneak into the closet to watch him sleep—just to make sure he was alright.

Thanks to good doctors and their wonderful church, things started to level out for Dad in 1957–1958. But the little talks with my mother never actually went away. She would usually warm up beforehand with three or more drinks of bourbon, and then the "talks" would start. This was always hard for me, but I just tried to get used to it. I knew Mom depended on her "little lady Kay " to help her cope, and although it was painful for me, I wanted to help. Our relationship from that point forward was always strained and uncomfortable. I was confused, and I needed her. I could see that she tried so hard to help Dad herself and that she was frustrated that she couldn't. She always took his silence and depressedion personally, which, unfortunately, just made things more volatile for everyone and more confusing for me. As a child I often looked at him and he seemed in a trance, even at my young age.

Mom did not go back to Charlotte. Her lieutenant was her life now, and he was in California. As much as she missed her family and ached for relief, where else would she go? So, there she stayed, and that was the right thing to do. But there is no doubt Dad's PTSD affected the whole family and that during those years in the 50s, she was just as lost and confused as Dad was. Those days were hard.

Mom was not easy to live with. She had a narcissistic streak, and even though she would never admit it, she believed that life was supposed to be all about her. Now that Dad was suffering from a "mental condition," it had to be all about him, which turned everything upside-down for her. He was supposed to be her provider and protector—the one to ensure her security and to keep her feeling safe. But that was not happening. She felt vulnerable and taxed beyond her ability to cope. Life wasn't supposed to be this way, and as much as she loved him, she resented him for not taking care of her the way he had promised in her mind.

As I grew up, I watched my Dad improve, and the little talks with my mother became less frequent over time. Looking back now, I hope they made her feel better. The little talks made me feel I was talking bad about my Dad.

Up until the end of her life, she never understood post-traumatic stress disorder or the need for therapy, and always resented the money they had spent on the psychologist and the doctors. She would never go to therapy; there was nothing wrong with her.

*****

In the spring of 1959, Crompton-Richmond transferred Dad back to Southern California.

The move brought several good changes for us as a family. Dad found a trusted therapist who was also a WWII veteran, and his family doctor gave him anti-anxiety medication. For years, he fought with addictions to cigarettes and alcohol, but because he was faithful to working with his trusted therapist, he experienced a great deal of healing and was able to get his life back.

Mom and Dad found a home to purchase in Fullerton, Orange County, California, where they had a full life with their daughters, friends, and the church. They volunteered for a lot of extracurricular activities at our schools and were active with charity balls and fundraisers in the community. Dad had a ball helping out at the YMCA's local fireworks stand every Fourth of July. I have such great memories of those days because it was one of the few times we got to see the "boy" in Dad once more. There were pool parties, birthdays, holidays, and lots of wonderful times to remember. They lived in the "Mad Men" era of the 1950s–1970s when the martinis flowed and good times were had by all.

In 1959, they joined the Fullerton Presbyterian Church and again became very active over the next few years. It seems they were never happier than when they had found a home in a local faith-based church.

Dad was a good salesman, and his career really flourished during these years in Fullerton. I'll never forget the day in 1964 when he came home early on a Friday afternoon with the news that he had finally landed an account with Levi Strauss. He was so thrilled that his face lit up, and he was grinning from ear to ear. It was wonderful to see him so happy.

Unfortunately, Dad's career with Crompton-Richmond came to an unexpected and abrupt halt in 1977. His hearing had been damaged when he was injured during the war, and over time, his hearing loss had become increasingly severe. On one occasion, he misunderstood the information he was given while taking a new order from Levi Strauss, and he recorded the order incorrectly. It resulted in a costly mistake for the company. In spite of the fact that they understood that it had happened due to his hearing loss, they were embarrassed, and they fired Dad shortly thereafter. It didn't matter that he had proven to be one of their premier salesmen or that he had brought in some of their largest accounts over the 26 years that he had worked for the company. It didn't matter that he had a family or that he was a war hero. In order to keep the Levi Strauss account and safeguard their bottom line, they determined that he was expendable.

Dad took it hard, and it was a while before he was able to recover from this blow. After leaving Crompton-Richmond, he dabbled in retail and real estate sales but never had an established career again. In a way, he was grateful to have a less stressful time over the following few years leading up to his retirement. He no longer had to worry about landing accounts, managing dye lots and orders, and meeting shipping dates. But in truth, he did miss the customers, the designers, and the opportunity to work with fabrics—all of which had been such an important part of his life.

In the 1990s, Dad attended a 17th Airborne reunion on the East Coast with Mom, where he hoped to find some of the men from his old unit. To his dismay, there was not one person he knew. "We thought that no one was left from your unit," they said. He did reunite with several fellow WWII vets who were glad to see that he was still alive after all of these years and that he had lived a full life. This was a sobering moment for Dad. His feelings were ambivalent, to say the least. On the one hand, he was thankful to be alive. However, once again, he wondered why he had been spared while the other men in his unit had not. Dad never did like talking about the war, but on more than one occasion. I did hear him say, "The real heroes were left behind on the battlefield."

Dad and Mom retired in Henderson, Nevada, in 1992. The cost of living was less expensive there, and they could also be close to my sister, Terry Lynn Green, who lived in Las Vegas. He loved gardening, and Nevada was a superb place to spend his retirement. He grew roses, irises, snapdragons (which he loved), and, of course, red carnations.

Mom was diagnosed with Alzheimer's in 1994, but Dad never left her side.

My Father taught me:

You are only as good as your word.

You learn more if you don't talk and listen.

Less is often more.

Love with love.

He would always give money to vagabonds on the street in Los Angeles, saying, "Things are not always as they seem."

My father, Dad Ward, died on October 16, 2001, from a stroke and related heart problems. Moments after we had stepped out of his hospital room to grab a quick supper, my 29-year-old son Gregory arrived from out of town unexpectedly and slipped into Dad's room. Sensing that the end was near, Greg held his hand and comforted him with the reassuring words that it was going to be alright. Before we had a chance to return, Dad had slipped into eternity, listening to Greg's voice, still holding his hand.

The angels cried the night he died. He was buried in the National Cemetery in Boulder City, Nevada, as a first lieutenant.

I miss him every day.

Thank you, Dad, with all my heart, for all the love in yours.
– author unknown

Mary Catherine Oliver Ward (Cath)

Mom moved to Los Angeles in June 1946 with her baby daughter, "Kay" (me), to start a life with Dad, the love of her life.

She found Los Angeles to be very different from Charlotte. She did well with this culture shock, and when she got homesick, she practiced her own advice and just kept her chin up and worked harder. This was the cure for all of her problems. Mom was outgoing and fun, and people liked her. However, she never learned to face her feelings or to deal with them in healthy ways. Time and time again, she just pushed them way down—away from her heart.

In the fall of 1946, Mom decided to go back to work in order to bring in more money. She had a built-in babysitter in the form of my Grandmother Ward, whom I adored. She found a job selling high-end clothes in the "Dixie Shop," a posh dress shop in downtown Los Angeles. It was a perfect position for her at the time—and with that sweet Southern accent, there was no doubt she was the perfect person for the job.

I think it is fair to say that she spent much of what she made on clothes for herself and for her family. When I was just three or so, Dad often took me along in our 1947 Chevrolet when it was time to pick Mother up from work. The first thing I would say to her was, "Mommy, what did you bring me today?" Bullock's Department store was right across the street from the Dixie Shop, and I knew that she often ducked into their little girl's department during her lunch hour. Thanks to all the lovely outfits they had there, I was always dressed like a princess with ruffles, bows, lace, organza, and more—little "Princess Kay." One thing was sure—no daughter of hers was going to grow up as she had: poor, deprived, and in rags.

Mother always said that she worked to help the family budget, and I'm sure that, to some extent, that was true. She was always careful with their money. The truth is that Dad supported his family extremely comfortably, and Mother never really had to work. But she liked nice things and didn't mind working to get them. She was a very social person and enjoyed the attention she received from folks who found her sweet, attractive, and intriguing with her North Carolina accent. She much preferred the company of intelligent adults in a productive atmosphere to the world of whiny, crying children and dirty dishes. So, for Mother, working was not so much a necessity for her family as it was a need for her own mental and emotional well-being. Whereas it is true that she took the job primarily to be able to contribute to the family budget, she had a generous heart and always found ways to spend a little of her hard-earned money on the people she loved the most. It was her way of telling them she loved them. In addition to keeping her little Princess Kay in frills and lace, she often purchased lovely things for her mother, her sister Becky, and her little sister, Betty Jean. She would pop them into the mail and surprise them with a new sweater, blouse, or skirt.

There is no doubt that Mother loved her girls and that she wanted to make sure we had many of the things that she had missed during her own childhood. Although she worked at a high end dress store in Millbrae Mall, she always found the time to serve as a classroom mother for various school parties and activities, participate in the PTA, and volunteer with the Girl Scouts of America, where she was a leader and neighborhood chairmen in the 1950s. With Mother so busy with her various activities, Terry and I were latchkey children, and we missed having Mother waiting at home for us when we came home from school. On the other hand, we were probably happier that way because she was happy working.

Mother worked her entire life and really found her niche in selling fine clothes to professional women. She was 72 years old when she retired.

Catherine and Frank were members of the First Presbyterian Church for 35 years until they moved to Las Vegas after their retirement. Mom loved her church life. She served as a deacon and worked on many committees over the years. And she sang in the Fullerton Presbyterian Church Choir until she was 72. She would say "When the hymns are sung, it is like praying twice."

Mother also loved to garden. Flowers were like a panacea to her. She had an innate talent for design and style, which never left her. Wherever she lived, it was beautiful.

Outwardly, Mom was very outgoing and always had an active social life. She was perky, sunny, and charmed everyone she met with her North Carolina accent. But behind her quick words of encouragement and her ready smile, there is no denying that she struggled with several inner demons. It is unfortunate that there were many different forks in the road when she might have benefited from some form of emotional support, but these were the paths not taken. She resisted any form of counseling or therapy, convinced that those services were designed to "fix" people who were weak or flawed. As a result, she carried a number of mental and emotional burdens over the years—many of which were unnecessary—and she was often highly critical of others. However, the day did come—well into her sixties—when Mom was finally able to accept herself and find peace in her life with her lieutenant. It was a good chapter in their lives when she found solace with Dad and he with her.

Both Mom and Dad worked, but they also took the time to have fun together. They often took days off for trips to the zoo, and they lunched at the Robert E. Lee, their favorite restaurant in Newport Beach. Terry had made her home in Las Vegas, and they always enjoyed taking trips to Las Vegas to visit her there. During these later years, Mom was much softer, kinder, and sweeter than she had been while we were growing up, and there is no doubt that her grandchildren really loved her. She would even babysit her grandchildren's dalmatian, "Buttons," when the family went on vacation.

Mother, when older, was not as angry as she had been in her younger days. Her narcissistic tendencies and insecurities mellowed in her elder years, and as her fears and anger diminished, her soul found a new peace. This was a great blessing for both of them during their last ten years together. After years of struggle, they were once again both happy in their love.

The love they had for one another was strong enough to last through Dad's deployment when he went to war, his PTSD, Mom's narcissistic personality disorder, Dad losing his job at age 55, and the drinking problem that had plagued her over the years. Their love was like a lifeboat in the swirling waters of a hurricane: when one was being sucked under the surface, the other grabbed on from a position of safety within the lifeboat—and held on tight! Most of the days were good, some excellent, and others bad, but one thing was sure: they always knew they would be together for the rest of their lives.

The strained relationship I had with Mother through the years vanished in the 1980s, and we became mother-and-daughter friends. We learned to enjoy things we had never shared in the past. I am grateful that we were able to create these new, fond memories because I can now look back on that time of forgiveness and love and cherish those days we had together.

Mom was diagnosed with Alzheimer's disease in 1993, right after they moved to Las Vegas. She was 74 years old. Dad showered her twenty-four-seven with care and love and never left her side. He was her protector, caregiver, and her link to the memories they had built together in times past. Dad may have lived through WWII and survived some dreadful years being haunted by his PTSD, but without a doubt, the hardest thing he ever had to do was watch the love of his life turn into a mere shell of her formerly radiant self. His beautiful bride was slipping away a little bit each day. This was his greatest battlefield: staying brave and strong by her side.

Some nights, she would thank him for taking such good care of her that day. To Dad, it seemed like a portal to the past, but to Mom, the past was short-lived. The greatest mercy, however, was that even in third-stage Alzheimer's, she always knew her lieutenant—Dad—and sometimes, he was the *only* one she knew!

Mary Catherine Ward had a deadly stroke on August 4, 1998. It was only one short week later that she left us, almost 55 years to the day from the moment she first met her lieutenant. For 55 years, they had lived out a commitment never to say "goodbye." Over the years of the life they had built together, it was always "So long," "See you later," or "Back in a bit!" But on that day, August 11, 1998, Dad finally had to say "goodbye" to his sweet Catherine, the love of his life.

She was laid to rest at City National Cemetery as a first lieutenant's wife.

Frank Royal Ward Senior (Papa Ward)

Francis Royal Ward Senior, or Papa Ward, had a smile that was attached to his heart. His talents were immense. At six years old, Frank Senior stood in front of the church congregation and read the morning newspaper from top to bottom. His photographic memory was a gift from God. He was a whiz at math, and his gifts never reached their full potential.

A true wordsmith, he was particularly an artist of verse. His heart gave him the words he wrote. In his poetry, he created beauty, love, and humor and inspired tears. The world would have been a kinder place if more of mankind had received the gift of his prose.

Papa Ward was a man of faith and a wonderful husband, father, and grandfather. He loved, and he was greatly loved. We lost Papa Ward to complications from a stroke in September 1967.

Anna Ethelda "Mama" Ward

My first memories in life were of Mama Ward. I just called her
"Mama" in the house on 53rd Street in Los Angeles, California.
From the time I was nine months old, my mother went to
work in order to help the family, and Mama Ward took care
of me. She was the one to raise me from the age of eighteen
months until I was three years old. It was at that point that
her health made it too difficult for her to chase a young child
around the house. She was an angel of love to this little girl,
and she taught me how to love.

Anna Ethelda knew how to love her family and her neighbors. She taught me not to judge others or to talk about them
unkindly, always to forgive, and always to remember that love
is all that matters. She didn't know why the white race should
have such superiority since the races of other colors outnum-
bered the white race two to one. In today's world, she would
probably be known as a "liberal," but if that was the case,
wasn't Jesus a liberal, too?

Mama lived I Corinthians 13:4–6:

*4 "Love is patient; love is kind. It does not envy; it does not boast,
it is not proud. 5 It does not dishonor others, it is not self-seek-
ing, it is not easily angered, and it keeps no record of wrongs. 6
Love does not delight in evil but rejoices in the truth. 7 It always
protects, always trusts, always hopes, and always perseveres."*

It is sad to note that Mama Ward never got her son back
after the war was over. During his time away, she missed her
boy desperately, and when he returned from the war, it was
as a wounded soldier and a changed man. After his period of
convalescence in a hospital two states away, they had barely
had a chance to rekindle family ties before Frank married his
sweetheart, a mere four weeks after he came home on leave. As

much as she mourned the loss of her boy and had no choice but to adjust to a new normal, she did gain a daughter-in-law and, in time, two granddaughters. There is an old saying that goes, "Your son is a friend until he takes a wife, but your daughter is a friend for the rest of your life."

One thing is sure. As a grandmother, she was a hard act to follow. I firmly believe that if everyone had a grandmother like Anna Ethelda Ward, the world would be a better place to be in.

Anna Ethelda Ward died in April of 1969. She was the best grandmother ever!

Clinton Ward

Clinton Ward was married a year or so after Frank. He married Prudence Ellingsworth, the girl next door. The couple lived in Whittier, California, right across the street from Frank and Catherine. They had one son, Michael Ward, in 1948 and one daughter, Linda Ward, in 1950.

Clint had a tremendous sense of humor. One day when he was hanging out in the garage with Frank, Frank kiddingly asked, "Hey there, Clint, how are you doing? Have you been getting any on the side lately?"

Clint's answer was, "Hell, France! It has been so long since I got any that I didn't even know that they moved it to the side!"

As I have mentioned before, Catherine had quite a lovely figure. When she wore a sweater, Clinton would joke, "Catherine, I sure do like that camel hair sweater you have on."

Clinton was born to be a writer. Whether he was writing a shopping list or a casual letter, his words always danced across the page in full color. It is a shame that he was never published; his talent with words would have been a blessing to this world. It was such a loss. Clinton B. Ward died in the 1970s.

Dora Mae Oliver

Dora Mae Oliver is the grandmother I did not know well. She was in Charlotte, and our family lived in California. She was always sweet and loving when I was able to visit her in North Carolina, and it was clear that she loved everyone. I will always regret that she could not travel to California to see us.

Mama Oliver never quite understood Catherine's obsession with weight and diet. During our visits to Charlotte, my mother often tried to restrict my diet. When I was only six years old, I remember Mama telling Mother, "Let that child eat what she wants to eat. Kay is on her vacation!"

She was the mother of three daughters and one son and the grandmother of four grandsons and one granddaughter. As I read through my parents' letters, I learned that she really did love her only granddaughter and missed her terribly when Catherine moved to California in 1946.

I will always remember Mama Oliver as a woman of God who lived her religion. I was sad to lose her so early in my life. She died of pneumonia in January 1961. She was 70 years old.

James Edward Oliver

Papa Oliver was a character who loved his family and worked hard. He was a man with less than a high school education who found his niche in the tools and trades. During the last part of his life, he lived with his son Bill. In the 1960s, he came to California to see Catherine and her family. It was then that they learned that he liked his bourbon and cigarettes. This was a huge surprise, as the Olivers had always been known as teetotalers. He liked to stay with Catherine because while he was away in California, he was always able to have his cocktails and "a big plate of those fancy appetizers before supper." He died in July 1972. He was 80 years old.

David Kelly

David Kelly was a Southern gentleman. He made me feel like I was the most important little girl in the world when he talked to me. He loved Frank like a brother, and they truly were brothers of the heart. I will cherish the memory of their times together for a lifetime. I was lucky to have David Kelly as my uncle until he passed away in January 2011 at the age of 96. What a gift he was!

Frank Markey

In 1952, my father was transferred with his family from Los Angeles to a new sales area in San Francisco. It was shortly thereafter that he learned that Frank Markey, his "brother" from the war, also lived in the Bay Area. As we know, the bonds of friendship forged in the service are especially meaningful and strong. The sights and sounds of war were never to be forgotten, and the experiences that these two friends had shared allowed them to understand things about each other that even their closest family members could not comprehend. Frank Markey had been captured in the Battle of the Bulge and remained a prisoner of war until his release after the Allies' victory in Europe. He was the only one that Dad could talk to about the nightmare they had faced in the Ardennes. Well out of earshot of their families, they would talk for hours. Sometimes, they even met at a local bar if they could steal a few minutes away from their wives. I remember times when the wives would fuss about it, but I have always been grateful that Dad had this special friend in his life.

Markey would always say, "I wonder what the poor people are doing today?" That question puzzled me at the time, but now I think I know what he meant. I know that he was thankful for those moments in time that he was able to spend with Dad—even if it was for just a cribbage game and spaghetti dinner with his old Army buddy, Frank Ward. Dad always said, "He is a good egg." As a little girl, I called him "Uncle Frank."

Frank Markey died in the mid-1980s.

Margaret Rebecca Kelly (Aunt Becky)

I spent most of my vacations as a child with the Kellys. They were my summer family, and I loved them dearly. Oh, how sweet my Aunt Becky was! I loved to visit her and loved having her for my aunt. She was my favorite and way "cooler" than my mother, or at least I thought so at the time. She was beautiful, and I loved listening to her talk. She always just sounded so sweet. On the other hand, she did have a prickly side, and I was careful to stay away from that side for sure. She taught me in her own way that "You can get more flies with honey than with vinegar."

Even though Catherine and Becky lived on opposite sides of the country (Catherine in California and Becky in North Carolina), they saw each other every year. In spite of the fact that there was a noticeably intense sibling rivalry between them, it was clear that they genuinely loved one another and that they enjoyed a bond that only sisters share. Rebecca was always perfect and even more of a perfectionist than Catherine, if that was possible. She, too, had a flair for design and fine clothes. The unspoken rivalry died only when Mother left us in 1998. Becky was always a class act—one very hard to follow.

She died in 2006 after being afflicted with both Parkinson's and Alzheimer's disease. She was the best aunt ever!

Terry Lynn Ward Green

My younger sister Terry was given the nickname "TNT" by her grandparents, and I always felt it was appropriate. As a baby, she would climb up the cabinets and help herself to whatever she wanted while she stood on the counter, smiling with those big blue eyes just sparkling and dimples gleaming.

When Dad was transferred to the San Francisco area, the family moved to a home in San Mateo. One day when I was only seven, I was told to watch her. But while she was "in my care," Terry decided to take a stroll. Yes, even though she was only eighteen months old at the time, she strolled down that busy street where we lived—all on her own. Boy, did I get in trouble!

Yes, Terry Lynn Ward was a very busy baby, and by the time she was eighteen months old, I learned that she was my responsibility. From the time she was two years old until she was six, she was very active and would not mind telling you that she was unhappy with the world and everything that was in it. In 1958, our family moved from San Mateo to Fullerton, California. She went into her tomboy stage with her "mischievous" little friends on Royer Street while we were living in Fullerton. She was always there when I got home from school. She was a latchkey kid until I got home. There again, she was my charge. As a teenager, I often resented the after-school duty, but if anyone ever crossed Terry Lynn, I was a "big sister mama bear." Kids can be so cruel to one another, but soon enough, she and her friends would make up and be friends again.

In Terry's middle teen years, she did not get along with Mother very well, and she often stayed with me for as long as she could. I was married by then, and if I could have, I would have had her live with us from 1968 to 1969. At age eighteen, right after graduating from high school in 1970, she married Richard Green, who was five years her senior and in the Navy. In 1971, they had twins—a boy and a girl—and moved to Northern California. I cried for weeks.

Terry had become a beautiful person by this time, and not only skin deep. She was kind and unassuming, honest, and damn right determined to do what she set out to do—maybe even a little stubborn. We were close and saw each other when we could. She was my baby sister—my only sibling.

In 1980, Richard had a job with an up-and-coming TV cable company, and they relocated to Las Vegas, Nevada. Their twins, Christopher and Shannon, were nine, and by then, their youngest, Johnny, was two. The family thrived in their new situation, and they lived happily for the next 29 years.

On February 5, 2009, Terry's daughter Shannon was a victim of domestic violence by her ex-husband. Shannon was shot ten times, and her ex-husband committed suicide. Somehow, Shannon survived, but Richard, Terry's husband, was murdered trying to save his daughter.

Terry had not needed her big sister for the previous forty years, but when this happened, she needed her "big sister mama bear" again. For three weeks straight, I ate with her, slept with her, cried with her, and made arrangements with her. It was such a senseless nightmare of violence and the only chapter in our lives that I was glad that our parents did not live to see.

Terry's strength in overcoming her husband's violent death has been remarkable. She still lives in Las Vegas, and considering the tragedy she has lived through, she is doing great. She is the grandmother of five grandchildren, not to mention the mother of three. Her capacity to take care of her family during and after that tragedy was incredible. Every day, she got up and put one foot in front of the other to keep her family together. She worked, she cried, she took care of her grandchildren, she took them on vacations, and she cooked thousands of meals for all of the Greens. She took care of Shannon and her doctor appointments. Shannon is still dealing with the aftermath of those injuries today. She grieved for her husband of 40 years, but while grieving the past, she never forgot to keep an eye on the future. She did it for her family. Yes, Terry found the faith and the strength to live. She is a hero to her children.

Mary Catherine Ward / Mortensen (Kay): Author's Note

When I began reading through these letters, I could not believe the number of things I did not know about my parents. As I read them and worked on the research for this book, it seemed as if I could reach out and touch them. It was like having a time machine back to the 1940s. I got to know them all over again, without them knowing me.

I found out the following:

I did not know they had only known each other for a few short days in August and September of 1943, leading up to Frank's deployment overseas. I thought they had known each other longer. Their love affair was a paper affair with letters and airmail stamps.

The hardest thing about writing this book was that I did not have a chance to ask Dad or Mom any questions. Indeed, there was no one to ask. All of their sisters, brothers, friends, and cousins were gone. Some days, I miss them terribly, even though both of them had passed away more than ten years before.

Their generation held the future of the world in its hands, and they knew it. I can't help but wonder if any other generation would have stepped up to the plate like the heroes of the 1940s. Catherine and Frank were brave beyond belief and did not even know it. In every situation that they faced, they always kept their chins up with determination. Every day of that tumultuous period, they plowed ahead, defending all that they knew to be true. Their strength and resolve came from a blind faith in the values that had always defined their lives and a deep faith in God.

There was an undeniable spark on that sandy beach in South Carolina on the day they met. A few short weeks later, they fell in love somewhere between the dance floor and the Olivers' porch swing. But it was through letters that their love deepened into a life-encompassing bond. Catherine was smitten with his words of love, and Frank was endlessly delighted with her naïveté, her sweetness, and her sassy little pout when she was upset. He learned quickly that his Southern gal would not mind letting you know it when she was unhappy about something. But it was also in her nature to promptly forget about it ten minutes later.

It is clear that Dad came home from the war for one reason: Mother.

I would love to have known the boy-man in Dad—the person he was before WWII killed the boy in him. From all the stories I have heard, he was a lot of fun before Hitler and the war stole his innocence and his carefree zest for a good time.

Catherine's mantra of "keeping your chin up and working hard" was her fix-all for anything and everything. It was the bedrock philosophy that gave her the strength to face the challenges of each day. She would say, "It will be alright—just don't think about it."

Now that I have read their letters, I understand so much more about their relationship. From the very beginning, Dad did all he could to protect his Catherine. He knew that she had led a rather sheltered life in North Carolina and that she wasn't quite as educated or worldly-wise as he was. Once they were building a new life together in the big city of Los Angeles, he took on the responsibility to quietly and discreetly protect her from herself, from others, and from the realities of the world they lived in—always and forever.

I learned how my nickname came to be "Kay." My cousin David could not say "Cathy" when he was little, so he called his Aunt Cathy "Kay" when he was two years old. To this day, I am still called Kay by my family.

As I read through their letters, I had a chance to get to know my mother as a 24-year-old girl—before she was my mother. She was sassy but sweet, thoughtful but often self-serving. As a young woman, she liked to flirt with the young men in her life, and she loved to have fun. But her quick temper and the mercurial quirks in her personality occasionally sent her young men away hurt and confused. They often left her, shaking their heads and wondering, "What just happened?"

She was faithful to her God, and her values and morals were above reproach. She had never been in a serious relationship before she met Dad. There was never any question: he was the only man she had ever loved in her life. She communicated best through letters. Even after they were married, she continued to write to him—all the way into the 1960s! She could be quite the tease and sometimes a little daring with her words, as we saw in her famous "Dear Jack" letter to Frank after he had hurt her foot in Myrtle Beach.

Never afraid to work hard and play hard, Mother had a strong independent side. She often gave of her time and energy to help others. I did not know that she had such a passion to work in the medical field. As a young woman in her twenties, it was there that she found purpose and happiness—and a way forward from the unhappy childhood she had suffered during the Depression.

Mom could be quite impatient, but I have to admire the patience she did show as she waited for Dad's letters—especially after he was wounded. She wrote to him every night, even when she did not have an address for him. He must have received a huge bag of mail once he arrived at Baxter Army Hospital! As I have mentioned in the early pages of their story, she was a hero in her own right.

My One Regret

It was Memorial Day of 1991, and Dad was grilling in their backyard. I always loved to grill with my dad; it was our special time together without mother being around. We would have bourbon cocktails and a smoke while he manned the grill. Although he had officially stopped smoking many years before, he never lost the desire for "just one." He knew that if he sneaked a smoke at the barbecue, the smoke from the pit would mask it, and Catherine would be none the wiser.

That day, he took one of my cigarettes, and to my surprise, he began to reminisce about the war. It was like a moment snatched out of time. I was married with two grown children of my own, but I had never heard him talk about the war before.

He had a faraway look in his eyes as he quietly recalled how he had seen his men die in the village streets of Belgium. I did not know why he was choosing this moment to tell me about this horrific, life-altering experience. I felt as if he was almost unaware of my presence, while he cracked open the window on this chapter of his young life. He stared into the fire as he quietly told me that he could still see the men dying on the snow banks at the Battle of the Bulge. He paused for a long moment, and I watched as an unbelievable wave of grief engulfed him.

Suddenly, he looked up. It was as if he had to look into my eyes to escape the wave of guilt that still haunted him—and to anchor himself once again in the present. "Kay, I saw nearly every man in my platoon killed in the most horrid of ways." He had to look back into the fire before he could continued to speak, of the images seared into his memory—of how the huge Nazi Panzer "beasts" had hit the village with artillery shells that shook the very ground beneath them. On that day, it had been cold to the bone, and the chaos and carnage were surreal.

he was choking back sobs. Finally, he looked up at me. His eyes were brimming with tears. "Why did I come home?" he blurted out in a tone that was both desperate and confused. "Why me?"

With huge tears in his eyes, he cleared his throat and struggled to get a hold of himself. For that brief moment, he was back on that battlefield alongside the men he had trained with, traveled with, joked around with, served with—and with whom he had almost died. In that stolen moment, he once again saw their faces so clearly and heard their laughter— laughter which was abruptly and mercilessly pierced by their screams as they paid the ultimate price on that bone-chilling day in a remote part of the world. It was clear that he was having a hard time coming back into the present. "Oh well," he stammered, "that was a long time ago. And so it goes. Your mother is going to want this meat soon." He cleared his throat once more and stared back at the embers as he mechanically took the steaks off of the grill. That was so Dad. Ever the hero who stood up to rise above any given challenge. And in those moments when he did not have an answer for something, how often would he say, "And so it goes."

As we walked back into the house, I realized that the pictures in his mind were as real to him as yesterday—not 45 years in the past. He never did tell me about being shot or the bullet that almost killed him and all of his dreams. That cold day in Belgium missed taking his life by one-eighth of an inch. I never knew the story behind his Purple Heart. But I did know that he felt that in the grand scheme of things, the ones who did not come home were the true heroes—and that the value of their sacrifice far outweighed the pain of his personal wounds.

He never spoke to me of the war again.

*****

Dad passed away in 2001. As we went through his things, we came across the trunk that I had asked about so many years before when I was just a five-year-old child. His concise but mysterious words drifted back to me through the years: "My life is in that trunk." and remembering the day, we helped him move to Las vegas. When we opened the trunk, we found many mementos: his uniform, his medals, his Purple heart, his dress uniform "Pinks," his dog tags, and the insignia pin that he had sent to Catherine. All of these items were precious, but the greatest treasure of all was the letters he and Mom had written to each other, all carefully bound and stashed away for safekeeping. As much as I wanted to read them, I just couldn't open even the first one—not yet. It would be more than a decade before I could bring myself to read them. I hadn't finished letting him go.

In 2014, thirteen years after Dad's death, I decided that

the moment had come. I was finally ready to read the letters that Frank and Catherine had exchanged during the war, from 1943 to 1945. Delighted, moved, and captivated by the amusing stories, the engaging day-to-day accounts, and the loving words that they shared, I felt obligated to share their story with a larger audience. It was in those moments that the idea for this book was born.

I had never realized the personal sacrifices that Dad had made to serve in WWII. He lived through seemingly endless weeks of strenuous physical training, exercises, and C-rations, interspersed with hours of loneliness and homesickness and outlines from time to time with periods of sheer boredom. In the Army, he learned to kill the enemy with weapons he otherwise never would have even thought of picking up, much less weapons with which he would develop the mastery of an expert. For weeks, he wondered when he would be called upon to use the specialized training that Uncle Sam considered so necessary in being prepared to fight this war. His mail was erratic, and he desperately missed Catherine, the girl he had fallen in love with on the way to war. Although every soldier was terrified of the German artillery shells that fell all around them, as an officer in the foxholes of Southern France, he was careful to mask his fear behind a façade named Duty. The half-dozen countries where they were stationed were sometimes strange, mysterious, and dangerous, and the weather conditions in those locations ranged between hot and sub-zero cold. It took a great deal of bravery to lead his men into that village in Belgium at the Battle of the Bulge—but it took even more strength and courage just to live out that one day in the wilderness of the Ardennes forest. It would have been easier to die.

It was not until I read the letters from the war and wrote *Catherine's Lieutenant* that I fully understood the *gravity* of that conversation with my dad on Memorial Day, 1991.

My biggest regret is that I never *thanked him* for coming

home, giving me this beautiful life, and my family, or thanked him for saving our way of life as we know it. But if I had, he probably would have said, "The ones you need to thank are the ones who did not come home. They are still in the fields of Belgium. We just did what we had to do."

*****

I do have an answer for Frank's question, "Why did I come home?" Dad, at that point in time in 2018, you had two daughters, five grandchildren, and nine great-grandchildren. Who knows what marvelous things these children will do? After all, they are related to *you!* It is because of you and your generation that these children of yours can live, learn, and thrive in this country with freedom.

*****

Although Frank and Catherine were the actual authors of *Catherine's Lieutenant*, let me close with a few words about myself – Mary Catherine Ward Mortensen or "Kay."

I am married to the love of my life, Larry Mortensen, and I thank him for the help and understanding he has consistently shown me while I worked on this book, *Catherine's Lieutenant*. We live in Southern California, enjoying our beautiful retirement and our well-blended families. We often go to visit Frank and Catherine at the National Cemetery in Boulder City, Nevada, when we travel through Las Vegas. We always take Mom a bouquet of red carnations and a shot of bourbon for Dad.

About Atmosphere Press

Founded in 2015, Atmosphere Press was built on the principles of Honesty, Transparency, Professionalism, Kindness, and Making Your Book Awesome. As an ethical and author-friendly hybrid press, we stay true to that founding mission today.

If you're a reader, enter our giveaway for a free book here:

SCAN TO ENTER
BOOK GIVEAWAY

If you're a writer, submit your manuscript for consideration here:

SCAN TO SUBMIT
MANUSCRIPT

And always feel free to visit Atmosphere Press and our authors online at atmospherepress.com. See you there soon!

About the Author